Welcome to THE EVERYTHING Family Guides

THESE HANDY, PORTABLE BOOKS are designed to be the perfect traveling companions. Whether you're traveling within a tight family budget or feeling the urge to splurge, you will find all you need to create a memorable family vacation.

Use these books to plan your trips, and then take them along with you for easy reference. Does Jimmy want to go sailing? Or maybe Jane wants to go to the local hobby shop. *The Everything® Family Guides* offer many ways to entertain kids of all ages while also ensuring that you get the most out of your time away from home.

Review this book cover to cover to give you great ideas before you travel, and stick it in your backpack or diaper bag to use as a quick reference guide for activities, attractions, and excursions you want to experience. Let *The Everything® Family Guides* help you travel the world, and you'll discover that vacationing with the whole family can be filled with fun and exciting adventures.

📖 TRAVEL TIP

Quick, handy tips

⚡ E-ALERT

Urgent warnings

☰ FAST FACT

Details to make your trip more enjoyable

 E-QUESTION

Solutions to common problems

Timeshares

Dear Reader,

I am one of those people who take every opportunity to visit new places. I have been all over the world, with some of my favorite spots being nearly literal polar opposites. I love icebergs in Alaska as much as warm waters in Fiji. I enjoy making campfire s'mores in British Columbia as much as drinking fine Bordeaux in France. I thrill at photographing giant tortoises in the Galapagos Islands as much as learning American history on New England's shores.

Indeed, I am one of those people who is forever looking for new experiences, and for that reason, I find timeshares intriguing. As a frequent traveler, though, I also find myself wanting answers to serious questions before actually buying one: Are they a good value? What exactly do they include? Where can I use them for vacations? How can I protect myself from a bad financial deal?

The answers I have found to these questions and more are in the following pages. I hope they will help to educate you about timeshares just as they have helped me, so that we all may continue to experience the many wonderful destinations our vast world has to offer.

Kim Kavin

THE

EVERYTHING®

FAMILY GUIDE TO

TIMESHARES

Buy smart, avoid pitfalls, and enjoy
your vacation to the max!

Kim Kavin

Adams Media
Avon, Massachusetts

For my parents, Marc and Donna Kavin

• • •

Publishing Director: Gary M. Krebs
Associate Managing Editor: Laura M. Daly
Associate Copy Chief: Brett Palana-Shanahan
Acquisitions Editor: Lisa Laing
Development Editor: Jessica LaPointe
Associate Production Editor: Casey Ebert

Director of Manufacturing: Susan Beale
Associate Director of Production:
Michelle Roy Kelly
Cover Design: Paul Beatrice, Matt LeBlanc,
Erick DaCosta
Design and Layout: Colleen Cunningham,
Jennifer Oliveira, Brewster Brownville

• • •

An Everything® Series Book.
Everything® and everything.com® are registered trademarks of F+W Publications, Inc.

Published by Adams Media, an F+W Publications Company
57 Littlefield Street, Avon, MA 02322 U.S.A.
www.adamsmedia.com

ISBN 10: 1-59337-711-8
ISBN 13: 978-1-59337-711-3

J I H G F E D C B A

Library of Congress Cataloging-in-Publication Data
Kavin, Kim.
The everything family guide to timeshares / Kim Kavin.
p. cm. -- (An everything series book)
ISBN 1-59337-711-8
1. Timesharing (Real estate) 2. Timesharing (Real estate)--Law and legislation. I. Title. II. Title: Family guide to timeshares. III. Series: Everything series.
HD7287.65.K38 2006
643'.12--dc22
2006014734

This publication is designed to provide accurate and authoritative information with regard to the
subject matter covered. It is sold with the understanding that the publisher is not engaged in ren-
dering legal, accounting, or other professional advice. If legal advice or other expert assistance
is required, the services of a competent professional person should be sought.
—From a *Declaration of Principles* jointly adopted by a Committee of the
American Bar Association and a Committee of Publishers and Associations

Many of the designations used by manufacturers and sellers to distinguish their products are
claimed as trademarks. Where those designations appear in this book and Adams Media was
aware of a trademark claim, the designations have been printed with initial capital letters.
This book is available at quantity discounts for bulk purchases.
For information, please call 1-800-872-5627.

Visit the entire Everything® series at www.everything.com

Contents

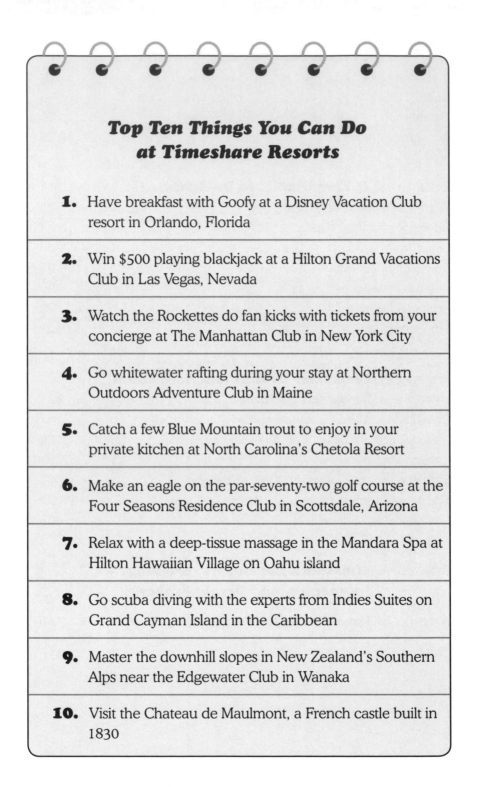

Top Ten Things You Can Do at Timeshare Resorts

1. Have breakfast with Goofy at a Disney Vacation Club resort in Orlando, Florida

2. Win $500 playing blackjack at a Hilton Grand Vacations Club in Las Vegas, Nevada

3. Watch the Rockettes do fan kicks with tickets from your concierge at The Manhattan Club in New York City

4. Go whitewater rafting during your stay at Northern Outdoors Adventure Club in Maine

5. Catch a few Blue Mountain trout to enjoy in your private kitchen at North Carolina's Chetola Resort

6. Make an eagle on the par-seventy-two golf course at the Four Seasons Residence Club in Scottsdale, Arizona

7. Relax with a deep-tissue massage in the Mandara Spa at Hilton Hawaiian Village on Oahu island

8. Go scuba diving with the experts from Indies Suites on Grand Cayman Island in the Caribbean

9. Master the downhill slopes in New Zealand's Southern Alps near the Edgewater Club in Wanaka

10. Visit the Chateau de Maulmont, a French castle built in 1830

Acknowledgments

Literary agent Jacky Sach of Bookends Inc. brought me this project and helped me to see it through. To her and everyone at Adams Media, thank you for the opportunity.

Ed Kenney at Marriott, Ryan March at Disney, and Jason Gamel at the American Resort Development Association were especially gracious with their time and deep industry knowledge. Thanks also to Lori Armon at Hyatt, Chris Bosch at Interval International, David Jimenez at Resort Condominiums International, and Lou Ann Burney at the American Resort Development Association.

Special thanks to Bill Rogers, Chris Nettleton, George Marine, and Mary Syer, all of whom generously shared the details of their timeshare-ownership experiences with me. Bill and Nancy Geigerich were particularly helpful in this capacity.

My parents, Marc and Donna Kavin, and my sister, Michelle Kavin, are wonderful supporters of everything I do—and excellent distractions when I need a break from writing. I love and appreciate them dearly.

Last on this list but first in my heart is Sean Toohey, who always understands when I am still typing long past midnight. He is the partner of my dreams.

Introduction

Americans, it seems, are falling in love with the idea of timeshare vacations. The concept of timeshares is nearly a half century old, having begun at a ski resort across the Atlantic Ocean in Europe in the 1960s. Timeshares did exist in the United States, too, back in the 1960s and 1970s, but they really didn't come into their own as a vacation powerhouse in America until the past decade. Europeans continued to invest their vacation dollars in timeshares for years, but the most recent worldwide studies show that it is now Americans who lead the timeshare buying craze—accounting for most of the $7.9 billion in United States timeshare sales that were recorded in 2004 alone.

According to the most recent studies, the median price for a week's use of a U.S. timeshare unit in 2004 was about $15,800—about 12 percent more than the previous year (and a good $5,000 more than a timeshare week in some other parts of the world). Nearly four million U.S. residents had a stake in the timeshare marketplace as of 2004, a full million more people than just two years earlier.

Still, even with such fast-climbing numbers, U.S. citizens account for less than half of the worldwide number of total timeshare owners. In fact, only a fraction of the number of U.S. citizens who can afford to buy a timeshare unit have actually done so.

Needless to say, the industry sees great potential for growth on the horizon. More and more timeshare resorts are being built, more and more brand-name companies like Marriott and Hilton are getting into the game, and more and more potential customers (like you) are asking questions about whether a timeshare might be a good vacation investment. A solid 85 percent of people who currently own timeshares consistently report that they are satisfied with their purchases, meaning that more and more word-of-mouth marketing is also pushing the industry into a period of what just may be even more tremendous growth.

There could be no better time to make use of all the information in *The Everything® Family Guide to Timeshares*. The following pages will explain all that you need to know about what timeshares are and how they work. You will learn how to buy, use, and sell units of various sizes; how to protect yourself against scams; how to locate the hottest properties on today's market; and more. You will get into the specifics of how the timeshare exchange game works, including how you can make the most of your particular unit's trading power and use it as a springboard to travel the globe. You will learn how to bring hidden fees into the light during sales presentations and how to get overly pushy salespeople off your back. You will even learn a few tips for buying off the resale market at substantially reduced prices.

Timeshares offer a wealth of vacation possibilities, whether you like to ski downhill trails in the mountains, snorkel off tropical beaches, or explore the world's most famous cities. Timeshares also can be smart financial investments that might save you thousands of dollars during a lifetime of travel. The question is, are timeshares right for you? And if so, how can you make the smartest possible decision about which unit to buy, where to buy it, and how to use it?

You will know the answers to those questions and more after reading *The Everything® Family Guide to Timeshares*. Welcome to what just may be the first step along a vacation path that will last you and your family for a lifetime.

CHAPTER 1

What Is Timeshare?

TIMESHARES ARE PART OF a nearly half-century-old business model. They have grown from an inauspicious beginning in Europe into a worldwide force controlling millions of vacations and billions of dollars. Still, the industry is eager to reach out to people from all walks of life and all income levels, hoping to tap the vast pool of remaining vacationers who can afford a timeshare but haven't yet purchased one. Will you buy into the global trend? First, you need to learn what the craze is all about.

History of Timeshares

The concept of timeshares is widely believed to have started in Europe in the 1960s, at a ski resort in the French Alps. The resort's owner believed that he could attract more business if he agreed to allow multiple owners to split the rights to use the rooms at his vacation property, instead of forcing wealthier individuals to purchase the more-expensive full rights to the rooms in their entirety. It worked, and a new vacation industry was born.

Nearly fifty years later, the concept of timeshares has spread from France to the entire European Union, the United States, Africa, Asia, Indonesia, Australia, the Middle East, the Caribbean, and just about everywhere else that people like to go during their vacations. Today, there are reportedly close to seven million timeshare owners around the globe, each with a stake in the more than 5,400 timeshare units that exist in forty-seven of the United States and about 100 countries in virtually every time zone on the planet.

You can now buy the right to use a resort room, like that one that started it all in the Swiss Alps, or even an evolution of that idea: a deeded property that gives you the right to pass your timeshare unit on to your children or grandchildren. Some timeshare companies are even allowing you the option of exchanging your accrued investment for things like airline tickets and cruise-ship vacations. Only time will tell just how much farther the industry will spread, but it certainly is showing no signs of stopping.

There have, of course, been some bumps along this path of expansion, and there continue to be scam artists out there selling worthless swampland to unsuspecting buyers. But for the most part, the timeshare industry has evolved into just that: a full-fledged industry. State laws, reputable timeshare exchange companies, and even a professional association of resort developers now exist where just a few decades ago there was nothing but *caveat emptor*—buyer beware. Internet communities have sprung up, too, allowing timeshare owners, buyers, and sellers to communicate with one another about past experiences. Even well-known hotel companies such as Marriott, Hilton, and Hyatt have gotten into the timeshare game.

≡FAST FACT

The average timeshare owner is fifty-four years old, and more than 80 percent of timeshare owners are married, according to industry leader Resort Condominiums International.

To understand what modern-day timeshare opportunities are all about—to grasp exactly where these resort vacations stand and how they grew to become what they are today—it is important to first take a look back at the timeshare industry's sometimes tangled roots.

The Early Days

For many people, the word *timeshare* is synonymous with scam. You get an instant vision in your mind of a greasy-haired, polyester-wearing salesman whose bad teeth make you extremely nervous every time he flashes that "trust me, baby" smile. This sleazeball typically offers you a deal that sounds just too good to be true for a fabulous vacation home in a destination where, he brags, it never rains and the temperature never drops below eighty degrees (with no humidity, to boot!).

 **E-ALERT**

A common misconception is that investing in a timeshare is the same as investing in real estate. This is simply not the case. A timeshare purchase is a way of locking in future vacation prices at current rates, not a way of investing money in the hopes of realizing huge appreciations in real-estate value.

The problem, of course, is that even in your vision, the salesman turns out to be just as big of a scumbag as he seems, and the deed you end up holding turns out to be good for nothing more than an undeveloped swath of swampland with a less-than-picturesque view of the local landfill.

This kind of imaginary tale, sadly, was reality for many unsuspecting timeshare buyers when the industry really wasn't an industry at all. Back in the 1960s and 1970s, it was a free-for-all for developers whose business practices were guided entirely by their own ethics and morals, which, in more than a few cases, turned out to be nonexistent. The sting that hard-working people felt after being duped out of their vacation savings left them bad-mouthing not just those unscrupulous developers, but timeshares in general for many years to come.

Even people who ended up working with reputable developers had gripes that festered over the years. The most frequently heard complaint about resorts that did, in fact, exist on beautiful beachfront land was that their timeshare units failed to appreciate in value at the same rate as other real-estate purchases—a fact that was likely very true, given that timeshares are not meant to be real-estate purchases at all. They may have been sold as a less-expensive alternative to making a costly real-estate investment, such as buying an entire waterfront vacation home, but many people failed to connect the financial dots and realize that buying a timeshare, or the rights to use a beachfront room for one week every year, is definitely *not* the same as owning the entire resort and thus seeing great gains in property value.

And so, timeshares in general developed an unsavory reputation. It is an albatross that, even today, the perfectly honest segments of the timeshare industry are still struggling to shed. Some even refuse to use the word *timeshare*, instead referring to their offerings as *vacation clubs* or even *vacation investments*. These marketing terms, while they may ring of calling an old dog by a new name, are actually quite valid, as they explain exactly what modern-day timeshares have grown to become.

Modern-Day Timeshares

There is much greater understanding in the world today that timeshares are investments in future vacations, as opposed to real estate itself. Part of this understanding comes from developers' very real need to market themselves more honestly if they want to continue to find customers, and part of it comes from the fact that more and more people are researching timeshares on their own as an alternative to paying ever-rising hotel rates and vacation-house purchase prices.

The timeshare industry, according to one study, saw a 116 percent increase in sales between 2000 and 2005. Sales of timeshares in the United States during 2004 alone accounted for $7.9 billion—almost as much as the entire world spent on timeshare purchases just a few years earlier, in 2002. The more people want to buy something, the more they tend to research it. Such is the case with timeshares and the corresponding spread of truthful information about them.

≡ FAST FACT

Even though timeshare sales in the United States brought in an estimated $7.9 billion in 2004 alone, industry experts say that less than 5 percent of Americans who earn enough money to purchase a timeshare have actually gone out and bought one.

It is true that some of the old timeshare sales practices remain, in particular the oft-lamented high-pressure sales presentation that tends to take place during a free vacation to the property being sold. (You will read more about those "fly-buy" techniques in Chapter 8.) There are also new incarnations of that greasy-haired salesman of old, such as people known nowadays as a resort's off-premises contact. This term refers to anyone who tries to lure you into a resort's sales presentation with the promise of free meals, theater tickets, and the like. Think of the guy standing on the Las Vegas Strip handing out blackjack vouchers to anyone who will go listen to his buddy over at the "hot new resort in town" for an hour, and you get the picture. These people are paid to put bodies into the sales-presentation seats, not to make business connections between you, the qualified buyer, and a resort vacation package that may or may not be right for you.

Luckily, as with any industry, the reputable companies that focus on customer-oriented sales practices tend to stay in business far longer than the shady operations, and eventually, a few brand names come to dominate the playing field. This is beginning to happen more and more often with timeshare resorts themselves, and it has already happened with exchange companies—the firms that control the trading of timeshare units among unit owners worldwide.

Exchange Companies

Exchange companies are businesses that create networks of time-share resorts and then oversee the exchanging of timeshare units between you, the owner, and other people who have bought time-share units at other resorts around the world. Most of the exchange companies have their own ratings systems to help you understand what you will be getting for your unit's exchange value, and many also offer things like unit upgrades, bonus time for extending your vacation at given resorts, and other timeshare-user perks.

Different exchange companies charge different fees—for membership, for exchanges in the United States and abroad, for adding bonus time to your ownership, and more—and they offer different services on the whole. Some handle exchanges only, while others also offer advertising and Internet support for timeshare renting and resale. The bigger exchange companies are part of huge worldwide corporations that also include car-rental companies, hotel properties, discount airline ticket Web sites, and more. If you join one of the bigger companies, your membership will include subscriptions to glossy magazines offering you access to everything from discounted cruise-ship vacations to vacation insurance.

The way exchange companies handle the actual exchanges can differ, too. Some force you to pay the exchange fee and deposit the week that you own into their system first, so other people can decide whether they want it, while other companies allow you to choose your exchange resort of choice first, then pay a fee and deposit the week you own afterward. (You will learn more about how these systems work in Chapter 12.)

Some people try to game the system by working with more than one timeshare exchange company at a time, but if you work with multiple exchange companies, you run the risk of trading away the single week you own to more than one person. If this happens, you would be liable for double or triple booking penalties from multiple exchange companies and, possibly, the resorts themselves.

Which exchange company should you choose? Often, it's not up to you. Some timeshare purchases include complimentary membership in one of the larger exchange companies, and some brand-name resort developers allow you to use only the exchange company with which they are affiliated. You should ask before buying any timeshare unit whether you will be forced to work with a particular exchange company and what penalties you might incur if you go outside the system in search of a better deal.

 **E-QUESTION**

If an exchange company doesn't own the resorts in its network, how does it make money?
It makes money by charging you—and every other timeshare owner—a fee whenever you seek to exchange your timeshare week for another person's. You sometimes also will have to pay annual membership dues as high as $80 to $100 and additional fees for additional services that you may want to use.

While there are several brand-name hotel developers getting into the timeshare business by offering their unit owners exchanges among only a handful of resorts, most developers are affiliated with the two exchange companies that continue to dominate the timeshare industry. The biggest is Resort Condominiums International, and its largest rival is called Interval International.

There are smaller exchange companies, as well, which you will read about toward the end of this chapter, but you should start your industry education by taking a look at its biggest players.

Resort Condominiums International

Often referred to as RCI, Resort Condominiums International is the world's leading timeshare exchange company. It had more than three million members as of 2004, and in that same year confirmed about 2.6 million timeshare exchanges—earning a fee of about $150 for each week of domestic exchange and about $189 for each week of international exchange. You don't need to be a math wizard to understand the huge financial power on which the company has built its brand.

As of this printing, Resort Condominiums International was part of the Cendant Corporation, which also owns the Avis and Budget rental car companies, the discount airline-ticket Web site *www .cheaptickets.com*, and hotel companies including Days Inn, Howard Johnson, Ramada Inn, Super 8, Travelodge, and Wyndham. Plans were in the works to break Cendant into smaller companies in early 2006, though only time will tell which division, if any, will include Resort Condominiums International in the future.

Resort Condominiums International itself has been around since 1974, when it incorporated in Virginia and opened its first office in Park Fletcher, Indianapolis. It had 453 members that year and didn't even publish its first resort directory until a year later. That year, RCI confirmed just 236 timeshare exchanges.

≡ FAST FACT

Your annual membership dues with Resort Condominiums International, as well as with Interval International, will get you on the mailing list for either company's travel magazine. Hold on to them, because the magazines sometimes mention resorts that are not yet in the exchange companies' online or printed catalogs.

Today, the Resort Condominiums International directory is so big that it is easier to search through the company's affiliated resorts via the Internet, at the company's Web site, *www.rci.com*. There are so many resorts to choose among—nearly 4,000 as of early 2006—that you have to start by selecting a continent, then a nation, then a state or region, and so forth. You can even search based on the activities you prefer, such as beach-going, golfing, and snow-skiing, as there are literally hundreds of resorts offering each. You also can search based on a resort's ranking, be it well-known for hospitality or for other forms of service.

Interval International

Interval International is the biggest competitor to Resort Condominiums International. The company's exchange network includes more than 2,000 properties in seventy-five countries around the world and nearly two million global timeshare owners. It has been in business since 1976, earning a solid reputation for treating its customers far better than those fly-by-night salesmen of old. As if to make the point, Interval International calls itself "The Quality Vacation Exchange Network."

The company's world headquarters is in Miami, Florida, though it maintains more than two dozen other offices worldwide. As of this writing, Interval International's exchange fees were slightly lower than those at Resort Condominiums International, with Interval International charging about $130 per week for domestic timeshare exchanges and about $150 per week for international timeshare exchanges. More than 850,000 timeshare exchanges were made through Interval International in 2004 alone, and the company boasts more than 1.7 million members.

Interval International is part of IAC/InterActiveCorp, which also owns Ticketmaster, the Home Shopping Network, and popular consumer-service Web sites such as *www.ask.com* and *www .lendingtree.com*. As of its last membership profile, Interval International's average U.S. member was about forty-nine years old, married, and earning $114,200 in household income. The average member spends about thirty-five nights each year traveling for lei-sure—a fact that is important in making timeshare purchase financially smart (which you will learn more about in Chapter 2).

The Interval International Web site, *www.intervalworld.com*, offers basic information about the company, but it has no searchable resort database available to nonmembers. You can, however, request a copy of the company's printed resort directory, which is more than 500 pages long and packed with resort listings and information.

Brand-Name Developers

Many of the timeshare resort developers out there today are brand names that you may already know, and most of them work with either Resort Condominiums International or Interval International in terms of offering their unit owners exchange services worldwide. In some cases, though, the developers themselves end up functioning in part like exchange companies because you often are allowed to trade your vacation time at one of their resorts for vacation time at another of their resorts—as opposed to trading it for time at a resort that was built by a different developer, which is the service that the big exchange companies offer. In alphabetical order, the timeshare divisions of these brand-name resort development companies include:

- Club Intrawest
- Disney Vacation Club
- Fairfield FairShare Plus
- Four Seasons Residence Club
- Hilton Grand Vacations Club
- Hyatt Vacation Club
- Marriott Vacation Club International
- Starwood Vacation Ownership
- WorldMark by Trendwest

These developers' in-house exchange options are a fraction of what behemoths like Resort Condominiums International and Interval International give their customers, but the big-name developers do offer something that nobody else can: a following with hotel users who know exactly what to expect from their brand names. As the theory goes, if you always stay at Hiltons when you travel, you are likely to enjoy the style and amenities when you exchange usage time at its timeshare properties, too.

Many of these brand-name timeshare resorts tend to be more expensive than other resorts around the world. Sometimes, this is because the brand-name resorts are offering better service and amenities, but other times, the higher prices are simply a reflection of the brand name's selling power.

Here is a more in-depth look at some of those smaller, brand-name resort development companies that are building timeshare resorts and allowing exchanges either in-house or through an affiliation with one of the bigger exchange companies.

Club Intrawest

Club Intrawest is part of the Intrawest Corporation, which has been around since 1976 and supports more than eight million travelers at its ski resorts each year. It is a Canadian company that owns nine resorts—in Whistler, Panorama, and Vancouver, British Columbia; Tremblant, Quebec; Blue Mountain, Ontario; Sandestin, Florida; Palm Desert, California; Kauai, Hawaii; and Zihuatanejo, Mexico.

TRAVEL TIP

When you become an owner through Club Intrawest, you purchase points that can be used toward vacations at any of the company's resorts, as well as at partnering resorts around the world. Should you want to explore becoming a member, you can stay at a partnering resort near your home and attend a sales presentation during a three-day Discovery Stay. Information about Discovery Stays and more is at the Club Intrawest Web site, *www.clubintrawest.com*.

Disney Vacation Club

The Disney Vacation Club began operations in 1991 with just one property: Old Key West at Walt Disney World in Orlando, Florida. Today, the exchange company has more than 90,000 timeshare owners with access to seven resorts, vacations aboard the Disney Cruise Line, stays at Walt Disney World hotels, and more. The Disney Vacation Club is affiliated with Interval International, which means you can exchange your timeshare unit for a vacation outside of the Disney brand, but the main reason the company exists is to win the business of parents and children who like to vacation at the Magic Kingdom, Epcot, and its other family-friendly destinations. In fact, the average Disney Vacation Club member visits Walt Disney World twice a year.

Timeshare prices, according to the company's Web site, *www .disneyvacationclub.com*, start at $14,700 per year. If yours is the kind of family that visits Walt Disney World once a year—and if you plan to return for at least a few more years in the future—you know that the ever-rising price of hotel rooms inside the Disney complex can add up to that and more before all of your children are grown. This is the philosophy that Disney had in mind when it created its timeshare division in the first place—though you must remember that those initial entry fees do not include annual maintenance fees, exchange fees, and other miscellaneous fees that you may be forced to pay. (More on those in Chapter 2.)

⚡ E-ALERT

As of this printing, the Disney Vacation Club had sold out all of the memberships at its resorts except for the Saratoga Springs Resort and Spa, which opened in May 2004 in Orlando. That's not to say you cannot buy a timeshare unit at a Disney resort through the resale market (more on that in Chapter 10), but getting one direct from the developer at this point is definitely a challenging proposition.

Fairfield FairShare Plus

Part of the Fairfield Resorts company, the Fairfield FairShare Plus program is a points-based system of timeshare ownership. It began in 1991 and is now a subsidiary of the Cendant Corporation, which also owns the Resort Condominiums International exchange company. Interestingly, more than 80 percent of Fairfield Resorts have been awarded RCI's highest ranking, the Gold Crown designation.

More than a half million members belong to FairShare Plus, taking advantage of more than seventy resorts in twenty-one U.S. states and territories. To learn more, go to the company's Web site, *www .fairfieldresorts.com.*

Four Seasons Residence Clubs

The Four Seasons program, as you might imagine based on the company's high-end reputation, includes top-of-the-line (and pocketbook) offerings for deeded properties at what is currently a five-resort network. Four Seasons Residences are available in North San Diego, California; Scottsdale, Arizona; Punta Mita, Mexico; Jackson Hole, Wyoming; and Peninsula Papagayo, Costa Rica. Some of the resorts, such as the ones in San Diego and Scottsdale, have already sold out their phase one development and are now taking orders only for units being built as part of phase two construction.

Spas and golf are the most prominently promoted resort amenities at each destination, except for Jackson Hole, which lacks a golf course because it is keyed to snow skiing and other wintertime activities. All five of the Four Seasons timeshare resorts do boast strong family packages, including on- and off-site childcare, programmed activities, and on-your-own family fun.

The company does not advertise pricing for its timeshare units, but you can make an appointment for a private showing through its Web site, *www.fourseasons.com.*

Hilton Grand Vacations Club

Based in Orlando, Florida, the Hilton Grand Vacations Club is controlled entirely by the Hilton Hotels Corporation and has been around since 1992. Its network includes twenty-seven resorts, and purchase of a timeshare unit automatically enrolls you in the Resort Condominiums International club as well as in Hilton Honors, a guest reward program that gives you access to 2,500 hotels around the world.

Resorts that Hilton has developed for its timeshare division include properties in Orlando and Miami Beach, Florida; Las Vegas,

Nevada; and Oahu, Hawaii. Resorts that Hilton manages as part of its timeshare program include additional properties in Florida and Hawaii, as well as one resort in Breckenridge, Colorado. The company created urban timeshare opportunities in 2002 when it opened The Hilton Club-New York, and its newest property, on the Big Island of Hawaii, was scheduled to open in early 2006.

Between the Hilton Grand Vacations Club and The Hilton Club, an affiliated program, the company has about 85,000 members so far. You can learn more at its Web site, *www.hiltongrandvacations.com*.

Hyatt Vacation Club

The Hyatt Vacation Club, which began operations in 1994, is affiliated with Interval International. The company is very close to the vest about its pricing and other information, as it wants you to contact Hyatt representatives directly to discuss its twelve resort properties:

- Beach House Resort, Key West, Florida
- Coconut Plantation, Bonita Springs, Florida
- Hyatt Aspen, Aspen, Colorado
- Hacienda del Mar, Dorado, Puerto Rico
- Highlands Inn, Carmel, California
- High Sierra Lodge, Incline Village, Nevada
- Main Street Station, Breckenridge, Colorado
- Mountain Lodge, Avon, Colorado
- Pinon Pointe, Sedona, Arizona
- Sunset Harbor, Key West, Florida
- Wild Oak Ranch, San Antonio, Texas
- Windward Pointe, Key West, Florida

You can find some information about each resort at Hyatt's Web site, *www.hyatt.com*. If you want in-depth materials, though, you will have to provide your name and contact information.

Marriott Vacation Club International

There are now a quarter million members in the Marriott Vacation Club, a following the company has built up since its entry into the timeshare marketplace in 1984. The timeshare units at its resorts are designed in one-, two-, and three-bedroom configurations, usually with full kitchens and private laundry facilities. It offers its units through different brand lines: Horizons by Marriott Vacation Club (typically the least expensive), Marriott Vacation Club International, Marriott Grand Residence Club, and The Ritz-Carlton Club.

The company has thirty-nine resorts in the United States, one in the U.S. Virgin Islands, and eight overseas. Among the U.S. properties, four are in Hawaii, six are in California, nine are in South Carolina, and ten are in Florida. The foreign resorts are located in Aruba, England, France, Spain, and Thailand. Marriott is also affiliated with Interval International, giving you access to all of that exchange company's resorts, as well.

For more information, check out the Marriott Web site, *www.vacationclub.com*.

Starwood Vacation Ownership

Starwood is the overarching brand that controls hotels under the well-known names Westin, Sheraton, Four Points by Sheraton, St. Regis, The Luxury Collection, and W Hotels. Its Vacation Ownership program began in 1980, and its network now includes more than 750 hotels and resorts in eighty countries. Timeshare units are configured with studio, one-, two-, and three-bedroom layouts and are as big as 2,800 square feet. Some of the resorts are affiliated with Resort Condominiums International, and others are affiliated with Interval International.

WorldMark by Trendwest

This is another points-based system in which you buy the right to use a certain number of points each year at any of the company's resorts. WorldMark by Trendwest is affiliated with the Resort Condominiums International exchange company, and your membership in WorldMark comes with a free first year of RCI membership dues.

Since the points-based system allows for two- or three-day vacations in addition to weeklong stays, this company promotes the fact that the majority of its resorts are within five hours' driving distance of major metropolitan areas in Washington state, California, Utah, Nevada, Colorado, Arizona, and Missouri. You can use your points at those resorts, for exchanges at other resorts worldwide, or for things like cruise-ship vacations, theme-park tickets, and more. Find out more by logging on to *www.worldmarktheclub.com*.

≡FAST FACT

In addition to being able to trade your timeshare unit purchase for longer vacations at Starwood's resorts, you also can use your accrued timeshare points for nightly rooms at any of its hotels or for services from affiliated airlines, credit card companies, and car rental agencies. To learn more, you can check out the company's Web site, *www .starwoodvo.com*.

Smaller Exchange Companies

While Resort Condominiums International and Interval International dominate the worldwide timeshare exchange marketplace—and while brand-name developers are working hard to get in on the game by affiliating with those two key players—there are also some smaller exchange companies worth considering if you plan to trade your timeshare unit usage for another person's.

These smaller exchange companies, in some cases, have been created by timeshare owners who want to do direct exchanges themselves without having to pay the larger exchange companies' fees. Sometimes, this means that the smaller exchange company simply charges a smaller fee, while at other times, it means that the smaller company merely connects you to other timeshare owners with whom you can make exchanges however you wish.

In still other cases, these smaller exchange companies are merely smaller versions of the larger companies, charging lower prices to undercut their mega-competition and even offering some of the same benefits that the larger companies do. These can include bonus time that you can buy in addition to the time you already own, and banking of weeks so that you can use two or three weeks' worth of time during one long vacation.

If you want to try to save a few bucks making timeshare unit exchanges and are not put off by what is perhaps a smaller selection of resorts or a bit more legwork on your part toward making an exchange, you may want to look into one of these smaller exchange firms. Keep in mind that because they have a smaller number of members than the larger exchange companies, they execute far fewer timeshare exchanges each year (sometimes one-tenth or less the amount of a company like Resort Condominiums International). For you, this may translate into some difficulties finding a taker for the timeshare unit you own, while in other cases, it may help you find a suitable trade for yourself much faster because you will have far fewer resorts to search among.

E-ALERT

When comparing smaller timeshare exchange companies with industry leaders, remember to take into account not just the per-exchange fees, but also the membership fees and any annual dues you will be asked to pay. If bonus time and banking of weeks is important to you, ensure that those services are available, as well.

Dial an Exchange

Dial an Exchange is a member of the American Resort Development Association, along with similar industry groups in Australia, New Zealand, Fiji, Europe, Canada, and Mexico. The company says its goal is to provide timeshare exchanges at a low cost with a minimum of aggravation, and it operates from offices in the

United States, the United Kingdom, Australia, and New Zealand.

The company charges no membership fee, and its exchange fees are based on your country of residence. If you live in the United States or Canada, for instance, you can make a domestic timeshare exchange for $99 or an international exchange for $125. Do note, though, that Hawaii—a popular U.S. exchange destination—is considered international under the Dial an Exchange program. Bonus time is available with this company, and you can bank your weeks for future use. The Dial an Exchange resorts are listed online at the company's Web site, *www.daelive.com.*

Hawaii Timeshare Exchange

Though this company's name hints at its geographical base, it does offer timeshare exchanges on the mainland United States and in international locations, as well. Joining is free, though you will be required to pay an annual membership fee. You can pay $50 per year, $125 for three years, or $199 for five years (if you pay the entire multi-year sums in advance).

You are allowed to bank your weeks for future use with Hawaii Timeshare Exchange, and upgrades are available for $175 plus the price of exchange. As of early 2006, internal exchanges—trading your week at your home resort for a different week at your home resort—cost $69, while external exchanges to other resorts cost $89. For a look at the resorts in the company's directory, log on to the Hawaii Timeshare Exchange Web site, *www.htse.net.*

Interchange Timeshare

Interchange Timeshare has been operating since 1988 and promotes itself as Australia's largest independent timeshare exchange company—though it does offer timeshare exchanges all over the world. The company charges no membership fee, no registration fee, and no other up-front fees except the cost of your exchange, which depends on your country of residence.

If you live in the United States or Canada, you would pay the same fees that Australian members did as of early 2006: $97 Australian dollars (about $71 U.S.) for exchanges in Australia, $132 Australian dollars (about $97 U.S.) for exchanges in New Zealand, and $143 Australian dollars (about $105 U.S.) for international exchanges. Bonus weeks are available for an additional fee of $100 to $350 Australian dollars per week (about $75 to $257 U.S.). To check out the timeshare resorts in the Interchange Timeshare directory, go to the company's Web site, *www.interchange-timeshare.com.au.*

Internet Exchange Services

Operating since 1996, Internet Exchange Services promotes itself as offering not just good deals on timeshare exchanges, but on buying and selling timeshare units on the resale market, as well. You are allowed to bank your weeks for future use with this company, and bonus weeks are available for as little as $79 per night. As of early 2006, exchange fees were $99 for domestic exchanges and $109 for international exchanges.

═══FAST FACT

The company's Web site resort directory does not list any international properties, but you can search to see what resorts are available in the United States. The site also will allow you to see the company's simple exchange-request form, so you will understand how the process works before becoming a member. To learn more about Internet Exchange Services, log on to the company's Web site at *www.internet-ies.com.*

Intervac

Intervac is not a timeshare exchange company per se, but it has been helping people from different nations to exchange homes worldwide since 1953. There is no reason you cannot use it as a timeshare exchange network, even though it is set up differently than most of the others that are described in this chapter. In fact, if you try Intervac with your timeshare unit and enjoy the experience, you can add your personal home or additional vacation property into its system, as well, for different levels of trades.

Memberships cost $50 per year for access to the Intervac United States directory and $70 for access to the company's international directory. If you join for two years and pay up front, you receive a 10 percent discount. With a three-year membership purchase, you will receive a 20 percent discount. The price of exchanges is determined by the people listing the properties, but the company claims you will save far more than you would by paying hotel rates (the same sales pitch given by timeshare developers). For more information about Intervac, log on to *www.intervacusa.com*.

OwnerTrades.com

OwnerTrades.com is exclusively for owners of Marriott Vacation Club timeshare units. The Web site promotes itself not just for exchanges, but also for resale and rental services. If you own a Marriott Vacation Club timeshare, you can list it for free on this Web site and have other owners contact you, but it will cost you $10 per year in membership fees if you want to be able to search the online database to find a resort at which you would like to take your vacation.

The Web site itself does not handle the exchange process; it merely puts two Marriott timeshare owners in touch with each other. It is then up to you, the timeshare owners, to make the trade yourselves—ensuring that all legal and other considerations are handled appropriately. To learn more, log on to the company's Web site at *www.ownertrades.com*.

Platinum Interchange

Platinum Interchange charges no membership fees or annual dues, and it is one of the bigger smaller exchange companies, doing tens of thousands of timeshare trades each year. The company charges $99 for domestic timeshare exchanges and $119 for international exchanges, with an upgrade fee of $87 if you want to trade your unit for one that is bigger or more in demand.

🧳 TRAVEL TIP

This company allows you the option of depositing the week you own into its system first, or requesting the timeshare resort you want to exchange for first. For more information, log on to the Platinum Interchange Web site, *www.platinuminterchange.com.*

San Francisco Exchange Company

Known as SFX, the San Francisco Exchange Company focuses on timeshare unit exchanges in the United States, Europe, Mexico, Canada, and the Caribbean. Platinum-level memberships cost $199 for three years, or $299 for five years, and entitle you to make exchanges at a rate of $129—no matter whether your trade is domestic or international. Platinum-level members also are entitled to a free upgrade in unit size, as well as a bonus week that can be requested from two years to just one week in advance.

There is no membership fee if you want to join at the gold level, but domestic and international exchanges are charged at a higher rate of $149. In addition, gold-level members do not get the additional benefits that platinum members receive. To learn more about the San Francisco Exchange Company, check out its Web site, *www .sfx-resorts.com.*

Timex Direct Exchange System

This company's Internet tagline is eye-catching: The site where timeshare owners can arrange exchanges themselves for about the cost of a cup of coffee. Membership is just $10, and it is good for three years' worth of exchanging any number of timeshare weeks that you own at your home resort. (Two weeks' worth of time exchanged over the course of three years amounts to $1.67 per exchange, or about the cost of that aforementioned cup of java.)

There are no additional membership fees. The company was created by a timeshare owner for use by other timeshare owners, and it has no brick-and-mortar offices. It is simply an Internet meeting place for timeshare owners from around the world—who arrange the exchanges themselves, including all the legal paperwork.

For more information about the Timex Direct Exchange System, go to the company's Web site, *www.timex.to.*

Trading Places International

This is another one of those bigger smaller exchange companies, arranging tens of thousands of timeshare exchanges each year (and claiming to be the third-largest timeshare exchange company in the world). The business is based in California. It began operating more than thirty years ago as a full-service travel agency and now specializes in everything from timeshare exchanges to timeshare resort management, rentals, and resale.

The company's philosophy is that 80 percent of timeshare owners want to exchange their units for the same 20 percent of other resorts in Hawaii, Mexico, and the United States, and so it focuses on servicing the resorts in those areas that it sees as high demand—as well as in exchanges for cruise-ship vacations. There is no mandatory membership fee to join, but you can receive a $30-per-week-traded discount, along with other discounts including unit upgrades, if you are willing to pay the $79 membership fee. If you sign up for a five-year membership, the cost is $314, an $81 savings over the year-to-year fee. The exchange fees themselves vary widely, from about $110 to $160. Learn more about Trading Places International by logging on to its Web site, *www.tradingplaces.com.*

TUG Direct Exchange

This Internet-based service is provided by the highly popular Timeshare User's Group, or TUG. It is exactly as its name explains: a direct-exchange service that brings together timeshare owners who wish to arrange exchanges among themselves. Timeshare units are available all over the world, and people are able to list their units on this Web site for free. If you want to enjoy the full benefits of the TUG Web site (and there are many, especially for first-time timeshare unit owners), you need to pay a $15 membership fee.

You can browse the direct exchange directory by logging on to the group's Web site, *www.tug2.net.* To get to the direct exchange page, click on "site index," then "direct exchange database" (to make a trade) or "direct exchange list" (to post your timeshare unit as available).

VacationEarth

The VacationEarth marketing message is that by using its services, you can exchange your timeshare unit for prime weeks that are unavailable through the "big two" exchange companies, Resort Condominiums International and Interval International. These weeks include yet-to-be-sold units in new timeshare resorts, foreclosed timeshare units, redline weeks (during which owners cannot use their units because of unpaid maintenance fees), and more.

VacationEarth, based in South Florida, charges $99 per week exchanged. The company does not list any membership fees. To find out more, check out the VacationEarth Web site at *www .vacationearth.com.*

CHAPTER 2

Is Timeshare Right for You?

NOW THAT YOU HAVE a general understanding of how the broader timeshare universe functions, it is time to figure out whether you want to become a part of it—and, if yes, how you might best fit in. There are fixed and floating weeks, deeded and right-to-use properties, and the all-important financial questions about whether a timeshare unit will actually save you money over the long term. This chapter will help you understand exactly what you are buying so that you can make the most of a timeshare purchase.

The Ideal Timeshare Owner

Close to 90 percent of timeshare owners who are surveyed say they are happy with their purchase, according to various studies that the timeshare industry promotes. It is safe to say that within that 90 percent—thousands upon thousands of people—there are people who are older, people who are younger, people who like to travel abroad, people who like to stay closer to home, people who like to visit new places each year, people who like to return to the same resort annually, and pretty much every combination in between.

So how do you know if you might fit in among those ideal timeshare owners, the people who say they are happy with their unit purchases? Start by taking a look at this list and seeing whether any of these statements describes you:

- You take a vacation for at least one full week every year.
- You spend a fair amount of your vacation budget on lodging.
- You would prefer to have larger vacation accommodations, such as a full kitchen, a living room, and additional bedrooms.
- You do not want to do year-round maintenance on a vacation house with your own two hands.
- You want to return to the same place year after year.
- You are willing to be flexible in changing your vacation resort, perhaps selecting two or three different resorts and visiting the one you are able to get an exchange for during a given year.
- You are willing to visit only resorts in your timeshare exchange company network for the length of your ownership—or trade your unit's value for other things that your ownership entitles you to, such as cruise-ship vacations and car rental discounts.
- You are willing to make a standard monthly payment for the next seven or ten years toward your vacation lodging, as opposed to saving money at your leisure and spending different amounts on your vacation lodging each year.

The odds are, if you are like most people, you do not see yourself in every single one of these statements. But if you see yourself in a fair number of them, timeshare unit ownership might be a good idea for you.

Ideal timeshare owners can be thirty years old or ninety years old. They can be golfers or skiers or sunbathers, and they can want to travel close to home or around the globe. The important thing to remember is that it is not whether you want to vacation that makes you an ideal timeshare owner. It is *how* you want to vacation that plays a much greater role—and how you want to pay for the vacations that you will be buying, timeshare or not, for the next decade or more.

What You're Buying

No matter which resort you choose, and no matter which exchange company you work with, it is important to know exactly what you are buying. There are different kinds of properties, different kinds of exchange systems, different kinds of fees, and so on and so forth. Your best bet is to go into any sales presentation with a sound understanding of timeshare basics, so that you will be able to focus on differences in the "small type" when it comes time to decide which unit you want to purchase.

In its simplest form, timeshare is exactly what its name implies: a sharing of time at a vacation resort. You are buying the right to use anything from a studio apartment to a three-bedroom villa for a given period of time each year, when other timeshare owners are not using it. Remember: This is not the same as buying the whole resort and watching it appreciate in value like a wholly owned waterfront home. This is a less-expensive alternative to making a massive real-estate purchase, one whose primary selling factor is that it is supposed to be a hedge against vacation inflation.

═ FAST FACT

Remember: When you buy a timeshare unit, you are essentially buying a financial hedge against vacation inflation, or the rising cost of hotel rooms. Do not expect to reap large real-estate investment gains from your timeshare purchase. Resale values can be 50 percent lower than original prices—or even less.

What does that mean? Basically, the sales pitch is that if you buy into a timeshare program, you will—over the course of ten or twenty years—end up spending less on your vacation accommodations than you otherwise would have if you had plunked down cash for hotel rooms during the same period of time.

The Marriott Vacation Club Web site offers an electronic calculator to help you understand this principle. It lets you plug in the amount of money you typically spend on hotel rooms during the course of a weeklong vacation, then adds 5 percent inflation to that number for each of the next ten, twenty, and thirty years. The resulting number—the amount you are estimated to be facing for hotel-room payments during the next three decades' worth of vacations—is what the company wants you to use for comparison when considering purchasing one of its timeshare units.

For instance, according to the calculator, if you spend $150 per night on hotel rooms this year, you can anticipate spending $251.32 per night in ten years, $409.37 per night in twenty years, and $666.81 per night in thirty years (based on a 5 percent per year inflation model). By taking one week's worth of vacation each year for the next thirty years, at those rates, the calculator shows that you will have spent $75,341.65 on hotel rooms. Some other examples from the Marriott calculator:

- If you currently spend $250 per night on hotel rooms, your thirty-year total for one week a year of vacation lodging will be $125,569.42
- If you currently spend $350 per night on hotel rooms, your thirty-year total for one week a year of vacation lodging will be $175,797.19.
- If you currently spend $450 per night on hotel rooms, your thirty-year total for one week of vacation lodging will be $226,024.96.

Those are certainly some big numbers, and they're exactly the kind of prices Marriott and other timeshare companies want you to consider when deciding whether to purchase a $25,000 or $50,000 timeshare unit. It may seem like a lot of money up front, but when you compare it with the numbers for those hotel outlays, timeshare suddenly looks like a much better deal. And, when you compare the amenities of a private villa against those of a typical hotel room, the deal looks even sweeter.

Beyond the Sales Pitch

There are, of course, other factors that you should consider beside the numbers. For starters, some people who bought timeshares during the past ten years have not seen a 5 percent per year rise in lodging costs in the locations where their units are based. In 2001 and 2002, for example, the monitoring company Ernst & Young reported 1 and 2 percent declines in the average rates of hotel rooms. This means that anyone who bought a timeshare before or during those years likely would have paid about the same amount, or less, for hotel rooms during that time period versus a timeshare.

Also, you must consider whether you actually believe you will keep—and use—your timeshare unit for twenty or thirty years. Timeshares, because of their high front-end costs, typically do not tend to become good bargains until they have been used for some time. If you buy a $20,000 timeshare unit at 15 percent financing and use it for only two years before selling it, you are going to have paid a heck of a lot more for two weeks of vacation time than you would have by just staying in hotels instead.

⚡ E-ALERT

When comparing the cost of a timeshare unit against the cost of renting hotel rooms for the next few decades, be sure to include additional costs that come with the timeshare, such as mortgage interest payments, annual maintenance fees, special assessments, and exchange fees.

Another factor is miscellaneous fees that you will be required to pay during your decades-long period of timeshare use. For starters, if you finance your purchase, you will have interest payments. These are typically higher than first-home mortgage payments, as timeshare developers set the interest rates themselves, sometimes in the neighborhood of 15 percent or even more.

You also have to factor in your timeshare unit's annual maintenance fees, which typically average from $200 to $600 per year. That may sound high, but when you compare those numbers with having to maintain your own vacation home year-round, the timeshare maintenance fees are nominal.

There are also special assessment fees that you will be required to pay from time to time, for things like major beachfront upgrades, golf course work, and the like. And don't forget those exchange fees that you read about in Chapter 1. As of late 2005, they were in the neighborhood of $125 per exchange.

Many of these fees and surcharges, of course, will rise along with inflation over the years, just as hotel prices are likely to rise. In some cases, you will come out ahead by owning a timeshare. But in other cases, you might not.

If you simply want to return to the same home resort year after year, and if you can get a good deal on a timeshare unit that you absolutely love, buying it may be a no-brainer. After all, buying a timeshare is, in part, an investment in the quality of vacations you hope to enjoy for many years to come.

That is also true if you want to exchange your timeshare unit for others: Your exchange company's rating system will give you some peace of mind about the quality of vacation and resort you will enjoy no matter where in the world you decide to go. Economically speaking, though, if you intend to make a lot of timeshare exchanges based on the long-term financing of a unit that you buy today, then your overall financial benefits will depend on several factors: how often you vacation, how much you tend to spend on lodging, whether you choose a high-priced area for your home resort, and what type of timeshare you buy.

Types of Timeshares

You already know how often you vacation and how much you tend to spend on your family's accommodations. Before you consider time-share resort destinations (which you will read more about in upcoming chapters), you should think about exactly what kind of timeshare you want to buy. Your choices will be deeded or right-to-use properties, which you will be able to purchase in either weeklong units of time or in points that are similar to airline frequent-flyer miles.

Deeded Properties

A deeded timeshare is exactly what it sounds like: a timeshare that comes with a deed. When you buy a deeded timeshare, you are gaining ownership rights to your timeshare unit. This—at least in the United States—usually means that you own your timeshare forever (or "in perpetuity," as the lawyers like to say), and that you can sell it or pass it on to your children or grandchildren just as you might with any other type of real-estate investment that you purchase. Deeded timeshares also often give you the right to rent your unit during years when you cannot use it.

Right-to-Use Properties

A right-to-use timeshare unit is also exactly what it sounds like: A timeshare that gives you the right to use somebody else's property for a certain number of years or for a specific number of times.

≡FAST FACT

Right-to-use timeshares do not come with deeds, and thus are not transferable upon your death. You may be able to rent your right-to-use timeshare during the years when you cannot use it, but you will have to check the fine print of your specific contract for details about that.

For instance, you might buy a timeshare unit that gives you rights to one week per year for the next twenty years. Or you might buy a timeshare unit that gives you the right to use it twenty times during the next twenty years, meaning you could use up all of your usage rights in one year if you wanted to vacation for five months straight.

No matter whether your timeshare unit is a deeded or a right-to-use property, you will be buying either time in the form of weeks or time in the form of points that you cash in.

Weeks-Based Systems

Timeshare units traditionally have been sold in the form of weeks, meaning that you buy the right to use your unit for a specified number of weeks each year (most often, one week).

Most timeshare units are designed for annual use, though there are some plans that allow you to become a biennial timeshare-unit owner. This means that you end up being able to use your timeshare unit every other year—usually designated as odd or even year usage. Biennial timeshares typically cost less than annual timeshares, simply because you are purchasing less usage time.

There are two kinds of weeks: fixed and floating. Each has its benefits and its drawbacks, depending on how you like to vacation.

Fixed Weeks

Fixed weeks are seven-day units of time that you own at your home resort and that do not change from year to year. If you buy the third week of the year at a Colorado resort, you can show up at that Colorado resort every third week of every year until the end of your contract, or forever if it is a deeded property. (You can see the weeks calendar that timeshare resorts use in Appendix B.) You sometimes will have to make reservations annually, just to let your resort and exchange company know that you do, in fact, plan to use your week, but short of that, you will have few other tasks in terms of using your timeshare unit each year.

A common misperception is that when you buy a fixed week, you absolutely must take your timeshare vacation during that week every year. This is *not* true. All that buying a fixed week means is that you own the same week every year. You still are entitled to trade that week for somebody else's week, during a different time of year, at another resort.

⚡ E-ALERT

Buying a fixed week of timeshare does not mean that you have to take your vacation during the same week every single year for the next thirty or forty years. It simply means that you own a specific week of time, which you are allowed to trade for other people's time-share units during any season of the year.

In fact, many people buy high-demand fixed week timeshares for the sole purpose of trading them. The week between Christmas and New Year's Day, for instance, is very popular in Orlando because children are out of school and many families want to visit Walt Disney World. If you are the person who owns that fixed week at a popular timeshare resort near the Magic Kingdom, you should have very strong trading power should you want to exchange your week for someone else's.

Other people with an eye on the worldwide marketplace might buy a high-demand week during the middle or end of August in Spain's Canary Islands, where many European travelers enjoy taking their vacations during that time of year. Americans who own such timeshares may never once set foot in them, but can trade them with the same kind of high demand as someone else might closer to home.

Investing a larger sum in a fixed-week timeshare in a popular location during a high-demand week, then, can essentially give you all the flexibility of—or even more than—a floating week timeshare.

Of course, if you really do want to return to the same destination at the same time every year, a fixed week makes the most sense for you. Some examples include families with small children that want to vacation during the summertime or elderly couples who want to escape to warmer climates during colder months.

Floating Weeks

When you buy a floating week timeshare, you are buying the right to one week of timeshare use, usually during a given season of each year. By seasons, the exchange companies do not mean spring, summer, fall, and winter. Instead, they mean high-demand, low-demand, and everything in between.

Different exchange companies have different names and coding systems for seasons of the year. Resort Condominiums International, for instance, uses red, white, and blue color codes to indicate high-, medium-, and low-demand seasons. Interval International also uses red to identify high-demand seasons, but uses yellow and green to indicate medium- and low-demand seasons, respectively.

Sometimes, a resort's timeshare units are all considered red. Las Vegas and Orlando are good examples. These are year-round hot spots for vacationers from all over the world, so the timeshare units are always in high demand. If you purchase a floating week during red season in Las Vegas, your vacation could occur any time of year.

Of course, floating week timeshare units make the most sense if you maintain a busy schedule that changes from year to year. But bear in mind that if you buy a floating week, you will have more vacation-planning tasks than a fixed-week unit owner. You will have to plan ahead and request your floating week of choice as early as possible in order to get the vacation time you want later in the year.

Points-Based Systems

Points-based systems are relatively new to the timeshare marketplace. They are similar to the airline frequent flyer and credit card company points systems in that you are essentially given a number of points in bulk that you can spend as currency on whatever you choose.

These points systems were introduced into the world of timeshares to accommodate owners who did not want to take an entire week of vacation each year. With the points, these people could cash in two or three days' worth of points one month, and then another two or three days' worth of points several months later, allowing for two long weekends instead of one long vacation.

In some cases, leftover points that aren't quite enough to purchase a vacation can be used for other things, such as car rentals, airline tickets, and the like. With brand-name development companies that also own hotels, such as Hilton and Hyatt, you may also be able to use timeshare points as payment for overnight hotel stays outside of your regular timeshare vacation period. Your individual timeshare contract should spell out these options. Keep in mind that they will vary depending on which resort and which exchange company you choose.

▮ TRAVEL TIP

Any timeshare unit you purchase under a points-based system will be, by its very nature, a floating week. You can use the points whenever you choose, for whatever you want, and you often will have the option of buying additional points each year that you can put toward things like cruise-ship vacations and other getaways.

The downside that some people see to the points-based systems is that the points may not keep up with inflation—a major reason for buying a timeshare in the first place.

Why not? It's simple: With a weeks-based system, a week is a week is a week. No matter what interest rates do during the next thirty years, the third week in August is still going to be the third week in August. On the other hand, with a points-based system, a purchase made in 2006 may entitle you to 10,000 resort points per year, which, in 2006, may be enough for one week of vacation. Who is to say that in 2026, 10,000 points will still be the equivalent of one week's vacation time? Just look to the airline frequent flyer programs as an example—tickets that used to cost 20,000 points sometimes now cost 50,000 points—and it's easy to see that points can go down in value just as easily as they can go up.

On the other hand, the value of points *can* go up—something a weeks-based system is not likely to do (unless the government changes our calendar to an eight-day week, giving you an extra day of vacation for the same price!). Some owners of Disney timeshare points, for instance, have seen the value of their points increase. How? The price has gone up for newcomers who want to buy the same amount of points today as those other owners bought for less money a few years ago. The folks who bought first are entitled to the same amount of points as their newcomer colleagues, but at a lower cost overall.

The point, then, is that points-based systems have more built-in uncertainty than weeks-based systems. The points-based systems are definitely a bit more of a financial gamble over the long-term, but that may be a gamble you are willing to take if you foresee yourself needing the flexibility of two- or three-day vacation choices that points-based systems offer compared with weeklong plans, which are always seven-day vacation periods.

Fractional Ownership Programs

If you travel more than a week each year for vacation, you may want to consider a fractional timeshare program. Fractional programs divide the year into fractions (hence the name), allotting a few weeks' to a few months' usage time per purchase. In other words, instead of buying a week or a week's worth of points, you can buy a month or two worth of time at your favorite resort.

It sounds higher-end than other timeshare programs, and it certainly can be. After all, two to thirteen weeks of vacation time each year doesn't come cheap, no matter how you finance it. In 2001, the average price for a fractional week of timeshare ownership was $34,000—but you may be surprised to learn that the average household income for Marriott Vacation Club fractional owners was just $130,000 (far from millionaire status). Certainly, there are some very high-end and far lower-end properties entering into the equations that produced those figures, but the point is that fractional ownership can be a viable time-share option even if you are not a recent lottery winner.

≡FAST FACT

Not all timeshare resorts offer fractional ownership programs. Overall, there are far fewer fractional ownership properties than there are traditional timeshare resorts, and many of the fractional properties are quite high-end.

Usually, the people who buy fractional timeshares either live in the same region as their resort or they plan to visit that place frequently. A good example would be snowbirds who want to spend winters in Florida and summers in New England. If you are of this inclination and want to spend three months a year in the same place, a fractional timeshare could be a smart financial option compared with ownership and maintenance costs on a second home.

Sometimes, fractional units are even used for business. This can make a great deal of sense over the long term in high-priced cities such as New York and London, where prime-location hotel rooms usually start around $250 or $350 per night. If you own a business in one of those cities, for instance, you can put clients up at your timeshare instead of being at the mercy of hotel prices day in and day out.

What's Not Included

Your timeshare purchase includes many things, including:

- A guaranteed week's worth of accommodations at a resort of your choosing every year

- The option of exchanging your timeshare unit for someone else's in a different location you've always wanted to visit
- The possibility of realizing substantial financial savings over several decades' time compared with outlays during the same number of years for hotel and motel rooms
- Vacation accommodations that often are larger and better-outfitted than standard hotel rooms
- Use of your exchange company's rating system to help you determine which worldwide resorts meet your demands and expectations
- The opportunity to own a vacation retreat without having to do year-round maintenance yourself

But there are some things—important things—that are not included in the base price of your timeshare unit. Many of these things are ongoing costs, as opposed to one-time fees, and it is important that you factor them into the price of your timeshare purchase when deciding whether it will be of good value to you over the long term.

Following is a look at many of the major additional expenses that go along with timeshare ownership. There are also smaller expenses and situational expenses that you many encounter when you decide to exchange, sell, or rent your timeshare unit, but you will learn more about those fees in later chapters.

Annual Maintenance Fees

Every resort charges timeshare unit owners an annual maintenance fee, usually in the neighborhood of $200 to $600. This fee covers everything from upkeep of the grounds to maid service and staff salaries. Sometimes, it also includes property taxes that are paid to the local government, but this is not always the case—and you should ask up front to determine whether you will be receiving a separate tax bill each year.

As prices for goods and wages tend to rise over the years, you should expect your annual maintenance fees to rise over the years, as well. A good rule before purchasing a timeshare unit is to ask the developer what the maintenance fees have been for several of the preceding years, so that you can anticipate whether a big upcharge is about to be levied.

Special Assessments

Special assessments are one-time fees charged to timeshare owners for things like capital improvements. Beachfront and golf-course timeshare resorts tend to have a fair number of special assessments, as their properties require more nonroutine maintenance than other types of properties. Things like beach erosion repair and replacement sod cost money, and those costs get passed on to you, the timeshare owner.

▌ TRAVEL TIP

You are not likely to see a special assessment charge every single year, but you should expect to pay one at least every three to five years. If a developer promises you no special assessment charges, you know you are being had. After all, who would want to vacation at a property that makes no improvements during twenty or thirty years of time?

Mortgage Interest Payments

If you finance your timeshare purchase, you will have to factor mortgage interest payments into the overall cost of your timeshare.

Do not expect to get a timeshare mortgage for the same low rate that you may have gotten on your primary residence mortgage. Most timeshare mortgages are held by the developers of the resorts, not by banks, and thus the developers can—and do—charge far higher interest rates. If you finance a $10,000 timeshare, an interest rate that high can add a good $5,000 to the overall cost of your unit during the course of your loan.

Exchange Company Fees

Exchange fees are the payments you must make to your exchange company every time you decide to trade your timeshare unit for someone else's. These fees are how companies such as Interval International and Resort Condominiums International make their money, as they do not own the actual resorts where you purchase your unit. Again, as these fees are the main way the exchange companies earn their profits, you should expect them to rise along with inflation during the course of your timeshare ownership.

⚡ E-ALERT

If you plan to make a lot of exchanges during the length of your ownership, be sure to also factor in your exchange company's annual membership fee, and any additional fees for other services you might use including timeshare unit upgrades and bonus-week purchases.

Conversion Fees

In most cases, if you own a fixed or floating week of timeshare use and want to convert it into points that you can use for something else (say, airline miles or a cruise-ship vacation), you will have to pay a conversion fee. This fee varies from resort to resort and from exchange company to exchange company, but generally, you will not be able to make those kinds of conversions for free.

Should you come up short on points after converting the timeshare you own, you usually will be able to purchase additional points to make up the difference. This can be helpful if your timeshare is worth 10,000 points, but the cruise of your dreams costs 10,500 points.

CHAPTER 3

What Kind of Property Best Suits Your Needs?

UNDERSTANDING THE FINANCIAL and legal aspects of timeshare ownership is the hard part. Once you decide that buying a unit is a good idea, you get to explore all of the exciting resorts that offer timeshares around the world. Whether you want a studio apartment or a three-bedroom villa, you can find it on the ski slopes, at the beach, on the links, or beyond. Put your imagination into high gear, because it is time to envision the vacation resort of your dreams.

Consider the Location and Amenities

The majority of timeshare resorts that exist today, and that are being built for future customers, are located on beachfront property. Why? Because that is where most people say they want to spend their hard-earned vacation time and money. If you want to catch a few rays and swim in the surf, you will find no shortage of timeshare resort options from South Africa to the Big Island of Hawaii.

Timeshare resorts are also being built to revolve around golf courses and spas, which are typically big draws for vacationers all over the world, and near places like Walt Disney World and Las Vegas, which draw massive crowds all year round. Every timeshare resort is built to suit its environment, which is important to consider when deciding which facility might be the best one for you.

Different types of resorts offer different amenities. A tiki bar, for instance, would be more suitable at a beachfront resort than a driving range, which may be among your must-have amenities at a golf course timeshare resort. If you are a winter-sports enthusiast, you may prefer downhill skiing trails to cross-country pathways, but you may not care whether snowmobiles are available for daily rentals. The important thing to remember as you sift through your timeshare resort options is that your resort should offer all of the amenities that will allow you to make the most of your vacation time there. The only one who knows what amenities you and your family need is, well, you. Take a few minutes to think about what kinds of activities you have enjoyed in the past and what you think you might like to do in the future, and then you can weed out timeshare resorts that lack those options.

TRAVEL TIP

While many resorts can be classified as beachfront, golf, spa, and the like, plenty of resorts offer a combination of vacation services and amenities. Some golf resorts, for instance, are located on the oceanfront where water-skiing and swimming are available. If your family has multiple interests, a multiple-amenity resort is likely to suit you best.

Not all beachfront resorts offer scuba diving, for instance, but that is all right if you are not a certified underwater explorer. By the same token, all urban timeshare resorts may not offer concierge services, but that is okay if you already know your way around town and prefer to make your own plans for the week with friends from the area. Some wilderness timeshare resorts lack televisions and Internet access, but you may find that a blessing if your goal is to tune out and get lost amid the forest animals for a week every year.

Here is a look at some typical resorts and the kinds of amenities they offer. Keep in mind that all of the resorts named in the following pages offer far more to see and do than what is mentioned under their particular activity heading. They are listed as examples of what is out there in terms of amenities—and how resorts can vary greatly in the ways that they provide them.

Beachfront Timeshare Resorts

Timeshare resorts that hug the oceanfront are being built everywhere from South Florida to South Africa. They are, by far, the most popular style of timeshare resort, and there is no end in sight to how many will be built worldwide.

Key features to look for when buying a unit in a beachfront resort include water views from a private balcony, beach bars that offer snacks or light meals that you can eat while in a bathing suit, self-controlled air conditioning units, and plenty of water-sports activities such as water-skiing and sailing. Horseback riding and scuba diving also are popular activities, though not usually ones that make or break a resort's reputation with the majority of timeshare users.

You also should check into the timeshare resort's policy regarding towels, because some resorts charge an extra fee for beach towel use. That will be a key additional charge in a beachfront environment.

Absolute Private Residence Club at Samui Peninsula, Koh Samui, Thailand

This Interval International resort, located on the southeastern seaboard of Thailand, has earned the exchange company's prestigious Five Star Award. The resort sits on a palm-fringed beach full of water sports, with a well-appointed spa housed in traditional Thai-style pavilions. Nearby amenities include tennis, golf, and scuba diving. You also can go on an elephant trek, visit the Big Buddha statue, or stand before the Na Muang Waterfall.

Temperatures are consistently warm all year round in this part of Thailand, though rainfall typically peaks during October, November, and December. If you get caught in heavy showers, you can always while away your time while indulging in award-winning Thai dishes and seafood specialties at the resort's Royal Siam Restaurant.

Beacon Island Hotel, Plettenberg Bay, Western Cape, South Africa

This Resort Condominiums International resort has earned the exchange company's prestigious Gold Crown ranking. It is located on Plettenberg Bay in South Africa—a longtime European getaway destination that is growing in worldwide popularity. The Beacon Island Hotel is on a private peninsula overlooking the ocean, and its amenities include a restaurant called the Captain's Cabin where you can dine next to expansive windows that buffer the breaking surf as it crashes up toward your table.

≡FAST FACT

Remember: Beachfront resorts are the most popular timeshare options worldwide, not just for travelers from the United States. That can be an important point when it comes time for resale or exchanges.

Even if you intend to visit a far-away beachfront property like this one only a few times during the tenure of your timeshare-unit ownership, you will have the benefit of being able to play into the worldwide exchange market and take advantage of European travel patterns.

Grand Seas Resort, Daytona Beach, Florida

Located directly on Daytona Beach in Florida, this Interval International resort has earned the exchange company's Five Star Award. It offers two outdoor swimming pools, one indoor swimming pool, a full-service health spa, a restaurant, a children's playground, a miniature golf course, a children's pool, and more. The resort is also within driving distance of the major Orlando theme-park attractions, as well as the Kennedy Space Center.

The resort boasts more than 800 feet of beachfront property, with activities including boating, snorkeling, scuba diving, and water-skiing. All of the timeshare units have full kitchens, whirlpool tubs, and sleeper sofas for your tagalong guests.

Hilton Grand Vacations Club at Hilton Hawaiian Village, Oahu, Hawaii

Located on the world-famous Waikiki Beach on the island of Oahu, this timeshare resort boasts three swimming pools, a spa and health center, multiple restaurants and lounges, nearby golf, and even a barber shop should you miss your appointment before leaving for your vacation. That is all very impressive, of course, but the real draw here is the beach and all of the water sports activities available on it.

This twenty-two-acre resort is landscaped in keeping with traditional Hawaiian themes, which is a nice selling point compared with other properties that simply plop a cookie-cutter building down into the middle of paradise.

The Westin St. John Resort and Villas, St. John

This Starwood timeshare resort is in the U.S. Virgin Islands on St. John, most of which is dedicated parkland—and spectacular beaches. Swimming, scuba diving, parasailing, snorkeling, windsurfing, fishing, kayaking, and more are mere footsteps away from the timeshare units on a private, 1,200-foot white sand beach.

One of the nice things about this beachfront resort is that it offers three restaurants and poolside lounges on site, meaning you never have to leave the compound for a change of scenery if that is your preference. On the other hand, this timeshare resort also offers Jeep rentals that will let you go exploring around the island, including its varied hiking and snorkeling trails. The point is that you and your family will have options outside of sitting on the beach every day (unless you want to do just that, which is okay, too!).

Golf Course Timeshare Resorts

You will find timeshare resorts built around lavishly sculpted golf courses everywhere from Arizona to Aruba. Some timeshare units line links-style courses, which overlook the ocean, while others are inland and offer pristine views of mountainsides and riverbeds.

Other key amenities to look for are the number of golf course holes (eighteen will do, but thirty-six unique holes are better), the golfing benefits that come with timeshare unit ownership (such as preferred tee times), and the view of the course from your unit's private balcony.

Marriott's Shadow Ridge

Located in Palm Desert, California, this timeshare resort has an eighteen-hole, Nick Faldo–designed golf course on site. It is a par-seventy-one course of 7,006 yards, challenging enough for most people but not so difficult that it will leave you hurling your brand-new irons into one of the many scenic lakes on the property. A driving range and putting green are also on site, and equipment rental and golf lessons are available at the Faldo Golf Institute on the resort's property.

What is nice about this Southern California timeshare resort for golfers is that in addition to the Shadow Ridge course, there are seven other nearby golf courses from which to choose a day of play—adding great variety to any vacation. Some are 18-hole courses, others are 36-hole courses; some are highly challenging, while others are easier designs.

Sheraton PGA Vacation Resort

This Starwood property is located in Port St. Lucie, Florida, about forty-five minutes north of Palm Beach. The resort is literally in the backyard of the PGA Village, which is owned and operated by the Professional Golf Association. For golfers, it simply doesn't get much better.

PGA Village includes three courses, two designed by legendary golfer Tom Fazio and one designed by equally impressive golfer Pete Dye. PGA Village also offers a historical center, a six-hole short course, three practice putting greens, a separate practice range, stations where you can receive videotaped analysis of your swing, a private instruction area for lessons with a PGA professional, a PGA golf shop, and a golf-themed restaurant.

🧳 TRAVEL TIP

When buying a timeshare unit at a golf course resort, pay close attention to the name of the golf course designer. Courses that were created through consultation with members of the Professional Golf Association—such as PGA greats Arnold Palmer, Jack Nicklaus, and Nick Faldo—will be more in demand than courses without such star power to their names.

In addition, the village includes the PGA Learning Center, a thirty-five-acre golf park where you can practice at chipping and bunker stations, learn workout techniques that will improve muscles specific to golfing, testing areas for different kinds of golf balls and the newest brand-name equipment, and more.

Willowbrook at Lake Harmony, Pennsylvania

This Interval International resort in Lake Harmony, Pennsylvania, has earned the exchange company's Five Star Award and is part of its Golf Resort Program, which includes discounted greens fees, discounted lessons, advance tee times, and more for the exchange company's members. There is a twenty-seven-hole championship golf course on site, and the 585-yard eleventh hole is said to offer one of the most spectacular views of the rolling Pocono Mountains in the entire Northeastern United States. Carts are provided, as the holes are generously spaced. The resort's dedicated Web site, *www.splitrockresort.com*, even has an interactive section where you can research each hole's layout before playing the course.

The closest airport is in Scranton, Pennsylvania, about thirty miles away. Additional amenities at the resort include boating, fishing, bicycling, tennis, and more. There are several restaurants on site, and organized children's activities are available.

Skiing Timeshare Resorts

Ski buffs have made winter-destination timeshare resorts popular in places you have likely heard of, such as Vail and Aspen, Colorado, but you can find excellent skiing and lovely resort accommodations elsewhere, too—sometimes as far away as New Zealand, in the South Pacific.

Key amenities to consider when looking at a timeshare unit at a skiing resort include private fireplaces for warming up after a day on the slopes, a good mix of downhill and cross-country trails, and indoor/outdoor whirlpool tubs for relaxing at night. Also be sure you understand the resort's policy on lift tickets, ski equipment rentals, and the like, so that you will not be surprised by additional charges.

Marriott's Summit Watch

Located in Park City, Utah, this resort offers two-bedroom villas with private fireplaces and alpine views. Snow skiing trails are just a mile away, and ski-equipment lockers are available on site. The resort also boasts a heated indoor swimming pool, hot tub, and whirlpool.

≡FAST FACT

Many ski resorts double as warm-weather getaways during the summer months, offering things such as hiking and mountain biking. These kinds of timeshare resorts are inherently more financially stable than one-season-only resorts, a factor worth noting when deciding which resort you want to pin your hopes on for the next decade or more of timeshare ownership.

Summit Watch is a year-round timeshare resort that, in the summertime, offers everything from hunting to horseback riding and fly fishing. These kinds of activities give it the feel of a wilderness timeshare resort, making it a natural choice if you are the type of person who likes to snow ski, but who wants options for other activities, as well.

The Lodge at Kananaskis

This Resort Condominiums International Gold Crown property is in the heart of the Canadian Rockies, in the province of Alberta. Your timeshare will allow you to ski the slopes of Mount Allan—site of the 1988 Winter Olympics—or the nearby well-known slopes of Fortress Mountain, Norguay, Sunshine, and Lake Louise. Cross-country trails and ski instruction are also within a couple of miles of the resort site.

One of the nice things about The Lodge at Kananaskis is that it serves as an all-year-round destination, with summertime activities including boating, golf, tennis, and horseback riding. The fact that it is doing business year-round is a nice peace of mind factor toward the resort's long-term financial stability.

The Ponds at Foxhollow

Located in the Berkshires town of Lenox, Massachusetts, this all-seasons resort offers downhill and cross-country skiing during the wintertime. It is near the Norman Rockwell Museum and Tanglewood (where the Boston Symphony Orchestra performs and holds a Jazz Festival each summer), and the resort itself has earned a Five Star Award from its affiliated exchange company, Interval International.

The Ponds sits on a 223-acre site and has just forty-eight condominium units, each with fireplaces and some with second bedrooms and lofts. Additional amenities at the resort include indoor and outdoor swimming pools, a sauna, an exercise room, and trails for walking, hiking, or bicycling. Wine and cheese parties are held in the library on Fridays, and local baby-sitters are available.

Spa Timeshare Resorts

Timeshare resorts specializing in spa treatments are popping up more and more frequently as the spa craze continues to broaden across the United States and the world. Many timeshare resorts offer spas in addition to their other amenities, but at a limited number of resorts, it is the spa itself that is the main attraction.

If a deluxe spa is your number one priority, look for a timeshare resort that offers not just facials and manicures, but also the newest treatments, including microdermabrasion and nonsurgical facelifts. The highest-end spas offer at least a half-dozen different styles of massage, plus body treatments including scrubs and polishing, soothing treatments, such as aromatherapy and steam baths, and beauty packages that can be purchased to create an entire day of pampering for men and women alike.

Marriott's Club Son Antem Golf Resort and Spa

The name of this timeshare resort in tourist-friendly Mallorca, Spain, is a sure tip-off that spa amenities are among the top on-site priorities—not just a tiny little throwaway back-room operation that the developer refers to as a spa to generate more business.

Available treatments include body wraps, body scrubs, facials, fitness counseling, foot baths, a lap pool, manicures, massages (and massage lessons), paraffin hand treatments, pedicures, a plunge pool, a steam room, and therapy baths. These are in addition to the sauna and steam rooms that are part of the on-site fitness center.

The Inn at Bay Harbor

This resort is in Bay Harbor, Michigan, on the shore of Lake Michigan's Little Traverse Bay. It has earned the Five Star Award from Interval International and offers a full-service spa and salon with treatments including massages, body wraps, facials, manicures, pedicures, bronzing, waxing, makeup application, and more. You can rent the entire spa facility for a group day of beauty or purchase gift certificates for packages including a three-and-a-half-hour men's treatment session (including a hot towel facial, a deep-tissue massage, a haircut, and more).

The Inn at Bay Harbor is also part of Interval International's Golf Resort Program, which includes discounted greens fees, discounted lessons, advance tee times, and more for the exchange company's members. A course is on site, along with other amenities such as bicycling and swimming.

Westgate Park City Resort and Spa

Located in the skiing mecca of Park City, Utah, this resort has earned the Five Star Award from its exchange company, Interval International. Most timeshare units have steam rooms and fireplaces inside, making them a nice complement to the world-class amenities offered by the resort itself.

Papillon the Spa specializes in treatments that incorporate Utah desert botanicals. Options include various massages, aromatherapy, body wraps, facials, manicures, pedicures, haircuts and styling, waxing, and more. There is also a youth menu for children ages nine through thirteen, with everything from shorter manicures and pedicures to a ten-minute massage. An additional menu for teens between ages fourteen and seventeen includes facials, twenty-five minute massages, and more.

Wilderness Timeshare Resorts

Wilderness timeshare resorts are woodsy retreats, the types of places people go when they want to unplug, unwind, and get lost amid towering trees in the heart of lush forests. They can be wintertime or summertime getaways offering everything from hiking to mountain climbing to bicycling. Horseback riding tends to be popular at these resort destinations, as does lake fishing.

The key to purchasing a timeshare unit at a wilderness-style resort is to find one that offers a bevy of activities—enough to keep an entire family busy for a week. Since these resorts also tend to be out of the way of civilization, you also should look for one that has multiple restaurants offering various styles of cuisine. In-house shopping areas will also be a plus, as will be complimentary transportation to and from the airport (which may be as far as an hour or more away in some cases).

Gala Fjellgrend

One of Interval International's Five Star Award properties, this resort is located about 135 miles from the airport in Oslo, Norway, close to the site of the 1952 Winter Olympics and within easy driving distance of fjord country and the glaciers. It is open all year round, with activities that include downhill skiing, cross-country skiing, bicycling, fishing, horseback riding, canoeing, and walking.

While this resort is based in Norway's cultural center, it is located in the heart of the Gudbrandsdalen Valley, high above sea level with views of Lake Gala and the Jotunheimen Mountains—giving it a feel of being truly in the heart of the wilderness. Private cabins are available to further enhance your out-of-the-way ambience with amenities that include fireplaces and direct access to the downhill and cross-country skiing trails.

Hyatt High Sierra Lodge

This timeshare resort is located in Incline Village, Nevada, near Lake Tahoe. While that does mean that it is not technically out in the wilderness, it does promote many activities that wilderness buffs tend to favor. These include hiking, bicycling, and jogging trails, along with skiing, snowboarding, fishing, horseback riding, and even hot-air balloon adventures. Golf, a spa, and a full-service casino are also among your options for vacation-time fun, and the timeshare units include natural gas fireplaces and master-bath whirlpool tubs.

📁 TRAVEL TIP

What is nice about a resort like the Hyatt High Sierra Lodge is that it offers all of the fun of the wilderness within spitting distance of civilization. If you are the type of person who likes to get out there—but not *too* far out there—a resort like this may suit you perfectly.

Lake Okanagan Resort

When bird-watching trails are part of a timeshare resort's sales pitch, you can bet you will enjoy more than a taste of the wilderness during your visit. Such is the case with Lake Okanagan Resort in Kelowna, British Columbia, Canada. It sits within 300 acres of designated parkland and has earned the Gold Crown designation from Resort Condominiums International.

The interesting thing about this resort is that its hiking trails, horse stables, and lakefront views give it a strong feeling of the wilderness, yet it also offers a golf course, tennis courts, and even a marina. And, should you tire of the great outdoors and want a bit more human social activity, there are nearly two dozen wineries in the area for tastings and tours.

Theme Park Timeshare Resorts

If you have ever visited a theme park like Six Flags, Universal Studios, or Disneyland, then you know the key to having good accommodations is a room that is in close proximity to the action. Timeshare units are no different: The most popular ones tend to be in the resorts that allow families the most time on the rides and attractions. Nobody wants to spend half their vacation time commuting to and from the roller coasters. Everybody wants to stay at the theme park until the minute it closes, and then have a short ride home to shower up before dinner.

When buying a theme-park timeshare unit, look for amenities including reduced-rate theme park admissions, extra theme-park usage hours, and complimentary transportation to and from the parks. Perhaps more so than any other types of timeshare, theme-park units tend to be most valuable when their usage time coincides with school vacations—a factor to consider if you are purchasing a fixed week.

≡FAST FACT

As you might imagine, Disney dominates the timeshare scene in places like Orlando, Florida, where it has its well-known cartoon characters wandering the timeshare grounds and adding to the magic of the vacation experience. For families, extra touches like this are of course hot selling points—ones that will make your timeshare unit all the more valuable during the long run.

Disney's Beach Club Villas

This timeshare resort is in Orlando, Florida, but it is designed to look like a (rather large) mid-Atlantic seaside home. It is within walking distance of Epcot and a boat ride away from Disney-MGM Studios. Your timeshare-unit purchase includes the same benefits that you would receive if you stayed at a Disney hotel, including extra hours at a different Disney theme park every day, a complimentary shuttle to and from Orlando International Airport, and complimentary transportation to and from the Disney theme parks, including the Magic Kingdom.

A nice thing about this resort is that since families with smaller children are the typical guests it offers many children's services on site and close by. These include a boardwalk-style game area, water slides, a game room, a playground, a supervised children's area for kids ages four through twelve (where Disney movies are shown, among other things), and a drawing room where you can sit with your kids while they color quietly during some much-needed downtime.

Hilton Grand Vacations Club at SeaWorld International Center

Located in the heart of the theme-park universe that is otherwise known as Orlando, Florida, this timeshare resort has earned the Gold Crown distinction from Resort Condominiums International. It was built to look like a seaside village in Bermuda, with timeshare units that overlook a private four-and-a-half-acre lake.

As with all good theme-park timeshare resorts, this one has many on-site activities and amenities that are designed to keep the entire family happy. There are two children's swimming pools in addition to several adult swimming pools, along with a game room and a playground. Organized activities are also provided for adults and children alike.

Sheraton Vistana Villages

Situated on International Drive in the heart of the theme park universe in Orlando, Florida, this ninety-five-acre Starwood Vacation Ownership timeshare resort is scheduled to complete construction on new one- and two-bedroom villas in early 2006. The resort offers discount tickets, not vouchers, to many of the local theme parks, meaning you can save a few bucks and also avoid the long lines at the admission areas.

The resort itself is well-suited for families, including separate adults' and children's swimming pools, barbecue grills, picnic tables, videotape rentals, a game room, a children's playground, and an interactive children's fountain. There is also an activity center on site that offers a host of organized children's activities.

Urban Timeshare Resorts

Urban timeshare resorts are a relatively new concept, but one that seems to be catching on. Especially in world-renowned cities such as New York, London, and Venice—where hotel rooms tend to be quite expensive—timeshares are becoming ever more popular as a long-term money-saving option.

One key amenity to look for when considering an urban time-share unit is concierge service. You, or anyone else using your time-share unit, will want access to all of the best restaurants, theater shows, and city-wide goings-on. A concierge will be key to ensuring that access, whether it is in the form of a last-minute dinner reserva-tion, front-row seats to a sold-out play, or admission tickets for an annual festival that draws visitors from near and far.

Also, if you are looking at a fixed-week purchase, consider what tends to be going on in your city of choice during various weeks of the year. Mardi Gras in New Orleans, Louisiana, is sure to be the most valuable week in that city, while New York City's annual JVC Jazz Festival is always a popular summertime tourist draw. On the world-wide stage, look for things like the Cannes Film Festival in France during the spring or Italy's annual Carnival of Venice, which is held in February.

Cordial Theaterhotel Wien

Located in the city of Vienna, Austria, this resort is directly next to the Theater in der Josefstadt and close by Ringstrasse Boulevard, which encompasses the historical old city of Vienna. You can explore much of what Vienna has to offer, including the Parliament building and St. Stephen's Cathedral, while staying at this Interval International Five Star Award resort.

There is a casino nearby, along with tennis courts and swimming pools. In a feature rarely found in United States timeshare resorts, pets are allowed here, as well. The biggest timeshare unit available is two bedrooms, sleeping six people with the pullout sofa.

Hilton Grand Vacations Club on the Las Vegas Strip

This is the third timeshare property that Hilton has developed in Sin City, a year-round hot-spot destination for worldwide travelers. It is due to be completed in the summer of 2006, offering a ten-acre site at the north end of the famed Las Vegas Strip. The fact that the conglomerate can support three separate timeshares in the same city tells you two things: The area is ever-growing in popularity, yet it is also perhaps approaching a future of being over-built. It is impossible to say what timeshare values in the city will be during the next decade or two (think about how Orlando looked ten or twenty years ago), but it is important that you understand the current situation clearly before making a timeshare-unit purchase.

💼 TRAVEL TIP

While the city of Las Vegas is, technically, an urban area, the resorts there have theme-park leanings, including not just wildly colored casinos and attractions but also swimming pools, fountains, and other outdoor amenities you might typically find at beachfront resorts. The same will be true of this new Hilton timeshare resort, making it an urban getaway with the flavor of many more vacations combined.

Pestana Rio Atlantica Hotel

This Resort Condominiums International Gold Crown property is in the sultry city of Rio de Janeiro, Brazil, proving that your timeshare vacation experience can be urban and exotic all at the same time.

The resort property is actually on Copacabana Beach, but it is right near the city center and just twenty-five minutes from the international airport. Its proximity to all the urban excitement is evidenced by its business center, nearly two dozen meeting rooms, and 250-person banquet facilities. That a timeshare resort can support so much business is a good sign that its design is in tune with the surrounding city environment—and that you will be able to make the most of all the nearby urban offerings during your weeklong vacation stay.

Other Timeshare Resorts

Just because a timeshare resort does not fit neatly into one of the categories described previously in this chapter does not mean you should overlook it. For many people, destinations are just as important as amenities, and simply getting to Hawaii will be just as valuable as being in the top-rated spa timeshare resort on the island of Maui.

Timeshare resorts that fit into this more generic category can also be great if you are one of those people who just wants to find a place where you feel comfortable so that you can return there year after year during your vacation time. The best-known golf course designers and newest spa treatments may be irrelevant to you, which is absolutely fine when considering which unit will make you happiest over the long haul.

Marriott's Village d'Ile-de-France

This timeshare resort in the French countryside offers private villas that can serve as your home base for exploring the region. Nearby restaurants serve classic French cuisine and regional wines, and the city of Paris is close enough that you can make day trips back and forth to visit the Louvre. The world-famous Versailles is also within day-trip distance.

The resort itself tries to be family-friendly, offering everything from finger painting to classes in the French language. The concierge can also help you arrange a trip to the nearby aquarium or Dali Museum, which offers painting workshops and other art classes.

Harborside Resort at Atlantis

Located on Paradise Island in the Bahamas, this Starwood timeshare resort is a colorful grouping of villas that are adjacent to the marina at the world-famous Atlantis Resort and Casino. The resort's amenities are listed in conjunction with those of Atlantis, meaning your timeshare unit will give you access to everything from the Atlantis resort's substantial indoor aquarium to its lazy river and Mayan water slides. There is a walkway from the Harborside Resort to the Atlantis grounds, as well as a courtesy shuttle. Or, you can stay at Harborside and enjoy its swimming pools, fitness center, and sculpted courtyards.

The good thing about a timeshare resort like the Harborside Resort is that it is in a location that is considered exotic—outside the borders of the United States—but it is still close to home, especially if your home is in Florida. That Paradise Island remains a popular vacation destination for many Americans is a good sign, too, for the future exchange value of your timeshare unit.

WorldMark Pinetop

At an elevation of 7,800 feet, this WorldMark by Trendwest resort is located about 200 miles from Phoenix, in Arizona's White Mountains—which boast the largest stand of ponderosa pine in the world. Hiking, bird watching, fishing, golf, and stargazing are among the most popular activities at this year-round Interval International five-star property, though the truly unique appeal is one of historical exploration.

≡FAST FACT

You can really get into the feel of the rustic Old West by taking day trips from this resort to Fort Apache, an 1870s Army outpost, and to the Casa Malpais National Historic Landmark, a sixteen-acre complex built around 1250 A.D. and formerly inhabited by Native Americans. The timeshare units themselves have gas fireplaces for warming up during the winter months.

Typical Timeshare Unit Layouts

Timeshare units, just like timeshare resorts, come in all shapes and sizes. They can be rooms within castles on the French countryside, apartments in high-rise buildings on the Florida coastline, cabins in the wilderness of the Canadian Rockies, rooms within hotels on the Las Vegas Strip, or even colorful villas lining the turquoise ocean in the

Caribbean. Each type of room will offer you a different environment and different amenities, hopefully in keeping with the broader theme of the resort and the area you are visiting during your vacation.

Having said that, virtually all timeshare units come in studio, one-bedroom, two-bedroom, or three-bedroom configurations. Sometimes you will have a full kitchen in the smallest of studio units, while at other times you will find far more amenities inside the larger timeshare units.

 **E-QUESTION**

Is a 3,000-square-foot unit always more valuable than a 2,000-square-foot unit?
While many resorts promote the square footage of their timeshare units, it is private sleeping capacity that will determine your unit's value in the world of timeshare exchange. A 3,000-square-foot villa with two bedrooms will often be considered an equal trade for a 1,500-square-foot unit that sleeps the same number of people.

Your goal in choosing a timeshare unit layout will involve one or more things: getting a layout that suits the needs of you and your family and getting a unit that will have good exchange value should you decide you want to trade it for a vacation elsewhere in the exchange company's system of resorts.

If you do not anticipate ever making an exchange, trading value will of course be of less importance to you than finding a perfect fit for your family's needs. But if you think you might want to exchange your timeshare unit for someone else's in the future, you might consider purchasing one that is a bit larger than you actually need, but that can be locked off to increase its trading value.

Single-Family Versus Lock-off Units

Lock-off units are exactly what they sound like: timeshare units that can be locked off, or divided into separate parts.

The two-bedroom units at Marriott's BeachPlace Towers in Fort Lauderdale, Florida, are a good example. Each unit is composed of two bedrooms with private baths, small kitchens, laundry machines, and/or a sitting area. Between the two bedrooms is a large living room and full kitchen that either bedroom can access, or that can be locked off from one or the other bedroom by simply closing and locking an adjoining doorway.

This means that two couples can share this unit, and its living room and full kitchen facilities, or one couple could use one of the bedrooms and the adjacent living room while the second bedroom remains locked off like an unused adjoining hotel room.

The benefit of owning such a unit—even if you believe you will never need both bedrooms—is that when you purchase a two-bedroom lock-off, you are essentially purchasing two possible weeks of timeshare use for the price of one. Why? Because if you lock off one half of your timeshare unit during any given vacation time, you are using only half of your timeshare value—meaning you have the other half left to exchange or use however you wish. You could, for instance, exchange your two-bedroom lock-off's value for two separate weeks of vacation in studio units at two different resorts.

⚡ E-ALERT

Even if a smaller timeshare unit is promoted as having a full kitchen, you would be wise to ask exactly what is included. Sometimes, a mini-refrigerator and two-burner cooktop are listed as full kitchens when, in reality, they are more limited resources than you might be expecting.

Of course, if you are traveling with a spouse and a few children, you may not want to lock off anything. Heck, half the fun of having a timeshare unit in the first place is being able to spread out and not feel trapped in the same room as the kids for a whole week of vacation. You actually may want to upgrade to a three-bedroom timeshare unit, for even a bit more breathing room.

By the same token, if you are traveling only with your spouse to the same destination each year, buying a lock-off unit may not make sense for you. You may want the coziness of a studio without the added expense and arrangement headaches of buying a two-bedroom unit and locking it off year after year for exchange purposes.

≡FAST FACT

Some people use the terms *lock-off* and *lock-out units* interchangeably, but the industry prefers the term *lock-off* to describe bedrooms that can be sealed off from the rest of a timeshare unit. Part of the reason is legal: You don't want to be accused of discriminating against someone by locking them out of timeshare accommodations.

The important thing is that you understand your options. Not all resorts have all kinds of timeshare unit layouts (many have only two-bedroom or smaller units, for instance), but the following introduction to classic accommodation plans will give you a broad understanding of exactly what's out there.

Hotel Unit

A hotel unit is the smallest timeshare that you can get. It sleeps no more than two people and often lacks things like a kitchenette, private laundry facilities, and personal balcony.

If your plan is to exchange your timeshare unit for vacations at high-end properties worldwide, a hotel unit is not your best bet, as its size gives it limited trading value. However, if you simply want a room to return to year after year, a hotel unit might work for you.

Studio

On average, timeshare studio units are about 500 square feet. (That is an *average* number; some are a good 100 square feet to 150 square feet smaller or bigger.) They typically sleep two people, maybe four with a pullout couch. Studio units may or may not have a kitchen and private laundry facilities. If cooking in your room or doing laundry is important to you, double-check your unit's layout or consider buying a one-bedroom unit.

One-Bedroom

One-bedroom timeshares begin to look more like apartments than hotel rooms, as they typically offer a living room and kitchen or kitchenette area in addition to a private bathroom off the bedroom. These units can sleep four to six people, though at least two will usually end up on a pullout couch in the living/dining area.

E-ALERT

Remember that if you purchase a bigger timeshare unit you will be required to pay higher maintenance fees than owners who buy smaller timeshare units. According to the American Resort Development Association, average maintenance fees for studio owners are $242, while three-bedroom owners are paying an average of $670.

Two-Bedroom

Two-bedroom timeshare units are where you really start to feel like you have graduated from an oversized hotel room into a full-fledged vacation villa. These units often include adjoining dining rooms and living rooms, as well as full kitchens and additional kitchenettes. Two-bedroom layouts are among the most desirable when making exchanges, and many resorts offer nothing larger—meaning that if you buy a three-bedroom unit at one resort, you may end up having to exchange it for a less-expensive two-bedroom unit elsewhere, since that is all that will be available.

Sleeping six or even eight people is the norm. The two-bedroom units at one resort, for example, are nearly 1,100 square feet and have second bedrooms that can be arranged with two queen-size beds in just the second bedroom, in addition to a pullout couch in the living room and the master bedroom bed.

Three-Bedroom

Three-bedroom timeshare units feel almost like small houses, running an average of 2,500 square feet and sleeping from eight to twelve people at a time in a combination of beds and sleeper sofas. You will rarely find more additional living space by way of lounging areas and dining tables, and three-bedroom units that are configured like villas often feel no different than full-size townhouses back home.

Sometimes, three-bedroom units are so large that they include multiple private balconies or terraces, which can be nice for dining at home when you want to make use of your full kitchen amenities.

CHAPTER 4

What Do Timeshares Cost?

IT'S A PRETTY BASIC QUESTION: What do timeshares cost? There are plenty of dollar figures out there in all price ranges for the units themselves on the new-construction and resale markets, but the true cost of a timeshare is the sum of its parts—including size, location, demand, ranking, and more. There are long-term costs to consider, as well, including taxes and inflation. Before you pay a single penny, make sure that you understand the real costs you are agreeing to endure over the long haul.

General Prices

The true prices of new timeshare units are a secret guarded more closely than a favorite poolside lounge chair on a sunny morning in the Caribbean. Resort developers are, after all, businesspeople, and they want to sell their timeshare units for as high a price as the marketplace will bear. Even brand-name developers such as Hilton, Hyatt, and Starwood refuse to publish the base rates for their timeshare units. You have to call one of their sales representatives—and give over a world of personal information—before you will be offered so much as a peek at a price.

Having said that, the most recent research by the American Resort Development Association shows that the average price for a week of new timeshare ownership (or the equivalent number of timeshare-usage points) is $15,789. The number is nonspecific in terms of the type of unit owned—one-bedroom, two-bedroom, etc.—nor is it specific in terms of the types of resorts where most of the new timeshare units were purchased.

Also mucking up the learning curve on true costs for new timeshares is that the $15,789 figure represents the cost of just the timeshare unit itself. It does not include the many extra fees that you read about in Chapter 2. The number also is an average, meaning there are brand-new timeshares selling for as little as $5,000 and as much as $50,000 or more.

≡FAST FACT

While the number of timeshare owners in the United States is just shy of four million, those four million people own nearly six million shares of timeshare weeks—meaning that some people are investing an average of $30,000 or more in multiple weeks of timeshare vacation.

The resale market is its own can of worms when it comes to determining the cost of timeshare units. You can find everything from resale units that are selling well above that new-timeshare average price of $15,789 to resale units trading on eBay for literally a couple hundred dollars (plus closing costs). And again, those numbers do not include extra fees such as maintenance costs and exchange company memberships, meaning the cost being quoted—no matter what it is—is still less than the real price burden you will bear over time.

If you want to be sure that you are paying a fair price for a new timeshare unit, your best bet is to narrow your search down to a few resorts that you like the most and then ask for prices that you can compare side by side. Even better, if the resorts you like the best are all in the same geographic area, you can take a mini-vacation to that place and attend three private sales presentations—giving you the opportunity not only to compare the numbers on paper, but how you feel inside the units themselves.

You can take the same approach to your research if you are looking at comparing costs on the timeshare resale market, but—as you will learn in Chapter 10—you will also have the benefit of Web sites where you can look to see what other people have paid for similar units in the same timeshare resorts. There is no "blue book" similar to the one you can purchase when trying to determine the appropriate cost for a used car, but there are enough consumer groups keeping track of resale prices that you will be able to make a decent assessment of how much you should be paying for a good number of resale timeshare units.

No matter whether you are trying to determine an appropriate cost on the new or resale market, all timeshare units are subject to key factors that drive their prices up or down. These include everything from the units themselves to where they are located and how nice other people have found them during previous vacations.

Key Cost Factors

Location, location, location. That has always been the mantra among Realtors selling homes to families all around the world, and the philosophy plays a large role in the cost of timeshare units, as well. Just as you want to find a house that is in good condition in a good neighborhood with low taxes, you will want to find a timeshare unit that is in good condition in a good neighborhood with low annual fees.

The difference with timeshares—more so than with primary residences—is that other people's opinions of your unit will have as much to do with its cost as anything else. Of course, such perceptions play a role in primary residence prices, as well, but usually only when you decide to buy or sell the home. With timeshares, the evaluations people make about a resort and the particular units within it can affect its cost day after day, week after week, and year after year. A unit that you can get for $12,000 today may cost you $13,500 if you procrastinate on making the purchase for a couple of months.

Why? Because resort rankings play a key role in setting timeshare unit prices. And those rankings exist in many different places, from exchange company databases to independent consumer group Web sites. A resort that people love (or that is in high demand, in the vernacular of the industry) will have timeshare units that can command higher prices than those at a resort receiving lackluster reviews from the people who have stayed there. As with anything, supply and demand are key. And since the timeshare industry is historically lower on supply than it is on demand, the truly high-demand properties may continue to skyrocket in cost.

 **E-QUESTION**

Where can I see resort rankings by people who have visited specific timeshare units?
Subscribe to TimeSharing Today, or become a member of the Timeshare User's Group. Each has a searchable database of rankings on its Web site, *www.tstoday.com* and *www.tug2.net*.

Other key factors that help to determine a timeshare unit's cost include unit size, location, and season of usage. They are important factors, to be sure, and they have their own bits of string that unravel as you begin to learn more about each of them.

Unit Size

When someone asks you the size of your house, how do you answer? If you are a typical American homeowner, you probably say something like, "We have a 2,500-square-foot colonial sitting on an acre of land." The number of bedrooms is rarely part of the equation; it is the square footage that gives most people an idea about how big your house actually is, which is why the square footage is usually one of the first things out of your mouth when asked.

It is an easy assumption to make, then, that square footage

plays a significant role in determining the cost of a timeshare unit. Unfortunately, this is the exact opposite of the truth. With timeshares, it is the number of private bedrooms and the total sleeping capacity that matter. A two-bedroom unit that sleeps four people in 1,100 square feet of space can cost the same as—or even more than—a two-bedroom unit that sleeps four people in 1,300 square feet of space, even though the latter timeshare unit will have a much more open and roomier feel to it.

Even better, a two-bedroom unit that sleeps six people (two on a pullout couch or an additional queen-size bed in one of the bedrooms) in just 1,000 square feet of space may have an even higher cost than the other two units, even though it is a physically smaller dwelling. The reason? It can sleep more people, therefore making it more attractive to a larger pool of timeshare owners who like to exchange their units every year.

In general, you can expect a hotel-style timeshare (basically a room with limited amenities) to cost the least, followed by studios, one-bedroom units, two-bedroom units, and three-bedroom units. Anything bigger than a three-bedroom unit will likely be the most expensive type of timeshare on the market, but since so few resorts have units that big, even the most costly four-bedroom unit may have a low exchange value after you buy it. There simply won't be enough other people with similar-size units for which you can trade at other resorts.

It is important that you factor that type of thinking into your overall cost assessment, since paying more for an extra-large, highest-cost timeshare unit may not allow you to get the usage you want out of it later on, in terms of exchanges. The *real* cost, then, will include all the extra money you could have saved by buying a smaller timeshare unit that would have gotten you exchanges for the exact same vacations in the future.

Location

Location is another key factor affecting the cost of timeshare units. If you want to return to your timeshare unit year after year, you will of course want to choose a vacation destination that you, personally, find more beautiful and relaxing than anywhere else in the world. The cost of a timeshare in that place may be high or low, but for your purposes, the only factor to consider is simply how well you like the destination.

E-ALERT

Sleeping capacity, not square footage, is a key factor in timeshare unit cost. It also is a key factor in timeshare unit exchange value. If you plan to make many exchanges, you will likely be more successful with a small two-bedroom unit than an extra-large one-bedroom unit—even if the one-bedroom has a higher original cost.

If you plan to make frequent timeshare-unit exchanges, though, you will have to think about location a bit differently. The cost of timeshare units in high-demand places—vacation destinations that a lot of people want to make exchanges *for*—is much, much higher than the cost of timeshare units in lower-demand areas.

What are the locations of highest demand? According to recent trends, they include (in alphabetical order):

- Hawaii
- Las Vegas, Nevada
- Mexico
- Orlando, Florida
- U.S. Virgin Islands

You will read more about these and other red-hot regions in Chapters 5 and 6. But for now, suffice to say that if you are looking for a timeshare unit in one of these locations, you are likely going to have to pay far more than you would pay for a same-size unit in, say, Branson, Missouri. It is not that Las Vegas or Orlando are, by their very nature, any better than a place like Branson for your personal vacation; it is simply that they are more in demand in terms of time-share exchanges, which means that the timeshare units there will cost more.

It is possible for you to find discounted timeshare units in even the most popular destinations—especially if you are looking on the resale market—but when shopping in these places, it is also important to remember that seasonal travel patterns will affect your unit cost, as well. There are high-demand and low-demand seasons everywhere—there are even highest-demand weeks in most places—and you need to factor annual vacation timing into each location that you consider.

High Versus Low Season

Every timeshare resort has high-demand and low-demand seasons, and those seasons correlate to higher and lower timeshare unit prices. A two-bedroom unit available during the summertime in Vail, Colorado, for instance, might cost several thousand dollars less than the exact same two-bedroom unit during the snowy wintertime, which is ideal for downhill and cross-country skiing—the favorite activities in that particular city.

Within high-demand and low-demand seasons, there are even highest-demand and lowest-demand weeks. Highest-demand weeks garner the absolute highest prices because they are the most in demand when it comes to timeshare exchange value. The week between Christmas and New Year's Day, for example, is a powerful—and costly—week to own in Orlando, Florida, because it is during that week that most children are out of school and most families can take their vacations. The week before Christmas, by contrast, may still be considered high season in Orlando, but the cost of that timeshare week is likely to be at least a little bit lower simply because it will have less trading power in the timeshare exchange system.

TRAVEL TIP

Timeshare homeowners' associations can be a great source of information about current prices for new and resale units. You can sometimes
get the telephone number for the president of a given resort's homeowners' association by calling the resort itself and simply asking.

So how do you know which weeks are high demand and low
demand in which parts of the country? The major exchange companies, Resort Condominiums International and Interval International,
each have their own systems for rating different time periods throughout the year. The assessments are based on previous years' demand
and are coded in resort catalogs in different ways. Some year-round
destinations—such as Orlando, Florida, and Las Vegas, Nevada—are
considered high-demand all year round. Others, though, have peak
and off-peak ratings.

Resort Condominiums International Seasons

Resort Condominiums International has a color-coded system for
rating its high-, medium-, and low-demand seasons. The colors are:

- Red (high demand)
- White (medium demand)
- Blue (low demand)

The exchange company's Web site, *www.rci.com*, includes a
searchable database that lists each timeshare resort in the RCI
network along with its amenities, nearest airport—and seasonal
demand color codes. Usually, a resort's information page will include
the exact weeks that are considered to be red, white, and blue. If the
resort is in a year-round high-demand destination, there will be a
designation stating that the resort is all red.

Interval International Seasons

Interval International, *www.intervalworld.com,* also uses a color-coding system to define its high-, medium-, and low-demand seasons. The colors are different than the ones used by Resort Condominiums International. Interval's colors are:

- Red (high demand)
- Yellow (medium demand)
- Green (low demand)

In addition, Interval International has created a Travel Demand Index that takes into account worldwide travel patterns to determine which weeks of the year are peak exchange weeks—no matter what color-coded season they are within.

The Travel Demand Index is a numerical system that is explained in the Interval resort directory, and then listed for resorts in each geographic region. Each week of the year is assigned a number that correlates to the amount of demand for timeshare use and exchanges. The higher a figure is above the number 100, the greater the relative demand is for timeshare use during that week.

≡FAST FACT

The highest-demand timeshare weeks may cost more for you to purchase than lower-demand timeshare weeks, but again, if exchange value is your utmost priority, they may be worth the additional price.

During a red season, for instance, demand for timeshare use may be at least 115 points during each week of the season—but there may be two or three weeks within the season when demand gets as high as 125 points. This may be due to holidays, school vacations, or annual festivals in the destination that draw a greater number of travelers.

Official Resort Ranking

How a resort is ranked in terms of amenities, services, and hospitality can also have an effect on the cost of its timeshare units. Both Resort Condominiums International and Interval International have their own, in-house ratings for resorts that consistently receive the best marks from timeshare owners. These resorts, then, become more in demand than other resorts that lack the highest-level ratings, and the cost of the units within them go up because more and more people seek to purchase and use them.

There are additional programs run by the exchange companies, such as golf packages, that also help to give some resorts a certain cachet that others lack. Here is a look at the rating designations used by the two largest timeshare exchange companies, Resort Condominiums International and Interval International.

Resort Condominiums International Ratings

There are three key ratings to consider when looking at the cost of timeshare units in the Resort Condominiums International exchange system:

- Gold Crown Resorts
- Resorts of International Distinction
- RCI Hospitality Award

Each of these ratings will factor into the price that a given resort can charge for its timeshare units, but the ratings are distinctly different in terms of what they measure.

Gold Crown Resorts

To earn the Gold Crown designation from Resort Condominiums International, a resort has to meet service and quality requirements as determined not just by RCI staff, but also through the comment cards that timeshare users submit after their vacations. The service and quality requirements are measured in all facets of the resort experience, including amenities, staff service, facilities, and maintenance. The exchange company claims that its requirements are the strictest in the entire timeshare industry. That may or may not be true, but you can be sure that when you buy a higher-cost unit in a Gold Crown resort, you are at least getting something that your exchange company promotes as being the best of the best.

Resorts of International Distinction

A Resort of International Distinction is the next best thing to a Gold Crown designation in the Resort Condominiums International system. These resorts are judged on service and quality, just as the Gold Crown properties are, and they are determined to have a good track record of leaving their timeshare users satisfied in everything from housekeeping to maintenance. Amenities, facilities, and other nonhuman factors do not contribute to this rating, as they do with the Gold Crown award.

≡FAST FACT

The RCI Hospitality Award is given to resorts that consistently do a good job with front-desk services, along with general staff hospitality. This is the least stringent of the Resort Condominium International ratings, but it does assure you that you will at least be well taken care of when you are in the resort's lobby.

Interval International Ratings

Interval International has just one quality and service rating: the Five Star Award. However, it also has a Golf Resort Program that makes some of its resorts more attractive to people who like to hit the links during their annual vacations. Again, the more attractive a resort is to as many people as possible, the more that resort can charge you for its timeshare units. For that reason, in trying to help you understand why some timeshares cost more than others, the Golf Resort Program is explained below—even though it is not technically a ratings program.

Five Star Award

The Five Star Award is given out annually to Interval International resorts that provide superior services, amenities, and facilities, and that the company deems highly desirable in terms of the destination itself, demand for exchanges, and the actual units being offered to timeshare owners. Since this award is given out annually, it is something that can be taken away—thus affecting the going price for timeshare units. If you are considering buying a timeshare unit at a Five Star Award resort, consider asking how many years in a row the resort has held the award. The answer will certainly affect the timeshare unit's cost, and it may help you to determine whether you are buying into a resort with a solid long-term history or a resort that is a newly anointed gem.

Golf Resort Program

Interval International's Golf Resort Program is a system by which, at some resorts, Interval members will have access to an on-site or nearby course, greens fees discounted by 20 percent or more, advance tee-time reservations, rental discounts of at least 15 percent, additional discounts on things such as golf lessons and cart rentals, and more. As explained earlier, the Golf Resort Program is not a quality ratings system, per se, but it will be a factor that drives certain vacationers to demand some resorts over others—and thus will have an effect on the prices that those resorts can charge for their timeshare units.

Unofficial Resort Reputation

Whether you are shopping for a new timeshare unit or for one on the resale market, you can take advantage of the ratings and rankings posted by consumer groups to evaluate which resorts have the best reputations—and, thus, can be rightly charging the highest costs for their timeshare units. In some cases, you can even find information about what other people have paid for similar units in the past.

Two good places to look for these ratings and reviews are the Web site of *TimeSharing Today* magazine, *www.tstoday.com*, and the Web site of the Timeshare User's Group, *www.tug2.net*. If you join these groups, you will have access to literally hundreds of comments and postings from other timeshare owners and users who have stayed at timeshare resorts worldwide. More information about each of these groups is listed in Chapter 19, along with additional places where you can research timeshare resort reputations and unit prices.

Remember Those Extra Fees

The true cost of a timeshare, as you learned in Chapter 2, is more than just the cost of the unit itself. If you want to try to analyze exactly how much you will be spending to use your timeshare unit during the next ten years or more, you must factor in many additional fees. Some you will be able to control, but others will be charged by home-owners' associations, exchange companies, and other groups that are outside of your purview.

E-ALERT

Keep in mind that extra fees are very likely to go up each year or two, and make those inflationary increases part of your overall budget when considering how much you can spend on a time-share unit itself.

The Big Fees

You learned about these fees in detail in Chapter 2. They include annual maintenance charges, special assessments, mortgage interest payments, and exchange company fees. These fees, when combined, are almost certain to make up the vast majority of your additional timeshare ownership costs. They will be lower or higher depending, in part, on the size of your timeshare unit, the number of exchanges you make annually, and the size of your mortgage amount.

Incidental and Usage Fees

Your resort itself may charge extra fees for everything from maid service to equipment use when you decide to take part in certain amenities and activities. Some of the items for which you may be charged an additional fee—every year, or even every usage—include:

- Beach towels
- WaveRunners and Jet Skis
- Tennis rackets
- Scuba and snorkeling gear
- Health club privileges
- Spa treatments
- Snow skiing equipment
- Horseback riding gear
- Golf club and cart rentals
- DVD and VCR movie rentals
- Dry cleaning

In addition, if you plan to make use of the full kitchen or kitchenette in your timeshare unit, your resort may have a shopping program through which you can order food, laundry supplies, and cleaning supplies and have them waiting for you upon arrival. This service will be at an extra cost to you, as well—and likely will cost more than if you had simply gone to the nearest grocery store or brought some items from home—but it may be worth the price in terms of convenience, depending on the length of your vacation stay and the distance from your resort to the nearest store.

Long-Term Cost Factors

When determining the cost of a timeshare unit, you also must take certain long-term factors into consideration. There are tax ramifications that will be individual to every owner, along with the costs that you will experience if you decide to add to your "timeshare empire" by purchasing additional weeks or points. There is also the long-term inflation factor to keep track of, simply to make sure you are actually saving vacation dollars as compared with the costs you would experience for the same vacations at hotels.

Tax Ramifications

In many cases, you will be able to treat your timeshare similar to the way you treat your primary residence each year during tax time. The information provided below is intended to be a guide—but you *must* check with a personal financial advisor to determine exactly how timeshare ownership will affect your long-term tax situation.

≡FAST FACT

The property taxes that you pay on your deeded timeshare, in general, are tax deductible, but you will not enjoy deductions for things like annual maintenance fees, special assessments, and the like.

Generally speaking, the interest you pay on your timeshare loan will be tax deductible—as long as you have purchased a deeded unit and not a right-to-use timeshare. The Internal Revenue Service typically allows for this deduction on one primary residence and one additional residence (which, in this case, would be your deeded timeshare unit). If you own more than one week of deeded timeshare at the same resort, you may be able to count all of those weeks as one additional residence, since they are in the same place, but you and your accountant will have to work through the finer points to be sure.

Further, when it comes time to sell your timeshare, any profit you make will be taxable. Given that most people do not earn a profit when reselling their timeshares, though, it likely will be more important for you to understand the tax ramifications of selling at a loss. In general, if you use your timeshare for personal reasons, your loss will not be tax deductible. If you use your timeshare for business—particularly as a rental property—you may, in some cases, be able to deduct any loss you sustain.

Since taxes and deductions are so personalized nowadays, it is important that you and your accountant discuss your specific situation before you purchase any timeshare unit. The guidelines explained here might be helpful, but they are no substitute for good firsthand knowledge about what you can expect throughout the duration of your timeshare ownership.

Owning Multiple Properties

The biggest long-term financial effect of owning multiple timeshare units is that you will be paying more for the privilege—and you will have to ensure that your payments are, over the long term, still lower than the amount of money you would have paid for hotel-based vacations in the same destinations.

Remember, these costs are not just the costs for the multiple weeks themselves, but also for multiple maintenance payments, special assessments, and the like. In some cases, you may be offered discounts on additional weeks during the time of your original purchase—discounts that can buffer some of the long-term expenses—but again, you need to be sure you are getting real long-term value for your "vacation investment." Owning multiple properties is a good financial idea only if you actually intend to use them, and if by using them you save money over what you would have otherwise spent on hotels.

Expected Resale Value

A lot of people think that timeshare units are like other vacation properties. The belief goes something like this: "If I don't use it, I can just sell it for a small loss, or maybe even for a profit." In truth, though, most people who sell their timeshares reap no more than half the original cost that they paid when their timeshare was new. If you buy a unit on the resale market and then try to resell it again, you may see less of a loss (or even a gain), but in general, new timeshare units hold their value about as well as new cars—dropping precipitously the minute you sign the papers.

E-ALERT

Be mindful when buying a timeshare in a red-hot development region. As with every other product in the world, timeshares are subject to the laws of supply and demand. You may get a high exchange value for a unit in a high-demand timeshare destination, but over time, you may see that value decline as more and more units become available and the marketplace becomes saturated.

Inflation . . . or Not

Perhaps the most important long-term cost factor to consider when buying a timeshare is inflation. Remember: The entire notion of timeshares being a smart financial purchase is that they will, over time, help you save money when compared with having to buy hotel rooms during a lifetime of similar vacations.

If that oft-stated inflationary projection of 5 percent, per year, increases on hotel rooms does not occur—and it has *not* occurred in recent years—you may be just as financially well off paying for hotel rooms instead of buying a timeshare at all. There are trade-offs, of course, in terms of room sizes and additional benefits, but when speaking strictly about long-term money management and the impact of a timeshare on your portfolio, inflation is going to be the key.

CHAPTER 5

Buying in the United States

WHETHER YOU WANT TO VACATION near New York, San Francisco, Chicago, or Honolulu, there are timeshare opportunities waiting to be had—no matter if you prefer to spend your relaxation time downtown, on the beach, on the links, or beyond. In fact, you need look no further than the United States for top timeshare properties even if you're hoping to buy a unit that will give you maximum trading power and that you can use to vacation around the globe for many years to come.

Red-Hot Regions

There is no doubt about it: The hottest timeshare destinations in the United States are developing pretty much in lockstep with the hottest vacation destinations from coast to coast. It just plain makes sense that places where millions of people choose to vacation each year would see the development of more and more timeshare opportunities. Why, some people believe, should you continue to pay hotel and motel rates in the same geographic spot when you can have roomier accommodations where you feel more at home every time you return?

To find the region with the fastest-growing concentration of timeshare opportunities, you simply have to look to the place with the most pulling power in terms of vacation experiences. Let your mind drift to the sunny Southeast, to the land built on the ears of a cartoon named Mickey and the loyal following of his band of Mouseketeers. The words are a siren song unto themselves: Walt Disney World.

Orlando, Florida

The city of Orlando—which has grown into a theme park paradise that now includes the Magic Kingdom, Epcot, Disney-MGM Studios, Disney's Animal Kingdom, Universal Studios, Islands of Adventure, SeaWorld, Busch Gardens, Cypress Gardens, and more—continues to draw upward of 50 million people a year who want to spend their vacation dollars in central Florida, according to the city's Tourist Information Bureau. Those fifty million people need places to sleep, of course, and timeshares are making more and more inroads into the hotel business that has traditionally dominated the marketplace. In fact, Florida has more timeshares than any other state—at least 350 as of late 2005—and Orlando, according to several sources, is the location for about half of those.

 **E-QUESTION**

What are the busiest tourist weeks of the year in Orlando?
When the kids are out of school and the weather is cold up North: The crowds are, well, the most crowded during Spring Break, Easter, Thanksgiving, and the Christmas holidays, according to the Orlando/ Orange County Convention and Visitors Bureau.

Las Vegas, Nevada

Hot on the heels of the family-friendly Orlando area, Sin City is quickly becoming a timeshare hot spot of choice. Las Vegas, Nevada, long considered an adults-only playground, has worked hard in recent years to transform its image by marketing vacations the entire family can enjoy. Posh hotels still revolve around glitzy, noisy casinos, of course, but today, you will also find baby-sitting services, shows you can enjoy with the kids, and family-friendly rates on everything from rooms to tours to meals.

E-ALERT

Hotel rooms in Las Vegas, Nevada, run the gamut in pricing from about $50 per night to well over $1,000 per night. When considering a timeshare purchase in a place with such a wide range, you must compare what you would normally pay versus what the timeshare would cost you over time.

Las Vegas, like Orlando, is a bona-fide premier U.S. vacation destination—luring some thirty-seven million people to the desert each year. Just think about how much money is being spent on hotel rooms and restaurant meals, and you quickly realize how investments in timeshare properties can begin to look like a long-term bargain.

Hawaii

Another red-hot region for vacations and, thus, timeshare development in the United States is the honeymoon haven of Hawaii. In the last recorded year alone, more than six million people visited the Pacific Ocean islands that lie between California and Japan—and spent upward of $10 billion during their vacations.

No doubt a large percentage of that cash went to hotel rooms, which average around $160 per night but that can be substantially higher on the popular islands of Maui and Kauai, where the natural beauty of the beaches and mountains is legendary.

Myrtle Beach and Hilton Head, South Carolina

Hawaii can be a good spot for golfers, too, but that sport has actually made South Carolina another burgeoning vacation and timeshare location in the United States. The areas surrounding Hilton Head and Myrtle Beach, in particular, are seeing more and more developers with timeshare projects who want to capitalize on the regions' increasing popularity.

More than two million vacationers spent about $1.5 billion in Hilton Head as of the last recorded year, while nearly thirteen million people chose Myrtle Beach as their vacation destination of choice. Again, that's an awful lot of people needing places to lay their heads, which is why timeshare opportunities are beginning to grow as fast as the foundations of local hotels.

▮ TRAVEL TIP

When looking to purchase a fixed-week timeshare investment in Hilton Head or Myrtle Beach—or in any coastal location from Maine to Texas—remember to consider when hurricanes typically strike. In South Carolina, for instance, the heaviest hurricane months are typically August and September.

Top Properties in the Northeast

The Northeast lacks an Orlando or a Las Vegas around which the regional timeshare universe revolves, but it does have something that many other parts of the country lack: great cities. New York and Boston, for instance, have been luring tourists from all over the world ever since the nation's founding several centuries ago. Northeast timeshares offer everything from beaches and horseback riding to snowmobiles and winter skiing. Here is a look at a few Northeast timeshares that continually receive high rankings from exchange companies and consumer groups alike.

Harbor Ridge, Southwest Harbor, Maine

This Interval International Five Star Award resort is in the midst of picturesque Acadia National Park. Summers are the busiest time of year here, but year-round accommodations are available if you would prefer a more secluded visit during the colder winter months. There are only forty timeshare units at Harbor Ridge, and each is designed as a luxury condominium. Most of the units have three-story, two-bedroom layouts and sleep as many as six people with the pullout couch. Some of the on-site amenities include tennis, indoor and outdoor swimming pools, a game room, and a fitness center. Restaurants are nearby, as is seasonal boating, cross-country skiing, bicycling, fishing, golf, and more.

The Manhattan Club, New York, New York

Located at West Fifty-sixth Street between Seventh Avenue and Broadway, this luxurious Midtown Manhattan timeshare is just steps away from Carnegie Hall, Rockefeller Center, the Museum of Modern Art, and the southern end of Central Park. The property is part of the Resort Condominiums International exchange system, which has awarded The Manhattan Club its Gold Crown distinction for amenities and services. The resort also is promoted as a Five Star Award–winner in the Interval International resort directory.

Suites are designed for four people and include elegant furnishings, marble bathrooms, refrigerators, microwaves, dishwashers, and more. The facility itself offers a concierge service, fitness center, business center, and valet parking—which is all-important in the middle of one of the busiest cities on the planet.

Marriott's Custom House, Boston, Massachusetts

The Custom House, part of the Marriott Vacation Club Resort network, overlooks Boston Harbor and offers elegant one-bedroom villas that can sleep as many as four people total. It is in the heart of this historic city, just steps away from favorite tourist destinations, including the Faneuil Hall Marketplace.

Each villa has a private bedroom with king-size bed, plus a queen-size sleeper sofa in the living room. A kitchenette is also included, with refrigerator, microwave oven, and dishes and utensils for serving four people. The resort has on-site laundry as well as valet dry cleaning, plus a bookstore, game room, florist, and more. Summertime, as with most of the Northeast, is typically the season of highest demand.

⎯FAST FACT

You may not think of major metropolitan areas when you consider time-share opportunities, but plenty of people do, which is why many developers are beginning to offer units for sale in cities across the United States. You also may not think that outlying suburbs are traditional vacation hot spots, but, in fact, timeshares are popping up in Northeast states including New Jersey, Connecticut, and New Hampshire.

Northern Outdoors Adventure Club, The Forks, Maine

The closest international airport to this wilderness resort is about ninety-four miles away in Bangor, which should tell you something about the kind of vacation you might experience at this Gold Crown Resort Condominiums International property. It is promoted as an excellent destination to enjoy during the fall, when the foliage is in full color, with activities such as whitewater rafting, snowmobiling, hiking, downhill skiing, and fishing.

Units come in one-, two-, and three-bedroom configurations, with the largest units sleeping six privately and eight altogether. Each have full kitchens, and some have fireplaces and/or private laundry facilities. The resort itself includes a restaurant, game room, sauna, swimming pool, and more. There are even conference facilities if you're considering using your timeshare for getaways as a team-building business tool.

Trapp Family Lodge, Stowe, Vermont

This Interval International Five Star Award resort is owned and operated by the Trapp family of *The Sound of Music* fame. It is a 2,800-acre mountaintop retreat that has Austrian-style guest houses, gardens, and live music. There is even an Austrian Tea Room on site, along with a dining room, fitness center, massage facility, and more.

The lodge is open year-round, with trails that can be used for hiking in the summertime or cross-country skiing during the colder winter months. Other activities include the use of indoor and outdoor swimming pools, fishing, tennis, bicycling, horseback riding, golf, and more.

Vacation Village in the Berkshires, Hancock, Massachusetts

This Resort Condominiums International Gold Crown property overlooks the Jiminy Peak ski area, which offers day and nighttime skiing at all levels. In the summertime, one of the popular activities is visiting Tanglewood for performances of the Boston Symphony. All of the timeshare units have fireplaces, air conditioning, and full or partial kitchens, depending on their size. The closest airport is over the state line in Albany, New York, about thirty-five miles away. Laundry facilities are on site, and a grocery store is about a mile away.

Resort amenities include children's and adults' swimming pools, exercise equipment, a playground area, and a hot tub. Nearby activities include boating, fishing, golf, horseback riding, live entertainment, restaurants, and a spa.

Top Properties in the Southeast

As discussed earlier in this chapter, much of the timeshare market in the Southeast revolves around the city of Orlando, Florida, because of the nearby Walt Disney World and other theme parks. Disney itself has gotten into the timeshare game with the Disney Vacation Club, which includes a handful of properties in Orlando as well as others in up-and-coming Southeast timeshare locations such as Hilton Head, South Carolina.

🧳 TRAVEL TIP

Whether you want to vacation with the kids and ride roller coasters all week long or try for par at a dozen golf courses a little farther up the Atlantic coastline, the Southeast has timeshare opportunities that will suit you.

Here is a look at a few Southeast timeshares that continually receive high rankings from exchange companies and consumer groups alike.

Chetola Resort, Blowing Rock, North Carolina

This Resort Condominiums International Gold Crown property is in the picturesque Blue Mountains and includes an on-site restaurant housed in a restored 1800s estate building. Hiking is a main activity, with twenty-six miles of trails adjacent to the resort. Other things to do include seasonal paddle-boating and trout fishing on the nearby lake.

Charlotte is the nearest international airport, about ninety miles away. Units are one- or two-bedroom, with the larger sleeping six people privately. All the units have full kitchens, private laundry facilities, and fireplaces. The resort itself offers tennis, a swimming pool, a game room, a health club, and more—including conference facilities for business travelers.

Disney's Beach Club Villas, Orlando, Florida

Pastel colors and Atlantic seaside décor contribute to the ambience at this timeshare resort—which is within walking distance of Epcot and a boat ride away from Disney-MGM Studios. Units come in studio, one-bedroom, and two-bedroom configurations. The smallest units, the studios, sleep four people—in one queen-size bed and one double-size sleeper sofa. Also in the studios are kitchenettes with microwave ovens, under-counter refrigerators, wet bars, and coffee makers.

The resort's amenities include Martha's Vineyard Lounge where you can sample fine wines, a dueling piano bar that hosts audience sing-a-longs, a boardwalk-style area called Wildwood Landing full of skill games such as Tin Can Knock Down, and more. There is also a marina on site offering rides aboard pontoon and canopy boats, as well as specialty cruises.

Disney's Old Key West Resort, Orlando, Florida

This timeshare resort has all the tropical ambience that made Key West so famous, right down to the steel-drum music and Jimmy

Buffett beats. There are four heated pools on site in addition to a kiddie pool, and the Disney Lake Buena Vista Golf Course is close by for duffers of all ages and skill sets. In addition to several eateries on site, guests can use the first-come, first-served barbecue grill areas to prepare inexpensive dinners.

Units at this resort come in studio, one-, two-, and three-bedroom configurations, with the largest timeshares sleeping twelve people on two levels that include one master bedroom, two guest bedrooms with two beds apiece, and one sleeper sofa in the living room. These large units also have full kitchens and private laundry facilities.

Ellington at Wachesaw Plantation, Murrells Inlet, South Carolina

This Interval International Five Star Award resort is just south of Myrtle Beach on the Wachesaw East Golf Course, former home of the LPGA (ladies' section) Myrtle Beach Golf Classic. There are nearly 125 championship golf courses in the area, including the one on site, which is part of Interval International's Golf Resort Program—giving members access to greens fee and lesson discounts, advance tee times, and more. Additional on-site activities include adults' and children's swimming pools, a playground, a hiking and exercise trail, a driving range, and a practice green.

Hilton Grand Vacations Club on International Drive, Orlando, Florida

This is one of two Hilton Grand Vacations Club timeshare properties in Orlando (the other one being at SeaWorld). The International Drive property occupies thirty-four acres right next to the Orlando Premium Outlets and is just minutes from Walt Disney World. Its atmosphere is Mediterranean, with touches of Tuscany throughout the décor—including a piazza, gardens, and lakefront walking path.

Units come in studio, one-, two-, and three-bedroom configurations, with the largest timeshares sleeping six people privately or eight people altogether. The one-, two-, and three-bedroom villas all have full kitchens, private laundry facilities, and air conditioning. The resort itself offers a children's playground, several swimming pools and whirl-pool spas, and picnic areas with barbecue grills. Parking is also on site.

Southwind Villas, Hilton Head Island, South Carolina

This Resort Condominiums International Gold Crown property boasts eight miles of paths. In addition to air conditioning, full kitchens, and private laundry facilities, each townhouse-style time-share unit also comes with a balcony and two bicycles for you to use on the resort's paths or as transportation to the nearby beach. The nearest grocery store is two miles away, and the nearest airport is about a forty-five mile drive from the site. Other activities include a sauna, swimming pool, whirlpool tub, and tennis courts. A golf course is nearby, as are opportunities to go boating, fishing, shop-ping and horseback riding.

The Highlands at Sugar, Banner Elk, North Carolina

Located on Sugar Mountain in the famed Blue Ridge Mountain chain, this Interval International Five Star Award resort offers year-round activities including hiking, white-water rafting, inner tubing, fishing, bicycling, canoeing, horseback riding, ice skating, downhill and cross-country skiing, golf, tennis, and more. There are caverns and attractions nearby to keep your kids happy, while the adults in your group might enjoy touring nearby antiques shops, crafts stores, and shopping outlets.

On site at this resort, you will find an enclosed heated pool, exer-cise room, redwood sauna, game room, children's play area, and more. Each of the one- and two-bedroom timeshare units includes a whirlpool tub, stone fireplace, balcony, and full kitchen.

The Villas at Disney's Wilderness Lodge, Orlando, Florida

Though it is located in central Florida, this timeshare is designed with the Pacific Northwest and the great American West in mind. It has a rustic look and feel thanks to Native American and wildlife motifs that permeate its décor inside and out.

There are studios, one-bedroom units, and two-bedroom units that sleep as many as eight people. The two-bedroom units are nearly 1,100 square feet and include one master bedroom with king-size bed, another bedroom with either two queen-size beds or one bed and one sleeper sofa, plus an additional sleeper sofa in the living room. Private laundry facilities and a full kitchen are also included in these units.

The resort amenities are designed with a rustic touch, as well, including spring pools that appear to have been carved from rock, a re-creation of the Old Faithful geyser, and a game room decked out with rocker-recliner chairs.

Top Properties in the Midwest

The Midwest is a vast region that offers everything from downhill snow skiing to summertime kayaking on sprawling lakes that grace gorgeous hillsides. Many timeshares from Minnesota to Missouri are considered all-year-round destinations, with winter activities taking hold during the colder months and summertime activities heating up with the summer sun.

🧳 TRAVEL TIP

You'll sometimes find casinos close by the top timeshare resorts, as well as live shows in places like Branson, Missouri, that are known across the world for their country music flair.

Here is a look at a few Midwest timeshares that continually receive high rankings from exchange companies and consumer groups alike.

Big Cedar Lodge, Ridgedale, Missouri

Located in the Show-Me state's famed Ozark Mountains, the Big Cedar Wilderness Club is a Gold Crown Resort in the Resort Condominiums International exchange network. The resort was built on the shore of Table Rock Lake and offers vacationers a chance to go biking, fishing, horseback riding, boating, water-skiing, and more. Nearby Big Cedar Lodge offers additional activities, including heated swimming pools, stables, a marina, a spa, and a fitness center. Also worth noting are the resort's conference facilities and handicapped-accessible units.

About sixty miles from the Springfield-Branson Regional Airport, this resort offers timeshare units in studio, one-, and two-bedroom configurations. The largest timeshares sleep six people privately, or eight people altogether. Some of the units have fireplaces, and all of the units include full or partial kitchens depending on their size.

Fairfield Branson, Branson, Missouri

A Gold Crown Resort in the Resort Condominiums International exchange network, the Fairfield Branson is off the beaten path and offers fishing, horseback riding, tennis, and golf. There are three sections to the resort, each within several miles of one another with shuttle service in between, as well as to Branson's main-strip nightlife. The closest major airport, Springfield/Branson Regional Airport, is about an hour away.

Timeshare units are in demand much of the year, save the coldest months of January and February. There are studios as well as one-, two-, and three-bedroom units, with the largest timeshares sleeping eight people privately and ten people in total. All of the units have private laundry facilities, as well as partial or full kitchens depending on the size of the timeshare.

Fairfield Wisconsin Dells at Tamarack, Wisconsin Dells, Wisconsin

Located in the town of Wisconsin Dells, this lakeside resort offers golf, downhill skiing, horseback riding, mountain biking, cross-country skiing, boating, hiking, and pretty much anything else you could imagine doing in the great outdoors. It is a previous winner of the Gold Crown Award from Resort Condominiums International, and it is now part of Fairshare Plus, a points-based timeshare exchange system run by Fairfield Resorts.

In addition to units of various sizes—all with kitchens and fireplaces, and some with whirlpool tubs—the resort offers indoor and outdoor swimming pools, a separate children's swimming pool, indoor and outdoor tennis courts, a game room, an indoor basketball court, and more.

Little Sweden, Fish Creek, Wisconsin

Log homes with vaulted ceilings and fieldstone fireplaces make up this Interval International Five Star Award resort, which is located in the heart of scenic Door County, Wisconsin. The décor is Scandinavian, with each two-bedroom timeshare unit sleeping as many as six people (including two on the pullout couch).

≡FAST FACT

On-site amenities of Little Sweden include bicycling, golf, a fitness room, a playground, a sauna, ice-skating, cross-country skiing, indoor and outdoor swimming pools, tennis, a whirlpool tub, and more. Nearby, you can go boating, fishing, and horseback riding or enjoy the quaint local shops, restaurants, state parks, summer theater, and festivals.

Premiere Vacation Club at Varsity Clubs of America—South Bend Chapter, Indiana

This Interval International Five Star Award resort is designed to reflect the Notre Dame community's history and spirit. It is located within driving distance of Chicago, Indianapolis, and Lake Michigan, as well as casinos, Amish country, and Midwestern vineyards. You also can visit the University of Notre Dame campus—where football rules—as well as the College Football Hall of Fame for a look at some of the teams the Fighting Irish have taken on over the years. The resort itself displays a large collection of college football memorabilia and originally commissioned sports art.

While there is no golf course on site, the resort is part of Interval International's Golf Resort Program—giving members access to greens fee and lesson discounts, advance tee times, and more at local courses. On-site activities include indoor and outdoor swimming pools, a fitness center, a playground, a sauna, and more.

Villas at Giants Ridge, Biwabik, Minnesota

There are no fewer than thirty-five alpine runs on Giants Ridge, along with hundreds of snowmobile trails and cross-country skiing routes. But don't let that fool you into believing this Resort Condominiums International Gold Crown resort is a winter-only destination—its summertime fun includes playing a PGA-designed 18-hole golf course or exploring adjacent Wynne Lake by paddleboat, fishing boat, kayak, or simply in your bathing suit.

The Duluth, Minnesota, airport is closest, about sixty miles away. Timeshare units come in studio, one-, two-, and three-bedroom configurations, with the largest units sleeping as many as eight people privately. Some of the units have fireplaces and private laundry facilities, and all of the units have full or partial kitchens, depending on their size.

Top Properties in the South

Many of the top vacation areas in the Southern United States—from Biloxi, Mississippi, to the world-famous city of New Orleans, Louisiana—were ravaged by Hurricanes Katrina and Rita in the fall of 2005. It is difficult to know when (and in some cases, whether) the timeshare resorts in this region will begin to function at their previous levels, but it is important to keep in mind as these destinations come back to life that resorts with previously high ratings are likely to regain ground faster, and return to top-notch service sooner, than other timeshare resorts. For that reason, resorts from storm-damaged areas are included on the following list of Southern timeshares that continually receive high rankings from exchange companies and consumer groups alike.

Chateau Orleans, New Orleans, Louisiana

Located in the historic French Quarter, this timeshare property is within walking distance of Jackson Square, Bourbon Street, and all the other attractions that have made this city of jazz come alive over the course of many decades. Demand is high at this property all year round, but especially during Mardi Gras every February, when the streets fill with revelers who flash their bosoms at the bead-dangling crowds on the balconies above.

Timeshare units at the Chateau Orleans come in studio, one-, and two-bedroom configurations, with the largest units sleeping four people privately, or six people total. All of the units have air conditioning, and some, depending on their size, have full kitchens and/or whirlpool tubs, as well. Public laundry facilities and a swimming pool are among the resort amenities.

Escapes! To the Gulf, Orange Beach, Alabama

This Interval International Five Star Award resort is located on the Gulf of Mexico near multiple golf courses and white sand beaches. There is a boardwalk connecting the resort's courtyard and pool area to the oceanfront, so you need not waste a step in getting to the swimming, snorkeling, and other water sports. Sailing, surfing, and saltwater fishing are among the most popular activities in the area, allowing you to work up an appetite before dinner at one of the many waterfront seafood restaurants nearby.

The timeshare units themselves are in one-, two-, and three-bedroom configurations, with some units offering the same number of bedrooms but different amounts of square footage.

▪ TRAVEL TIP

A typical three-bedroom unit at this resort is 1,660 square feet with two bathrooms, while there are also three-bedroom units in the resort that are 1,720 square feet with three and a half bathrooms. Be sure to ask for the extra space if you think it might be important to you and your family.

Gatlinburg Town Square, Gatlinburg, Tennessee

Nestled in a valley that borders the Great Smoky Mountains National Park, this Interval International Five Star Award resort is minutes from the local theme park attraction, Dollywood. Most of the timeshare units have their own fireplaces and private balconies, while the resort itself has a heated indoor swimming pool, an exercise room, a playground, and a waterfall on site. Nearby, you can also take part in fishing, horseback riding, and—during the colder winter months—ice skating and downhill skiing.

The timeshare units at Gatlinburg Town Square come in efficiency, one-bedroom, two-bedroom, and three-bedroom configurations, with the largest units sleeping eight people. The closest airport is in Knoxville, Tennessee, about forty-five miles away.

Hyatt Wild Oak Ranch, San Antonio, Texas

The indoor/outdoor family pool with two water slides is sure to keep the kids busy while adults enjoy this timeshare resort's Hill Country Golf Club—twenty-seven holes designed by Arthur Hill—and state-of-the-art health spa. There's also an 800-foot-long river pool on site if you'd prefer to float along while taking in the views.

Timeshare units come in studio and one-, two-, and three-bedroom configurations, with the largest units using sleeper sofas to accommodate as many as ten people. Most of the largest units have private balconies, and all of them include full kitchens, private laundry facilities, and whirlpool baths.

Inverness at South Padre, South Padre Island, Texas

Inverness at South Padre is an elegant high-rise resort right on the beach overlooking the Gulf of Mexico. Deep-sea charter fishing is a favorite vacation activity, and other options include golf, tennis, horseback riding, and shuffleboard. Demand is high nearly year-round for timeshare units in this location.

≡FAST FACT

The nearest public airport is about forty miles from the resort in the town of Harlingen, which itself is about a two-hour drive south of Corpus Christi.

Timeshares are available in studio and one-, two-, and three-bedroom configurations, with the largest units sleeping eight people privately. Only some of the units have full kitchens and air conditioning, but all contain at least a kitchenette and/or a microwave oven.

Silverleaf's Lake O' the Woods, Flint, Texas

This East Texas resort is on the wooded shoreline of Lake Palestine, about 100 miles from Dallas, and offers rustic cabins with access to a lighted tennis court, a fishing pier, nature trails, miniature golf, a playground, and more. Jet Skis are available for rent, and horseback riding is an option, as well.

Each of the timeshare cabins on the property has one bedroom and sleeps four people privately, or six people in total. There is air conditioning in each cabin, as well as a full kitchen. High season is from late April through late October, and again during the Christmas holiday week.

Top Properties in the West

Gambling and golfing are the top draws in the Western United States, with timeshare resorts from Las Vegas, Nevada, to Scottsdale, Arizona, luring vacationers with warm winter weather and hot night-life entertainment. Spas are also a big draw at many of these vacation properties, giving couples a chance to split up and have some alone time while being pampered by the staffs of their choice.

Following is a list of Western United States timeshares that continually receive high rankings from exchange companies and consumer groups alike.

Fairfield Las Vegas at Grand Desert, Las Vegas, Nevada

Less than a mile from The Strip, this timeshare resort has adult and children's swimming pools on site, as well as a health club, a game room, and exercise equipment. As most of your entertainment will take place on The Strip itself—everything from gaming to live shows to gourmet dining—the resort offers limited eating options, including a snack bar.

E-ALERT

Demand is high all-year round for timeshare use in this hot spot of a city, so you'll have to book or buy early if you want to enjoy the amenities.

Timeshare units at the Fairfield Las Vegas at Grand Desert include one-, two-, and three-bedroom configurations, with the largest units sleeping as many as ten people privately. All of the units have private laundry facilities and air conditioning, and some units have full kitchens and/or fireplaces.

Hilton Grand Vacations Club at the Flamingo, Las Vegas, Nevada

This Resort Condominiums International Gold Crown property is right on Las Vegas Boulevard and offers timeshare units in studio and one- and two-bedroom configurations. All of the units have air conditioning, and some, depending on their size, also include full kitchens and/or private laundry facilities.

There is a casino on site, with additional amenities including a health club, swimming pool, tennis court, spa, and children's pool. Live shows take place nightly on stage, and a shopping area is just steps away from the timeshare units.

Park Plaza at Beaver Creek, Colorado

This timeshare resort, an Interval International Five Star Award-winner, is located in a resort community in Vail Valley that includes shops, restaurants, and an eighteen-hole golf course. In addition, Vail Valley itself encompasses more than 2,310 acres of ski slopes and trails, perfect for wintertime skiing enthusiasts or summertime hikers.

The timeshare units at Park Plaza are configured as two- and three-bedroom units, with some of the two-bedroom units sleeping six people and others sleeping as many as eight. On-site amenities at the resort include an indoor pool, a whirlpool, a steam room, and a sauna, while nearby offerings include fishing, theaters, horseback riding, and tennis.

Four Seasons Resort Aviara, North San Diego, California

One- and two-bedroom timeshare units are available at this posh resort, which has a Spanish Colonial-style ambience. Each of the units has multiple balconies and/or terraces, and the larger units' kitchens feature refrigerators, ranges, and dishwashers.

PGA superstar Arnold Palmer designed the eighteen-hole, par-seventy-two golf course on site, taking full advantage of the natural lagoon to create challenging water hazards. There are also four hard and two clay tennis courts on site, all lighted for night use. If you prefer to be pampered, you can enjoy a massage, facial, body wrap, or other service at the luxury spa.

Four Seasons Resort Scottsdale, Scottsdale, Arizona

This resort sits on forty acres in the Sonoran Desert and houses the Troon North golf complex, which includes two separate par-seventy-two courses that are so exceptional, they were given five-star ratings by *Golf Digest* magazine. The public is allowed to play here on nonmember days, but timeshare owners may reserve their tee times as much as ninety days in advance, thus virtually guaranteeing whatever time on the green suits your fancy.

≡FAST FACT

Each two-bedroom villa is designed in traditional adobe architecture and includes a full kitchen, landscaped terrace or shaded balcony, and deep tub. Phase I of the development is entirely sold out, but Phase II units were still available at press time.

In-villa massages are available if you don't care to take advantage of the full-service spa, which also offers facials, body wraps, hair styling, and more. A pool and fitness center are also on site, and local activities include helicopter tours, bicycling, hiking, fishing, hunting, parasailing, mountain biking, and skeet shooting. There is also a children's club called Kids for All Seasons that provides partial- or full-day activities for little ones between the ages of five and twelve.

Sedona Summit, Sedona, Arizona

The Grand Canyon and a local Hopi Native American reservation are among the places you can explore with a stay at this resort in Red Rock country. Tours take place on foot, in Jeeps, and in hot-air balloons, all able to be arranged by the personnel at this Interval International Five Star Award timeshare resort.

On-site amenities include a playground, swimming pool, Jacuzzi, fitness center, and activities center. Nearby you can enjoy bicycling, horseback riding, shopping, and more. The largest timeshare units are two bedrooms sleeping six to eight people, and the smallest available are efficiencies good for two to four people. The nearest airport is in Phoenix, about 125 miles away.

The Ridge Tahoe, Stateline, Nevada

Summertime on Lake Tahoe offers a bevy of water-sports fun, while winters in nearby Carson Valley include some of the most scenic downhill skiing you'll find in the United States. Both seasons are high-demand times for The Ridge Tahoe, which offers all of that and more.

The resort's indoor recreation complex includes a swimming pool, a weight room, and courts for playing racquetball, badminton, and tennis. There is also an outdoor tennis court on site for summertime use, as well as a private gondola that will carry you to the Heavenly Valley Ski Resort during the colder months.

Timeshare units at this property are all two-bedroom vacation homes that sleep six people total. Each of the units has a full kitchen and a fireplace, and some of the units also have private laundry facilities. The closest major airport is in Reno, Nevada, about sixty-five miles away.

Top Properties in Puerto Rico and Hawaii

Hawaii, as mentioned previously in this chapter, has long been a hot spot for vacation and timeshare properties because of its natural beauty and its longtime reputation as an exotic honeymoon destination of choice. But don't let your imagination stop there. When it comes to traveling outside the continental United States, you'll also have some luck with well-respected properties in Puerto Rico—where, unlike other tropical islands, you can fly direct from many major United States cities.

Following is a list of timeshares that are within the United States, but outside the mainland, and that continually receive high rankings from exchange companies and consumer groups alike.

The Bay Club at Waikoloa Beach Resort, Kamuela, Hawaii

Located on the Big Island of Hawaii, this Resort Condominiums International Gold Crown property is graced with tropical waterfalls and garden pathways that simply ooze island lifestyle. Championship golf courses and white sand beaches are both within walking distance, as are a pair of championship tennis courts and two outdoor pools.

▥ TRAVEL TIP

Demand is high all year round for The Bay Club's timeshare units, which come in one- and two-bedroom configurations that sleep as many as six people privately. All of the units are air conditioned with full kitchens and private laundry facilities. In addition, the resort's amenities include a playground and an exercise facility.

Embassy Vacation Resort Kaanapali Beach, Maui, Hawaii

This Interval International Five Star Award resort is on the west end of Maui in the town of Lahaina. One- and two-bedroom timeshare units are available, sleeping a maximum of six people. There are gazebos in the resort's atrium, as well as tropical gardens and waterfalls around the grounds, all designed in keeping with traditional Hawaiian themes.

On-site amenities include a game room, a miniature golf course, a beachside barbecue area, a fitness center, shopping, boating, scuba diving, an outdoor swimming pool, and a sauna. Nearby, you can enjoy a playground, fishing, and championship golf courses.

Hilton Grand Vacations Club at Hilton Hawaiian Village, Oahu, Hawaii

Located on the world-renowned Waikiki Beach, this twenty-two-acre resort is manicured with swimming pools, gardens, and waterfalls that combine to create a romantic, tropical ambience. The resort's offerings include Mandara Spa and holistic health center, as well as three swimming pools, a beauty salon, and transportation to nearby golf courses.

▐█▌ TRAVEL TIP

The largest of the villas holds eight people maximum, while the studios are recommended for only two guests apiece. Rental car parking is available, as well, but for an additional fee.

Timeshare units are configured as studios, or as one-, two-, and three-bedroom villas. Most of the villas have private balconies, and all have air conditioning, full kitchens, and washers and dryers on each floor.

Kona Coast Resort, Kailua-Kona, Hawaii

This Big Island resort has earned a Gold Crown ranking from Resort Condominiums International for its one-, two-, and three-bedroom timeshare units. Each is air conditioned with a full kitchen and private laundry facilities, and the largest units can sleep eight people in privacy.

Resort activities include deep-sea fishing, scuba diving, sunset cruises, and shopping. There is a poolside restaurant on site, as well as live entertainment. Golf and boating are within a mile or two of the resort.

SMVC at Paradisus Puerto Rico, San Juan, Puerto Rico

This Resort Condominiums International property is the only one listed as Gold Crown on all of Puerto Rico. It is part of the Sol Melia luxury resort complex on Coco Beach, along the island's northeastern coast.

≡FAST FACT

It's important to note that this resort has a mandatory all-inclusive policy, which typically includes all of your meals, airport transfers, resort activities, and perhaps more.

Demand is high all year round for the timeshare units, which come in one-, two-, and three-bedroom configurations. All of the units have air conditioning, and some, depending on their size, also have full kitchens. Resort amenities include a casino, golf, fishing, boating, a game room, a swimming pool, laundry facilities, wind surfing, water skiing, and more.

The Cliffs Club, Kauai, Hawaii

Located in the town of Princeville, on the north shore of Kauai in the Hawaiian Islands, this Interval International Five Star Award resort spans more than twenty acres. Its on-site amenities include four tennis courts, a swimming pool, two whirlpools, a sauna, and a putting green with a sand trap. Nearby, you can enjoy full-length golf courses, boating, a full-service spa, fishing, horseback riding, scuba diving, and more.

The timeshare units at The Cliffs Club are configured as one-, two-, and four-bedroom units (no three-bedroom units are listed), and each has a lanai and ceiling fans to help you beat the heat. Garden and ocean views are available, so be sure to request waterfront if that is important to you.

CHAPTER 6

Buying Outside the United States

ABOUT TWO-THIRDS OF THE 5,400 or so worldwide timeshares are located in towns and cities outside the United States. They can be found in places as diverse as the treasured European city of Paris, France, the up-and-coming global power of Beijing, China, and the South Pacific tropical paradise of Nadi, Fiji. Buying timeshare units outside of U.S. borders can be a good option, for sure, but there are some considerations to keep in mind if you want to make the most of your vacation dollar.

Understanding the Worldwide Marketplace

In many ways, buying timeshare units outside of the United States is a lot like buying them inside the nation's borders: You need to make sure you are doing business with a reputable company, you need to do your homework about the resort—and the particular unit—that you are buying, and you need to buy at a price point that makes sense in comparison with the expected ten-year price range for hotel rates in your chosen destination. Having said that, the broader worldwide marketplace does present such a varying array of timeshare options that you would be wise to do a bit of extra research before buying.

Overseas Legal Considerations

For starters, as with any timeshare unit purchase, you need to consider how you plan to use your vacation property. If you intend to return to the same location year after year, you will want to choose a destination that, at a minimum, has a stable government and some sort of legal protections in place for timeshare buyers.

For instance, if you want to buy a timeshare unit within a country that is a member of the European Union (with France, Spain, and Italy being popular options), you can rest assured that those nations have been in existence for centuries, and that their governments—and thus legal systems—are unlikely to be upended by military coups anytime in the near future.

Also, timeshare developers in the European Union are required by law to give buyers the same kind of rescission, or cooling off period, that buyers in the United States are entitled to receive. In fact, in the European Union, the law states that you, the buyer, must not be asked to pay any money at all before or during the ten-day cooling off period, which, in theory, allows you at least a few extra days to go over the clauses of your signed contract in the most detailed way possible before any cash changes hands. If you change your mind about the deal during the rescission period, you can—by law—get out of the contracts that you signed.

European Union law also states that you, the buyer, have the right to receive a brochure and written contract in the language of your choice, as well as in the language of the country where your timeshare unit is located. That's a significant right—especially if you're looking to buy a timeshare unit in a nation such as Greece, where every word of the contract could be spelled out in the Greek alphabet.

These types of assurances are not always available for timeshare purchases in some other parts of the world. In fact, in many nations, you cannot even make a deeded timeshare purchase. Some places offer only right-to-use timeshare deals, which expire after a given time period or a given number of uses and leave you with no legal right to your unit (as explained in Chapter 2). This is not always a bad thing—and can sometimes make a timeshare option more affordable in general—but it is important that you understand what you are buying and what protections the local and federal law will give you should problems arise.

☰Ɛ☰ E-ALERT

Beware of overseas timeshare developers who refuse to give you anything but a local-language copy of their brochures, contracts, or other important paperwork. If you cannot get copies of documents in English, or in another language you understand, you would be wise to walk away from the deal before signing anything.

Your best bet, no matter which nation you choose for your time-share purchase, is to check with the federal and local agencies that regulate consumer purchases. Some good places to start include the U.S. Embassy in the nation where you are considering a purchase. A list of worldwide embassies is available at the U.S. Department of State's Web site, *http://usembassy.state.gov.*

While you're on the U.S. Department of State's Web site, you might also check out its travel and living abroad section, *http://state .gov/travel.* It includes a page devoted entirely to travel warnings, which tell U.S. citizens which nations the government recommends avoiding. (At the end of 2005, there were more than two dozen nations listed.) This section of the Web site also includes a link to Consular Information Sheets for many of the world's nations. These information-rich resources include everything from a nation's general description to an overview of its criminal laws, medical facilities, transportation services, and more.

In addition to researching your timeshare's nation through the United States government, you also may consider contacting attorneys and timeshare experts in the overseas nation of your choice. These people will have a more in-depth understanding of the complexities of timeshare law in their own nations, and thus may be able to provide you with more detailed information than a federal-level government agency. If your overseas resort has an office on United States soil, that can be a good place to start when seeking out overseas experts.

Overseas Financial Issues

Foreign currency rates are another thing that can have a major impact on your overseas timeshare purchase. For starters, there is the exchange rate. In some cases, you will be asked to pay for your timeshare unit in the currency of the nation where it is based, instead of in United States dollars. Over a mortgage term of ten or fifteen years, the exchange rate can add up to major savings, or major extra expenditures.

The United States dollar has traditionally been strong throughout the world, but in recent years it has experienced weakening against the European Union's euro and the United Kingdom's pound. This has made taking vacations in that region more expensive for United States citizens, while in other nations, such as the South Pacific's Fiji, the dollar remains strong, worth almost twice as much as a local dollar—making vacation purchases there relatively less expensive. In still other worldwide locations, including the Bahamas, the local currency is linked to the United States dollar at a one-for-one rate, meaning expenses there will cost about the same as they would at home.

📖 TRAVEL TIP

Be sure to check the strength of the United States dollar compared with the strength of the currency in the nation where you want to purchase a timeshare. A good way to do this is by using the free Universal Currency Converter at *www.xe.com/ucc.*

Also keep in mind that when you are using your foreign timeshare, you will have to purchase sundries, food, drinks, and everything else during your vacation with the foreign currency, as well. You also may be taxed differently than local citizens might be, again adding up to either additional savings or additional expenses during the course of your timeshare contract. The average timeshare vacationer spent about $210 per day in U.S. currency during Caribbean vacations in 2003, most of it on dining and shopping, according to a report by Resort Condominiums International. Imagine how that amount could rise or fall in accordance with the strength of the U.S. dollar.

No matter which country you are considering for a timeshare unit purchase, be sure to compare the long-term expenses of buying goods and services with the foreign currency against the power of your earnings in United States dollars. The last thing you want is to lose the potential savings power of your timeshare to a dollar that is traditionally weak in your vacation nation of choice.

Overseas Vacation Patterns

Another factor that will affect the success of your overseas time-share unit purchase is worldwide vacation patterns. If you are considering buying a timeshare unit that you will return to year after year, this factor will not be as important to you as it will be to a buyer looking at a timeshare unit to be used for exchange. If you are considering buying a unit overseas that you can trade for other vacation destinations around the globe, vacation patterns become a primary concern.

Why? Just as there are hot spots within the United States where you can buy a timeshare to maximize your exchange power, there are also hot spots around the world where you will get more exchange power than if you buy elsewhere. Some of these destinations, and others that seem to be growing into the hot-spot category, include:

- Bahamas
- Dominican Republic
- Mexico
- Netherlands Antilles/Greater Caribbean
- Coastal Spain
- U.S. Virgin Islands
- South Africa

Each of these destinations is growing in general tourism numbers—not just in American tourism numbers—which makes it logical that an increase in timeshare demand would follow. That's what understanding worldwide vacation patterns is all about.

Consider, for instance, the city of Paris, France, which upward of forty million people a year visit during their vacations. That's a staggering five million people more than live in the entire state of California, making Paris the type of worldwide destination hot spot that Orlando, Florida, is in the United States.

By contrast, you might look into the tourism statistics for Fiji, which boasts lush tropical islands and has always been a dream destination for travelers from around the globe. It might be a place you have always wished you could visit, the kind of place you keep posters of and watch television shows about every chance you get. Still, though, even with its romantic reputation, Fiji draws only about 500,000 tourists a year (not counting cruise-ship passengers). That's a fraction of the number of people booking vacations in Paris on an annual basis.

Thus, when you compare Paris with Fiji, you can see that as a potential timeshare unit owner looking to make exchanges, you are likely going to have more demand for a unit you purchase in the City of Lights than you will for a unit in the exotic South Pacific, even if the timeshare in Fiji is bigger, better-outfitted, and, perhaps, in what you consider to be a more paradisiacal setting.

If you really enjoy visiting Fiji and want to return every year, a timeshare unit there might be the right thing for you to purchase. However, if you're hoping to trade your timeshare vacation time for another unit elsewhere in the world, you will probably have a better chance of getting what you want if you can offer other vacationers a timeshare unit in Paris, where demand is far stronger.

Do keep in mind that if you want to return to the same place year after year, there are worldwide deals to be had in emerging timeshare regions. South Africa, for instance, had about 180 timeshare resorts as of 2004—and a unit's per-week price was only about $2,700 (one of the lowest averages for new timeshare purchases anywhere in the world, according to Resort Condominiums International). This means that if you enjoy a resort in South Africa and want to keep going back, you can do so for far less expense than you might find when purchasing a similar timeshare unit in the more developed markets of the United States and Europe.

E-ALERT

If you are purchasing an overseas fixed-week timeshare that you hope to trade for other vacations, keep in mind that holidays and special events are often key to worldwide vacation demand. If you own a week in Cannes, France, during the middle of winter, you will have less luck trading for the vacation of your choice than if you owned a fixed week in mid-May, when the Cannes Film Festival takes place.

Overseas Weather and Geography Concerns

Last, when considering an overseas timeshare purchase, you must keep in mind the resort's geographical location and all that it brings with it.

The Caribbean, for instance, has a wonderful reputation as a warm-weather destination of choice for vacationers from all over the world. However, some of the islands in the Caribbean are better developed than others, which means they have better infrastructures and businesses in place. If you want to eat fresh fruit at your timeshare resort for breakfast every morning, remember that it will probably cost you more to buy it up in the hills on the far side of Antigua, for instance, than it would in downtown St. Martin, near the airports where planes full of fresh produce land.

Geography is also a key concern in terms of weather. Again, a good example is the Caribbean, where hurricanes tend to devastate several different islands each year. Purchasing a timeshare unit in Grenada, for instance, might sound like a good deal nowadays because there are many properties to be had. Dig a little deeper, though, and you learn that the reason there is so much availability is that the island is rebuilding from the battering that came with Hurricane Ivan in September 2004. More than 85 percent of the island's buildings were damaged or destroyed, meaning many timeshare owners—if they owned right-to-use timeshares instead of insured, deeded properties—were left with absolutely nothing from their investment. You may not want to pick up with an investment where those poor souls left off.

═FAST FACT

According to the National Oceanic and Atmospheric Administration, your timeshare's chance of suffering a direct hit by a hurricane in the Caribbean during the month of September is anywhere from 2 to 12 percent, with the chances increasing the closer you get to the center of the Caribbean Sea.

Last, when considering geography in your overseas timeshare purchase, you would be wise to factor in the cost of your family's transportation to and from the resort. As fuel prices continued to surge worldwide in early 2006, discount airfares were becoming harder and harder to find. A round-trip ticket from New Jersey's Newark Liberty International Airport down to Bermuda, for instance, was in the neighborhood of $700 per person.

If you're considering buying a timeshare unit in a place with limited airport services, keep in mind that prices for plane fare will continue to rise along with worldwide energy prices. Those costs could easily take a big chunk out of the overall savings you can expect to enjoy by purchasing a timeshare in the first place.

Finding International Timeshares

Mexico, Spain, and the U.S. Virgin Islands are some of the hottest locations outside the United States for timeshare purchases these days, but if none of those areas appeal to you, there are still plenty of options among which you can choose.

Since your safest bet is to purchase an overseas timeshare that is part of a larger, worldwide exchange company—such as Resort Condominiums International or Interval International—those are the top properties that will be discussed throughout the rest of this chapter. You very well may be able to find reputable developers working outside of these networks in foreign lands, but working within the existing system is the easiest route that most people tend to choose when buying timeshare units overseas.

The Caribbean

There are as many timeshare units sprinkled around the Caribbean Sea as there are islands themselves. From Puerto Rico and the Dominican Republic all the way west to Jamaica and the Cayman Islands, or all the way south to Barbados and beyond, timeshare resorts are popping up to offer tropical getaways for couples, families, and even large groups. The U.S. Virgin Islands—particularly the islands of St. Thomas and St. John—appear to be among the most up-and-coming timeshare destinations in this region, which makes sense because they are already luring vacationers by the thousands as part of major cruise ship itineraries.

Here is a look at a few Caribbean timeshares that continually receive high rankings from exchange companies and consumer groups alike.

Casa del Mar Beach Resort, Oranjestad, Aruba

All of the units at this Resort Condominiums International property are air conditioned with full kitchens, should you prefer to cook for yourself with supplies from the on-site grocery store instead of grabbing a poolside snack or making reservations at the resort's restaurant. Touring the architecturally renowned city of Oranjestad is a favorite pastime, as of course are water sports such as swimming, water-skiing, boating, and more.

The Casa Del Mar Beach Resort has a child-care facility as well as a children's pool, playground, and game room, making it a good choice for families. Horseback riding and an adults-only casino are within a few miles of the resort.

Indies Suites, Grand Cayman Island

Indies Suites, a Resort Condominiums International Gold Crown property, is across the road from Grand Cayman Island's world-famous Seven Mile Beach. All of the timeshare units are air conditioned, and some have full kitchens. A complimentary continental breakfast and a complimentary sunset cruise are included in the price of your timeshare purchase.

TRAVEL TIP

As the island is famous for its five-star underwater scenery, the Indies Suites is an excellent choice for divers and snorkelers who want to enjoy every single minute of "down time" they can.

Red Sail Sports oversees the water sports at Indies Suites, and the company has a fine reputation on Grand Cayman for providing excellent scuba diving instruction and excursions.

Royal Islander Club la Plage, St. Martin

Just a mile from the international airport on St. Martin, the Royal Islander Club la Plage is a Resort Condominiums International Gold Crown resort. All units are air conditioned, and some have full kitchens. The resort boasts the largest freshwater swimming pool on the half-French, half-Dutch island, and it is close to activities including a casino, golf club, horseback riding, and more. A comedy club is on site, as are a restaurant and plenty of beachfront lounge chairs.

The Royal Islander Club la Plage is a large facility, and the staff requires a bit of extra time to perform the day's room cleanings.

This time crunch is passed on to you, in the form of early checkout times—no later than 10 A.M. on your day of departure.

Sand Acres Beach Club, Christchurch, Barbados

The Sand Acres Beach club boasts air-conditioned timeshare units, each of which has a full kitchen and a balcony overlooking the crystal-blue Caribbean Sea. The resort is just five miles from Bridgetown, a shopping district where you can find everything from English china to Asian silks and antiques. Nonmotorized water sports are included in the price of your timeshare unit, and for an additional fee you can participate in everything from scuba diving to guided fishing excursions.

Sand Acres Beach Club is just five miles from the Grantley Adams International Airport, and there is a restaurant on site. The nearest golf course and spa are two and three miles away, respectively.

The Royal Sea Aquarium Resort, Curaçao

This Interval International Five Star Award resort is located on a private island next to the world-famous Curaçao Sea Aquarium and Dolphin Academy. The aquarium has a unique design that is right on the beach and continually refreshed with new seawater, and some of its offerings include encounters where you can snorkel or scuba dive with stingrays, sea turtles, sharks, sea lions, and many different kinds of colorful fish.

If you would prefer to enjoy your leisure time at the resort—which offers only two-bedroom timeshare units that sleep as many as six people—you can make use of amenities including an outdoor swimming pool, a separate children's swimming pool, boating, fishing, scuba diving, and more. Golf is nearby, as are horseback riding, tennis, a casino, and shopping.

The Village at St. James's Club, Antigua

The St. James's Club is located on a private 100-acre estate far across the island of Antigua from where the cruise ships dock and the bulk of tourism takes place. This Interval International Five Star Award resort is near the yachting centers of Falmouth and English Harbours, destinations that sailors seeking a private slice of paradise have savored for years. You can enjoy a bit of it yourself in one of the hotel-style, one-bedroom, or two-bedroom timeshare units that are available.

≡FAST FACT

Close by the St. James's Club you'll find Nelson's Dockyard, which was built starting in 1725 to protect Royal Navy warships. You can also take a hike up to Shirley Heights, a former lookout post that now hosts a Sunday night sunset-and-steel-drum party led by the locals.

On-site amenities include boating, a casino, a fitness center, fishing, a playground, scuba diving, an outdoor pool, tennis courts, water-skiing, a Jacuzzi, and more. You can spend a few dollars in the nearby local shops or go horseback riding.

Virgin Grand Villas, St. John, U.S. Virgin Islands

The Virgin Grand Villas, which have earned the Gold Crown designation from Resort Condominiums International, are also known as the Westin St. John Resort and Villas. Each timeshare unit is on the resort's forty-six-acre tropical garden site and is air conditioned with a full kitchen and private laundry facilities.

Six lighted tennis courts and an outdoor pool are among the places you can hang out at the Virgin Grand Villas when you're not lounging on the resort's swath of oceanfront beach. There is child care available on site, as well, for those times when you want to hit the exercise room or relax in the sauna or hot tub.

Windjammer Landing Villa Beach Resort and Spa, Castries, St. Lucia

A Resort Condominiums International Gold Crown Resort, the Windjammer Landing Villa Beach Resort and Spa is an optional all-inclusive timeshare vacation spot that overlooks the sparkling turquoise sea from a classic Caribbean hillside. The resort is just five minutes from St. Lucia's international airport, and its units offer varying combinations of air conditioning, full kitchens, and private laundry facilities.

Ocean water sports are the main draw at this timeshare resort, though the site also offers tennis, fishing, adult and children's swimming pools, a playground, and live entertainment. There is a restaurant on the property, and golf and horseback riding are both within about three miles.

The Bahamas/Bermuda

The Bahamas—from the Abacos to the Exumas—and Bermuda to their north have long been popular vacation destinations for American travelers because of their proximity to the United States. They offer much of the same tropical sun and fun that you can find in the Caribbean, but without the longer airplane rides that are required to enjoy a vacation in the heart of the Caribbean Sea.

Here is a look at a few Bermuda and Bahamas timeshares that continually receive high rankings from exchange companies and consumer groups alike.

Harborside Resort at Atlantis, Nassau, Bahamas

This Interval International Five Star Award resort works in conjunction with the nearby Atlantis Resort and Casino to offer you the best of both worlds: a turquoise-water paradise and the hot nightlife of a thriving resort town. Timeshare units at the Harborside Resort come in one- and two-bedroom configurations, sleeping as many as eight people in total. On-site amenities include an outdoor swimming pool, fitness room, and whirlpool tub, while nearby you can enjoy boating, a spa, fishing, golf, shopping, and more.

📖 TRAVEL TIP

Much of the draw at the Harborside Resort is thanks to the amenities at the nearby Atlantis resort, which has entertainment for the whole family—from craps tables to music concerts to Mayan water slides. Be sure to ask about discounted, or even free, admissions when you reserve your timeshare exchange.

Paradise Harbour Club and Marina, Nassau, Bahamas

The Paradise Harbour Club and Marina, located on the beautifully named Paradise Island Drive, has earned the Gold Crown distinction from Resort Condominiums International. Complimentary water taxis and bicycles are available should you wish to cross the bridge and visit the shops in Nassau, where many items are available for you to purchase duty-free.

All of the timeshare units at this resort are air conditioned, and some have full kitchens, as well. Laundry facilities are on site, as are a restaurant, conference facilities, and child-care services. Water sports are the main activity, with everything available from swimming to fishing to scuba diving. A casino, golf course, and tennis courts are nearby.

Royal Oasis Vacation Club, Freeport, Bahamas

The Royal Oasis Vacation Club has earned the Gold Crown designation from Resort Condominiums International. It is part of the

Royal Oasis Golf Resort and Casino, which is just three miles from the nearest international airport. All of the timeshare units are air conditioned with full kitchens. Laundry facilities and a grocery store are available on the resort's property.

In addition to the golf course and casino on site, you can enjoy a million-gallon swimming pool that includes two water slides, a swim-up bar, and a waterfall. The resort also has a health club, game room, sauna, and tennis court. The beach is nearby, along with everything from fishing to water skiing to scuba diving.

Sandyport Beaches Resort, Nassau, Bahamas

A Resort Condominiums International Gold Crown property, the Sandyport Beaches Resort is a small operation run by Festiva Resorts. It has just seventy-two rooms, all of which are air conditioned and some of which also have full kitchens and/or private laundry facilities.

The resort is just three miles from the international airport at Nassau, though the property's size means on-site activities are limited. There are adult and children's swimming pools, along with a restaurant, tennis court, and beach. You can use the local bus in order to enjoy the nearby casino, golf course, scuba diving, wind surfing, and other activities.

The St. George's Club, St. George, Bermuda

This resort is on the northeastern tip of Bermuda, about a mile from its private beach and beach club. Moped rentals are available on site for exploring the island when you're not making use of the resort's three outdoor swimming pools (one heated) or three tennis courts (two lighted for night play).

All of the timeshare units at The St. George's Club are air conditioned, and some have full kitchens and/or private laundry facilities. There is a grocery store on site, as well as a full-service restaurant. Golf is also available at the resort, and there is a health club for workout buffs. The island's international airport is about three miles away.

Mexico

There are timeshare units available virtually everywhere from the Mexican coasts to the country's interior, from the far northwest fun spot of Tijuana to the southeastern scuba mecca of Cozumel. Here is a look at a few Mexican timeshares that continually receive high rankings from exchange companies and consumer groups alike.

Club Baccara, Cancun, Mexico

This boutique resort, with just twenty-seven villas, offers a refreshing alternative to the sky-scraping resorts found all along the Cancun beachfront. It was developed by Avalon Resorts, which also operates vacation properties in nearby Isla Mujeres, Mexico, Acapulco, Mexico, and the nation of Panama. Club Baccara, the smaller of two Avalon resorts in Cancun, has earned the prestigious Five Star Award from Interval International.

 **E-QUESTION**

What are the most popular locations for timeshares in Mexico?
Cancun, to the east, and Puerto Vallarta, to the west, are the hottest timeshare destinations in Mexico these days. This makes sense because visitors have been introduced to the areas over the years by cruise ships that call on the same ports.

Club Baccara's timeshare units are configured in efficiency, one-bedroom, two-bedroom, and three-bedroom layouts, sleeping anywhere from two to six people. On-site amenities include a restaurant, outdoor swimming pool, and whirlpool tub. Nearby, you can find bicycling, boating, a fitness center, fishing, golf, shopping, scuba diving, tennis, water skiing, and more.

Occidental Grand, Cozumel, Mexico

This Resort Condominiums International Gold Crown property is on the southwest part of Cozumel Island, right on the beach called

San Francisco. It is a mandatory all-inclusive resort, with your time-share purchase or exchange including meals, transportation, and possibly some resort activities. All of the timeshare units have air conditioning.

Scuba diving is the main draw here, as the resort is only a five-minute boat cruise from Palancar Reef. Other activities on site include children's and adults' swimming pools, a game room, exercise equipment, live entertainment, a hairdresser, a spa, a restaurant, tennis courts, and a playground area. Horseback riding is off-site, but nearby.

Omni Cancun Hotel and Villas, Cancun, Mexico

This Interval International Five Star Award resort is also part of the exchange company's Golf Resort Program—giving members access to greens fees and lesson discounts, advance tee times, and more at neighboring golf courses (there are none directly on site). However, there are plenty of activities available on the grounds, including a fitness center, shopping, a sauna, scuba diving, an outdoor swimming pool, tennis, a whirlpool tub, and more. Nearby, you can also find boating, bicycling, fishing, horseback riding, and water skiing.

Timeshare units at this resort come in three configurations: efficiency (sleeping two to four people), one-bedroom (sleeping four to six people), and two-bedroom (sleeping six to eight people). There are several theme restaurants on site, including La Paloma, which serves Mexican; the Pina Colada beach bistro, serving drinks and light dishes; and Da Vinci's fine dining, serving Italian food, seafood, and more.

Pacifica Club, Ixtapa, Mexico

The Pacifica Club is located about twelve miles from the Ixtapa-Zihuatanejo International Airport. All of its timeshare units are air conditioned, and some have full kitchens. The Pacifica Club is a mandatory all-inclusive resort, with your timeshare fees including meals, transportation, and possibly even activities and drinks.

The resort is on the beach and offers a swimming pool, as well. There is child care on site, along with a playground and a snack bar, making this resort worthy of consideration for family vacations with small children. Nearby activities include fishing, golf, tennis, water skiing, and scuba diving.

The Royal Mayan, Cancun, Mexico

The Royal Mayan has earned both the Gold Crown distinction from Resort Condominiums International and Five Star Award status from Interval International. It is part of the well-respected Royal Resorts family, which also includes The Royal Caribbean and The Royal Sands timeshare resorts in Cancun.

≡FAST FACT

The Royal Mayan sits on the Caribbean shore, with a lagoon-side marina where you can rent sailboats, water-skiing packages, and Jet Skis. All of the units are air conditioned with full kitchens, and there is a grocery store on site in addition to the resort's snack bar and full-service restaurant.

One of the favorite activities at the Royal Mayan is taking part in tours of the ancient Mayan ruins at Tulum, Chichen-Itza, and Coba. When you're done with those, you can relax in the Royal Mayan's adults' and children's swimming pools or play on the tennis court. Nearby activities include boating, fishing, golf, live entertainment, shopping, and scuba diving.

Aventura Spa Palace, Puerto Aventuras, Mexico

This adults-only, all-inclusive property has earned the Gold Crown distinction from Resort Condominiums International. All of its timeshare units have air conditioning, a double whirlpool tub, and a private balcony, and most units have ocean views.

The resort itself has 103 treatment rooms where you can enjoy anything from a basic massage to specialty treatments including hydro-reflexology and inhalation therapy. There are also whirlpool tubs and full-fitness facilities on site, and your timeshare purchase or exchange includes unlimited drinks and healthy meals.

At forty-eight miles away from the international airport in Cancun, the Spa Palace is certainly outside of the city's go-go party atmosphere. Because of its relative seclusion, it offers many activities and facilities on site, including a game room, hairdresser, live entertainment, restaurant, sauna, shopping area, snack bar, swimming pool, tennis court, and more.

Vacation Internationale Vallarta Torre, Puerto Vallarta, Mexico

This resort is two miles from the nearest international airport, right on the beach overlooking Banderas Bay. Air conditioning is not available in all of the timeshare units, but full kitchens are. A grocery store and laundry facilities are on site.

Amenities at Vacation Internationale Vallarta Torre include a swimming pool, restaurant, hot tub, and snack bar. Less than a mile away, you will find all of the other activities the resort offers, including horseback riding, scuba diving, a health club, a sauna, boating, water-skiing, and more. The closest golf course is about six miles away, and an eighteen-hole course is about fifteen miles away.

Western Mediterranean

Spain is the up-and-coming destination for timeshare purchases in the Western Mediterranean, particularly the nation's southern shore and its longtime vacation paradise of the Canary Islands. Urban timeshares are also becoming more high-demand in this part of the world, especially in tourist-friendly cities such as Venice, Italy. Here is a look at a few Western Mediterranean timeshares that continually receive high rankings from exchange companies and consumer groups alike.

Chateau de Maulmont, Randan, France

This castle, which sits on a hill within twenty acres of ancient forest, was built in 1830 with views of the Bourdonnais Mountains. Today, it is a Resort Condominiums International Gold Crown property that features a restaurant, indoor and outdoor swimming pools, a sauna, and more. All of the timeshare units have kitchens, some of them full and others partial.

The Chateau de Maulmont is near the town of Vichy, which has a famous eighteen-hole golf course along with countless fine restaurants. Other nearby activities include boating, cross-country skiing, shopping, squash, tennis, and wind surfing.

De Vere Resort Ownership, Belton Woods, England

This 500-acre estate in rural Linconshire boasts two championship golf courses with views of the rolling English countryside. The resort has earned Five Star Award status from Interval International, and it participates in the exchange company's Golf Resort Program, which offers discounted greens fees, discounted golf lessons, advance tee times, and more to Interval members.

Clay pigeon shooting is among the more unusual activities offered on site, along with bird watching, fishing, horseback riding, and tennis. There is an indoor swimming pool, too, along with a sauna, whirlpool tub, and fitness center. The timeshare units are configured in two- and three-bedroom layouts, sleeping six or eight people privately. The nearest airport is in London, about 140 miles away.

Eden Bay Resort, Malta

This Interval International Five Star Award resort is located on St. George's Bay. It is within walking distance of the trendy Sliema and St. Julian's, and it is a short drive from Malta's capital, Valletta (the airport is just ten miles away).

At the Eden Bay Resort itself, your timeshare unit will have satellite television, a full kitchen, a DVD player, and a balcony overlooking either the bay or the hotel's gardens.

💼 TRAVEL TIP

If you choose to exchange for one of the efficiency, one-bedroom, or two-bedroom timeshare units, you will also have access to many of the amenities of the adjacent InterContinental Malta, which has a swimming pool with panoramic views, a full-service spa, shopping, six restaurants and bars, a business center, and a fitness club.

Holiday Club Katinkulta, Vuokatti, Finland

The Holiday Club Katinkulta has earned the Gold Crown designation from Resort Condominiums International. Each timeshare unit has a fireplace, private sauna, and terrace barbecue, and some of the units also have private laundry facilities and-or full kitchens.

this isa an all-seasons resort, with summertime activities including swimming, hiking, fishing, horseback riding, and boating. An eighteen hole-golf course is on site, along with outdoor tennis courts. During the winter, you can enjoy cross-country and downhill skiing or relax in the resort's indoor leisure center, which includes a sauna, swimming pool, tennis, squash, badminton, golf practice range, game rooms, restaurants, and bars.

Kilconquhar Castle Estate and Country Club, Fife, Scotland

This Interval International Five Star Award resort is located in the East Neuk of Fife, which has one of the driest climates in the British Isles. The world-renowned St. Andrews golf course is just seven miles away, along with the British Golf Museum. You can tune up your game at the resort itself, which offers a driving range, putting green, and discounted fees for members of Interval International.

Other amenities available on the 130-acre estate grounds include horseback riding, tennis, squash, snooker, table tennis, an indoor swimming pool, and a fitness center. Nearby, you can take part in boating, bicycling, shopping, scuba diving, ice skating, and water-skiing.

Las Rosas, Canary Islands, Spain

This property is on the southwest coast of the island Tenerife, about a ten-minute walk from the town of Los Gigantes. The resort's hillside location is known for its sweeping views—and for its moderate to difficult hiking, which you should keep in mind if anyone in your family has difficulty walking. Each of the timeshare units is two floors with a full kitchen. Laundry facilities are available on site.

The resort has children's and adults' swimming pools, live entertainment, a snack bar, and a restaurant. Many water sports activities are nearby, though the nearest water-skiing and wind surfing is about seventeen miles away. Golf, too, is about that far from the resort.

Marriott's Marbella Beach Resort, Marbella, Spain

Part of the Marriott Vacation Club Resort network, this Costa del Sol property offers one-, two-, and three-bedroom villas that accommodate as many as ten people at a time. All of the villas have private balconies and/or patios as well as full kitchens and private laundry facilities. Master suites have king-size beds with oversized tub/showers. There is a grocery store on site.

The resort often receives high marks for family vacations, as it offers on-site baby sitting, a game room, indoor and outdoor children's swimming pools, and Compass Kids Club activities. Near the resort, you and your children can enjoy a game of miniature golf or a day of family-friendly water park fun.

For adults, Marriott's Marbella Beach Resort has a fitness center, a full-service restaurant, a beachside bar, four different swimming and lap pools, and a sauna. Nearby activities include golf, horseback riding, Jet Skiing, hiking, scuba diving, tennis, and more.

Palazzo del Giglio-Residenza Alberghiera, Venice, Italy

This property is one of precious few Resort Condominiums International Gold Crown facilities in Italy. The resort is in the heart of Venice near St. Mark's Square and the Rialto Bridge. All of its timeshare units are air conditioned, and some units offer partial kitchens (others offer no cooking amenities at all). Laundry facilities are on site for use by multiple guests at once.

E-ALERT

Activities you will find nearby include a casino, golf, live entertainment, restaurants, a swimming pool, and tennis courts. You may not have time for any of those, though, if you visit your timeshare unit during carnival time, which is in mid-February. You'll be having fun in the streets with the rest of the crowds.

The resort itself offers few amenities and activities, as the whole point of staying in Venice is to get out and explore all that the city has to offer.

Eastern Mediterranean

The Eastern Mediterranean—stretching across the Adriatic Sea from western Italy to Croatia, Greece, and Turkey—does not have the same hard-earned history of safe, worn-path tourism as some western Mediterranean countries do. However, with the quelling of ethnic wars in the former Yugoslavia, and with the Greek and Turkish desire to become more in line with the thinking, economics, and policies of the continent's western-driven European Union, the Eastern Mediterranean has begun in the past decade to take tourism quite seriously. As more and more people have begun to take summer vacations everywhere from Athens to Istanbul and in between, timeshare opportunities have popped up, as well.

Here is a look at a few Eastern Mediterranean timeshares that continually receive high rankings from exchange companies and consumer groups alike. Note that there are no Interval International properties listed. While the exchange company does work with multiple resorts in Greece, Turkey, Croatia, and beyond, none had earned the company's Five Star Award as of this printing.

Club Mykonos, Greece

The draw on Mykonos—as on most of the Greek Isles—is lounging on pristine beaches and exploring the charm of historic towns. Club Mykonos is positioned to offer both, with many of its timeshare units overlooking its stretch of Ornos Beach and with the main town's shops, cafes, and mountainside-climbing architecture less than two miles away. Tennis courts are also nearby.

≡FAST FACT

Club Mykonos is named for the beautiful Aegean island on which it was built. It is situated just three miles from the nearest airport, and all of its timeshare units are air conditioned. Some have full kitchens, as well. Laundry facilities are on site, as are a snack bar and full-service restaurant.

Ev Turkbuku, Bodrum, Turkey

This Resort Condominiums International Gold Crown property is in the town of Bodrum, which used to be the ancient city of Halikarnassos. It is a popular area on the Aegean coast near the now-submerged ancient port of Mindos, which you can still see through clear waters.

All of Ev Turkbuku's timeshare units are air conditioned with full kitchens, though you will likely enjoy dinners in town, as there are many fish restaurants to sample. Child care, a playground, and a children's pool are available at the resort if you want to leave the little ones behind and go enjoy the nightlife in town. Or, you can stay at the resort and enjoy the adults' swimming pool, spa, sauna, game room, restaurant, and exercise equipment.

Galaxia Vacation Club at the Marine Palace Suites, Crete, Greece

This family-friendly resort on Crete's northern coast has earned the Gold Crown distinction from Resort Condominiums International. All of its timeshare units are air conditioned with full kitchens, and a grocery store and laundry facilities are available on site. The closest airport is about forty miles away.

Galaxia Vacation Club boasts that it offers the best scuba diving in all of Crete. For nondivers who want to be in the water, activities include water sports at the beach such as swimming and wind surfing or lounging at the resort's children's and adults' swimming pools. Other resort offerings include a game room, live entertainment, playground, sauna, spa, whirlpool tub, and tennis courts. A snack bar and full-service restaurant are on site, as well.

Paradise Kings Club Paphos, Cyprus, Greece

The Paradise Kings Club Paphos has earned the Gold Crown distinction from Resort Condominiums International. It is on the southern side of Cyprus, just six miles from the nearest airport, with timeshare units that have private balconies, satellite television, and Internet access. Some of the units are air conditioned, and all of them have full kitchens. There is no grocery store on site, but one is nearby.

There are children's and adult swimming pools at this resort, along with a health club, exercise equipment, steam and sauna rooms, a beauty spa, a playground area, a game room for the kids, and a whirlpool tub. Once you've worked up an appetite, you can nosh at the resort's snack bar or enjoy full service at the on-site restaurant.

Pefkos Village Holiday Club, Rhodes, Greece

This Resort Condominiums International property is a couple hundred feet from the beach on the outskirts of Pefkos village, on the southeast side of the island of Rhodes, about 34 miles from the nearest airport. Timeshare units are designed as two-story bungalows and apartments that have air conditioning. Some units also have full kitchens, and a grocery store is on site for buying supplies. The resort has earned a high rating for hospitality.

Amenities at the resort itself include a snack bar and full-service restaurant, live entertainment, a swimming pool, and tennis courts. At the nearby beach you can enjoy boating, fishing, scuba diving, water-skiing, wind surfing, and all other forms of water sports. The closest golf course is about nine miles away.

More Exotic Locations

From Africa to Asia to Australia, timeshare opportunities are out there waiting to be had. You can do everything from ski down the slopes in Whistler, British Columbia, to explore downtown Beijing, China, or take a safari in northern or southern Africa. Here is a look at a few exotic timeshares that continually receive high rankings from exchange companies and consumer groups alike.

Beijing Shihao International Hotel, Beijing, China

Located in the heart of this international city, this Resort Condominiums International Gold Crown Property offers tours to the Great Wall of China, Ming Tombs, the Summer Palace, and more. The list of on-site amenities is extensive, including children's and adults' swimming pools, a sauna and spa, exercise equipment, a game room, a hairdresser, a health club, a playground, a snack bar and full-service restaurant, and shopping. Timeshare units are air conditioned, and some of them also have full kitchens. There is a grocery store on site, and laundry facilities are available, as well.

TRAVEL TIP

According to the president of one major exchange network, China and the Middle East are expected to be the next regions to see major growth in timeshare development.

Edgewater Club, Wanaka, New Zealand

Heli-tours of the area are one of the unique activities you can enjoy at this Resort Condominiums International Gold Crown Resort. It is situated at the foot of the nation's Southern Alps and offers year-round activities. Popular ski areas are nearby for wintertime fun, while rafting and trout fishing tend to capture tourists' imaginations during the summertime.

All of the timeshare units at the Edgewater Club have full kitchens and private laundry facilities, and a grocery store is about two miles away. Some of the timeshare units have lakefront views. The resort is family friendly, with on-site child care and a playground. For the adults, amenities at the resort itself include boating, fishing, a full-service restaurant, a sauna, tennis courts, and a whirlpool tub. Within about two miles of the resort, you can enjoy golf, horseback riding, live entertainment, and more.

Gokarna Forest Golf Resort and Spa, Kathmandu, Nepal

This Interval International Five Star Award resort is about five miles from the airport in Kathmandu, using the spectacular Himalayan mountains as a backdrop for its golf and spa amenities. The eighteen-hole golf course meanders through almost 500 acres of untouched forest, and because the resort is part of the Interval International Golf Resort Program, members will receive advance tee times along with discounts on greens fees, lessons, and more. The Harmony Spa adapts traditional Ayurveda treatments for modern-day uses, with options including massages, body wraps, facials, and reflexology.

You can take nature walks on the resort's trails, which are home to deer, monkeys, birds, and more. Also on site are a fitness center, restaurant, sauna, whirlpool tub, and indoor swimming pool. Nearby, you will find an outdoor swimming pool, horseback riding, tennis, bicycling, shopping, live theater, and a casino.

Hilton Sharm Dreams Resort, South Sinai, Egypt

This Resort Condominiums International Gold Crown property is in the Naama Bay area and boasts seven swimming pools plus three on-site restaurants. The city of Sharm El Sheikh is nearby, with countless cafes, shopping malls, and access to Red Sea snorkeling and scuba diving. Safari trips by way of motorcycle or camel are also an option amid the sandstone mountains.

Timeshare units at the Hilton Sharm Dreams Resort are air conditioned, and some have partial kitchens. Laundry facilities are on site, and a grocery store is nearby. Amenities at the resort include children's and adults' swimming pools, a game room, a casino, live entertainment, a playground, and a spa. Nearby activities include boating, fishing, golf, squash, tennis, water-skiing, and wind surfing.

Hotel Santa Clara and Las Bovedas de Santa Clara, Cartagena, Colombia

Timeshare units at this resort are configured in hotel-style, efficiency, and one- and two-bedroom layouts, and the resort's services have earned it an Interval International Five Star Award.

≡FAST FACT

Once a convent, the Hotel Santa Clara is a restored seventeenth-century building that is now regarded as a historic national monument inside the legendary walled city of Cartagena de Indias. There are two buildings on the property, the hotel and Las Bovedas, and both offer views of the Caribbean Sea.

On-site amenities include a fitness center, restaurant, outdoor swimming pool, sauna, and whirlpool tub. Nearby, you can enjoy boating, a casino, live theater, fishing, golf, shopping, horseback riding, scuba diving, tennis, and water-skiing. You also will have the privilege of beach club services in the nearby Rosario Islands.

Mabula Timeshare, Bela Bela, South Africa

This game reserve timeshare is in the foothills of Waterburg, about two hours by car from Johannesburg. More than 300 bird species and several of Africa's Big Five animals (lion, elephant, rhinoceros, leopard, Cape buffalo) are on site at this Resort Condominiums International Gold Crown property, and live snake demonstrations are held weekly.

All of the timeshare units have fireplaces, and some have partial kitchens, as well (though the nearest grocery store is about thirty-four miles away). Laundry facilities are available on the property. On-site amenities include child care, exercise equipment, a game room, horseback riding, a sauna, squash and tennis courts, a swimming pool, and a restaurant.

Mariner Shores Resort and Beach Club, Miami, Queensland, Australia

This Resort Condominiums International Gold Crown property is on Queensland's Gold Coast, which offers beaches, shopping, nightlife, restaurants, a casino, water sports, and more. All of its timeshare units have full kitchens and private laundry facilities. A grocery store is nearby, though not on the resort property itself.

The resort is just eight miles from the nearest airport and offers exercise equipment, fishing, a game room, a sauna and spa, a swimming pool, tennis courts, and a whirlpool tub. Nearby, you can find boating, golf, live entertainment, and restaurants.

Marriott's Phuket Beach Club, Phuket, Thailand

Boasting access to Mandara, one of the top-rated spas in all of Asia, this resort is situated on Mai Khao beach. It has a sushi bar on site, along with an Italian restaurant, an international cafe, and a pool bar. Also on the resort property are two adults' swimming pools and one children's pool, a hot tub and whirlpool tub, a miniature golf course along with chipping and putting greens, hiking trails, a spa, a sauna, tennis courts, and more.

Timeshare units are referred to as villas. Each has two bedrooms, a full kitchen, a private balcony or terrace, ocean or garden views, air conditioning, private laundry facilities, and satellite television.

This resort is family-friendly, with on-site activities for the whole family including batik-making classes, children's diving and snorkeling instruction, and child care services.

Rincon del Este, Punta del Este, Uruguay

This Interval International Five Star Award resort is located in Punta del Este, on Uruguay's easternmost seashore. It is a sophisticated beach destination where yachting regattas, offshore racing, and a variety of arts and crafts festivals take place each year. The shops are filled with the latest in American and European couture, much of it delivered by way of the nearest airport, which is just thirteen miles from the resort.

E-QUESTION

Can I find golf at this resort?
Golf is nearby, and the Rincon del Este resort is a member of Interval International's Golf Resort Program—meaning members get discounted greens fees and lessons, advance tee times, and more.

Timeshare units at Rincon del Este are configured as efficiencies, one bedrooms, two bedrooms, and three bedrooms. On-site activities include bicycling, a fitness center, table tennis, indoor and outdoor swimming pools, a restaurant, a steam room, tennis courts, and a whirlpool tub. Nearby, you can find boating, a casino, fishing, horseback riding, scuba diving, and water skiing.

Risata Bali Resort and Spa, Bali, Indonesia

Located on South Kuta Beach, this Resort Condominiums International Gold Crown property is part of the Tuban network of resorts, which pledge a commitment to protecting the environment. There are 139 timeshare units, each of which is air conditioned and some of which also have full or partial kitchens, depending on their size. Laundry facilities are available on site, as are a snack bar and a full-service restaurant.

Amenities at the Risata Bali Resort and Spa include children's and adults' swimming pools, exercise equipment, a health club, and a spa. Nearby activities include boating, fishing, golf, horseback riding, scuba diving, shopping, tennis, and water sports such as wind surfing and water-skiing.

CHAPTER 7

Your Timeshare Contract

AS WITH ANY MAJOR PURCHASE, buying a timeshare will require you to sign a contract. The good news is, you can learn a whole lot about them before you have one in your hands. The bad news is, they vary widely throughout the industry and there is no standard form that you can review beforehand. Your safest bet is to learn as much as you can about the ideas behind the contract before it's time to sign. That way, you can ensure that you are actually getting everything you should.

The Cold, Hard Facts

Remember when you bought the house where you and your family live? If your experience was like that of most people, your attorney sat down across from you at a long table. Although he was no more than two feet away, he could barely see your face above the towering stack of paperwork that separated the two of you.

He probably walked you step by step through the signing process, explaining in ways that seemed plausible at the time—but that you cannot recall to this day—what every single sheet of paper represented before you put your name at the bottom in ink. "This one is for your mortgage." "Sign here for the state disclosure form." "Here, you are giving up the right to ever again name a dog after your favorite television character . . ."

The paperwork went on and on, with you signing away at every turn—content in, or at least somewhat calmed by, the notion that your attorney was there to protect you and knew what he was doing. If anything was amiss, you figured, your attorney would either catch it on the spot or straighten it out immediately afterward. Either way, you could focus on things like hiring moving vans and packing boxes instead of on things like legal clauses and state regulations.

Unfortunately, this is not usually the case with timeshare contracts. Nine times out of ten, you will find yourself purchasing a timeshare unit at the end of a sales presentation—with nobody present except you and the salesman. You will, in effect, have to work as your own attorney, ensuring that every single word is correct in the paperwork before you sign it.

 **E-QUESTION**

Can I take timeshare contracts home for my attorney to review?
Sometimes, yes, if you insist. But the timeshare salesman's job is to get you to leave his presentation as an owner, not a person who is thinking things over. If you take an extra day or two to consult an attorney, you may lose out on developer discounts and bonuses that can be worth a great deal of extra vacation time and discounts.

Now, of course, the odds are that the law is not your chosen profession. And you certainly aren't going to call Harvard and take a few classes before you head off to sit through a timeshare sales presentation. So, how can you best protect yourself? The easiest way is to start by learning a few basics about timeshare contracts as they exist not just with the developer of your choice, but throughout the entire industry.

They're Nonnegotiable

First on the list: They rarely are open to changes. A timeshare sales-man who will let you negotiate the major points of your contract is like a shooting star. Be sure you see it as it crosses your horizon, because the odds are that you are experiencing a once-in-a-lifetime moment.

Truth be told, contracts are written by timeshare developers for the protection of timeshare developers. If they were meant to pro-tect you, then you would be the one writing them. And because the developer's goal is to make his sales as ironclad as possible, he usu-ally pays a team of attorneys quite handsomely to make his timeshare sales contracts as negotiation-proof as possible.

While demand for new timeshare units is not exactly staggering, it is good enough that the developers have no incentive to waive or change any of the clauses that they have paid so much money to have written into their contracts in the first place. You can ask for— and sometimes get—a change made in a minor clause, but the big stuff that you are likely to be most concerned about is probably not open for discussion. Don't waste your time even thinking about it; focus on the things that you can control, which you will learn about later in this chapter.

They Vary from Developer to Developer

The fact that everyone from Hyatt to Hilton to Starwood has their own kind of contract frustrates even the most savvy, long-term time-share buyers. This is not an industry where the phrase "you've seen one, you've seen 'em all" even begins to apply. You can be the happy owner of Disney and Marriott timeshares, then sit down at a Club Intrawest sales presentation and not understand half the clauses in the contract that the salesman gives you.

Even more frustrating is the fact that very rarely will any devel-oper send you a copy of their contract in the mail so that you can review it. Often, the only way to see a company's contracts is to sit through their sales presentation—or even agree to buy a unit.

≡FAST FACT

Developers guard their contracts closely, as proprietary information. The secrecy is so pervasive throughout the industry that sometimes competing developers will send people to pose as buyers at another developer's presentation, just so they can get a look at what kinds of clauses are in the other developer's contracts.

They Vary from Exchange Company to Exchange Company

Your timeshare unit contract is probably not the only one that you will be signing on the day that you buy into a resort. You also will be asked to sign an exchange company contract.

As you learned in Chapter 1, there are many different exchange companies out there. And just as with the myriad developers in the timeshare universe, every one of the exchange companies has its own set of contracts, as well. This means yet more clauses to consider, and even more terminology to weed through as you ensure that you are getting what you were promised during the sales pitch.

They Vary from Association to Association

You may not be asked to sign a homeowners' association contract on the same day that you purchase your timeshare unit, but usually, it will be mentioned in your contract as being an incorporated addendum—meaning that you are agreeing to follow whatever it says, even if it is not put on the table before you that day.

The problem, of course, is that homeowners' association rules and regulations vary from resort to resort, just as they do from complex to complex when in the world of primary residence condominiums. And again, for you, that means ever more clauses that you will have to decipher to ensure that you are getting everything that you think you are getting.

They Vary from State to State

Because the timeshare industry is largely regulated on the state level, as opposed to the federal level, many of the contracts differ substantially from state to state. Some states, such as Florida, have far more substantial timeshare laws than other states, such as New Jersey—where fewer timeshare resorts exist.

There are also major differences in rescission periods that are required from state to state, and it will be up to you to ensure that you understand the laws as they exist wherever you are buying a unit. You will learn more about that later in this chapter.

You Rarely Will Get the Whole Package

If, at the time of your sales presentation, a timeshare developer were to give you every single piece of paper that relates to the contractual obligations between you and him, you and your exchange company, you and your homeowners' association, and you and the state, he would be handing you a stack of paperwork about a hundred pages tall. Talk about a way to get potential clients to walk out the door!

E-ALERT

Make sure that you look for clauses in your timeshare unit contract that refer to "addendums," "other documents incorporated herein," and similar clauses that add paperwork you are not seeing to the agreement that you are being asked to sign. If you see something being added contractually, but not being shown to you, demand a written copy of the extra paperwork immediately for your review.

For this reason, developers typically ask you to sign a document that is maybe ten or so pages long—but that includes clauses that incorporate other documents into the contract itself, such as exchange company and homeowners' association agreements.

Often, if you ask for these additional documents, the salesman will have them, but they will be difficult for you to comb through in the short amount of time that you are likely to have that day. This is where your rescission period becomes important, because it allows you a few days to look through everything—once you know that you have to ask for it in order to actually read it.

Your Single Most Important Question

You could drive yourself insane trying to remember all the legalese and timeshare jargon that may or may not show up in the contract you are asked to sign. Nobody is expecting you to be a lawyer, even though it may feel that way when you are searching through documents that you will not always understand 100 percent.

The best thing that you can do to make smart decisions at a sales presentation is not to bone up on the specifics of contractual law, but to take detailed notes about everything that the salesman says will be included in your timeshare unit purchase. Then, when it comes time to sign on the dotted line, go item-by-item down your list and ask the salesman that single most important question: "Would you please show me where it says that in the contract?"

Salesmen in all industries are notorious for making promises that they later "forget" when the promised item turns out not to be in the written contract. Timeshare salespeople are no different: Make sure that you ask the salesman to point out—in the written contract itself—every single thing that he has promised you verbally.

In some cases, the salesman will say, "Oh, that's not in this contract with the developer, but you will see it in the contract that comes with your homeowners' association membership after we finish our purchasing process here." Your reply to this kind of a brush-off statement should always be: "That's fine, but then I am going to need you to show me a copy of *that* document, so that I can see where it says that in the contract."

Never, ever, *ever* take a timeshare salesman's verbal promise that you will be entitled to something that he cannot show you in writing.

If he says something is itemized elsewhere, demand to have a copy—and even get him to date and initial it, if you can. This goes for everything, even details that you might otherwise think are too small to be worth considering.

Sweat the Small Stuff

One of the biggest mistakes that you can make when going over your timeshare contract is failing to sweat the small stuff. Your job is, quite simply, to know what you are buying and to make sure that it is spelled out in writing. You cannot count on the salesperson to get even the most basic information correct. His job is to get you to sign the paper, not to ensure that it contains everything to which you think you are entitled. Remember: It is your responsibility to check all the little details for accuracy—on every single line of the contract—before you sign it.

This applies to mathematics, as well. You would be a fool to trust a salesman's math, what with the way he probably has been throwing numbers around the room throughout his presentation.

📰 TRAVEL TIP

Never assume that details of any magnitude can be left out of a written contract. If you are buying a two-bedroom, two-bathroom unit, make sure that's exactly what the contract states. If it simply reads "two-bedroom unit," the developer could stick you with one, or even no, bathrooms and be perfectly within his legal rights.

Bring a calculator with you to the sales presentation, or ask to borrow the salesman's so that you can double-check his figures after he writes them into your contract. You may be shocked to discover an error that could have cost you an extra $5,000 or $10,000!

Following is a list of "small" details that you should be sure to check before signing anything. If there are other specifics that you know you want to have in your timeshare unit, add them to this list before going into the sales presentation—and double-check them all against the contract *item by item* to make sure that what the salesman says is actually down on paper.

- Timeshare unit price
- Length of mortgage term
- Mortgage interest rate
- Number of points you are buying (in a points-based system)
- The word "fixed" or "floating" in a weeks-based system
- Fixed week number and/or calendar dates (if you are buying a fixed week)
- Resort name and location
- Timeshare unit square footage
- Number of bedrooms and bathrooms
- Existence of patios, decks, fireplaces, etc.
- Oceanfront or garden view
- Annual maintenance fees
- Annual property taxes (if not included in maintenance fees)
- Exchange company regulations and fees
- Homeowners' association regulations and fees
- Your rights as an owner, including renting your timeshare, bringing pets on your vacations, reserving fixed or floating weeks during certain annual dates, and using a different exchange company if you so choose
- Penalties for mortgage default, nonpayment of maintenance fees, nonpayment of special assessments, and the like

Again, this list is a good starting point for anyone seeking to buy any kind of timeshare. Your job as a consumer is to tailor the list to your own specific needs. If a salesman says there will be three televisions in your unit, for instance, make sure that is stated outright in the contract. If you are buying a unit at a ski lodge and the salesman says you will get free lift tickets during your first year, make sure it is written down.

The handful of moments just before you sign your contract is the time when you will have the most power as a consumer. Be sure you wield that power to your greatest advantage.

Addendums and Other Documents

As you learned earlier in this chapter, timeshare salespeople like to keep the paperwork they give you to a minimum. They believe, perhaps rightly so, that bombarding you with stacks and stacks of documents will make you far less likely to sign a deal—so they put only what they absolutely have to down in front of you for signing. Usually, the documents number around ten pages total.

In reality, the number of rules and regulations that you are agreeing to abide by is likely more in the one-hundred-page range. The way salespeople get around this is to have your contract refer to other documents, stating that they are addendums or "incorporated herein." That's a perfectly normal thing in terms of a sales tactic, but it behooves you to ask for copies of everything up front. Never, ever agree to sign a contract that incorporates addendums without a chance to review those addendums with your own two eyes.

≡FAST FACT

You can find references to addendums that are incorporated into your timeshare contract by looking for words like codicil, appendix, extension, rider, adjunct, attachment, postscript, option, accessory, auxiliary, and supplement. If you see one of these words in your contract, the odds are that they are part of a clause that refers to additional paperwork that you have yet to be shown.

What might be in those other papers? Things like a developer's Right of First Refusal, which means that if you decide to sell your timeshare unit, you have to sell it back to him, instead of on the open market, if he so chooses. You also might see clauses about pets, noise restrictions, barbecue restrictions that apply to balconies and terraces, and other things that will affect the way you are able to use your unit.

If you are buying a timeshare on the Gulf Coast, in Florida, or in the Carolinas, you also might pay special attention to any Acts of Nature clauses. Hurricanes have been especially destructive in recent years, and you will want to know your rights and responsibilities should your resort get leveled by wind or rain from a Category Five storm.

Terrorism clauses are also likely to be part of contract addendums. It is of course impossible to say how likely or unlikely a terrorist attack is in any part of the United States, but you should be aware of your rights and responsibilities should your resort end up being damaged by suicide bombers or other weapons.

 **E-QUESTION**

How has hurricane damage affected the timeshare industry in recent years?
In 2004, the four hurricanes named Charley, Frances, Ivan, and Jeanne reportedly affected more than one-quarter of the timeshares in America. At least thirty of those resorts, most in Florida, could not reopen until 2005—just in time for hurricanes Katrina, Rita, and Wilma to devastate them, and additional resorts, all over again.

Differences from State to State

In every one of the fifty United States—as well as in territories including Puerto Rico—there is a different set of laws regarding timeshares.

States that have a lot of resorts in them, such as Florida, Nevada, and California, tend to have not only laws designed to protect your rights as a consumer, but also laws that affect how the developer must work with you when trying to make a sale. Other states that have fewer timeshare resorts in them, such as South Dakota, Oklahoma, and West Virginia, tend to have fewer laws regarding a developer's behavior and, sometimes, less-stringent laws that protect you as a consumer.

≡FAST FACT

If you want to look through the laws that regulate developer and consumer rights in the state where you are buying a timeshare, contact the state's Real Estate Commission. The commission should also be able to tell you the length of the state's rescission, or cooling-off, period.

For your purposes in buying a timeshare, though, the most important thing that varies from state to state is the length of your rescission period. This is the cooling-off time that you are given by state law to change your mind after signing a contract. If, during your rescission period, you decide that you have made a bad deal, you have a certain amount of time to get out of your contract. That amount of time is what varies from state to state, as defined by different laws.

How much do rescission periods vary? In some states, you get ten full days, while in others, you get just three. The range is wide even among states where timeshares are the most popular:

- **Arizona:** seven days
- **California:** seven days
- **Colorado:** five days
- **Florida:** ten days
- **Hawaii:** seven days
- **Missouri:** five days
- **Nevada:** five days
- **South Carolina:** five days
- **Texas:** five days
- **Utah:** five days

Do your homework before going into a sales presentation so that you will know exactly how much cooling off time is available to you in the state where your resort is located. If nothing else, the information will give you greater peace of mind when it comes time to sign the contracts.

CHAPTER 8

Free Timeshare Vacations

IF YOU ARE A HOMEOWNER, earn at least $35,000 per year, and have taken a vacation in the past five years or so, the odds are that you have received an invitation to a partially paid or all-expenses-paid vacation courtesy of a timeshare developer. The catch is that you have to give up an hour or two of your vacation time to listen to their sales pitch. Is accepting the invitation to one of these "fly-and-buy" deals a good idea? Or are you setting yourself up for a financial fall?

The Pitch

The typical timeshare sales pitch could show up in your mailbox, or in your e-mail in-box, or in the form of a telemarketer's voice over your telephone (usually right around the exact moment that you put a hot, steaming plate of dinner onto the table, of course). In truth, the method of delivery really doesn't matter so much as the words being used, and they usually go something like this:

> Congratulations, James Smith! You and your spouse have been selected to receive a complimentary three-day, two-night vacation package at the luxurious Dream Resort on the paradise island of Aruba! Your package includes round-trip transfers to and from the airport to your private two-bedroom villa, which comes complete

with a full kitchen, washer/dryer, and more! You will have full access to all of the Dream Resort's amenities, including five swimming pools, an eighteen-hole golf course, and a seven-mile beach! Plus, you will receive free vouchers for four gourmet meals at the five-star Italian restaurant located inside the Dream Resort complex!

Sounds pretty awesome, right? As if you've finally won something worthwhile after all those years of throwing worthless lottery tickets into the trash along with your I'll-never-have-to-go-to-work-again hopes and dreams.

It actually could be true—if you're in the market for a timeshare unit like the Dream Resort on Aruba, and if you don't mind paying for whatever is missing from the fine print (in this case, airfare costs are notably absent). On the other hand, if you have not been shopping for a timeshare and you receive such a pitch out of the blue, you might be inclined to think it is part of a scam. And you might be right.

Are They Scams?

The short answer to this question is: It depends on the offer. The more detailed answer includes a little bit of history about how these free vacation/sales presentations came to exist in the first place.

Back in the 1960s and 1970s, when timeshares were a brand-new concept that almost nobody in the United States had ever heard of, developers felt they needed a hook to get people interested in listening to their ideas. Some of these developers were above-the-board businessmen who gave away a free night's stay to entice people like you into listening to their sales pitch. It was much like the marketing methods used by banks in those years: Open a checking account, take home a free toaster—just a little something extra for your time and the opportunity to earn your business.

Other developers, though, were hucksters who didn't care whether you could afford their timeshare product or not. They simply wanted to get your body into their pressure-cooker presentation and bully you until you agreed to fork over whatever amount of cash they wanted. If they couldn't get you to open your wallet, they would bring somebody else into the room to work you over. And if he, too, failed to get you to cave, a third sweaty-toothed bully would be waiting in the wings to deliver the knock-down punch.

This is the image that most people still have today of timeshare presentations, and in some cases, the fear is valid. In many cases, the sales presentations you will be forced to sit through will be high pressure, and you will not be able to leave until you have complied according to the terms of your free or reduced-rate vacation.

Companies that market timeshares know that the notion of a high-pressure sales pitch is likely to turn you off from visiting their resort at all, so they sometimes conveniently "forget" to mention that it will be part of your vacation package. This does not mean you will be able to forgo the experience. It simply means they are saying whatever they must say to get you to agree to visit the resort in the first place.

 **E-QUESTION**

If my telemarketer promises me that I won't have to sit through a sales presentation during my free vacation, can I believe her?
Absolutely not. You almost always will be required to attend an hour- or two-hour-long sales pitch during your trip.

On the other hand, many of today's timeshare sales presentations are far more respectful than the ones you or your parents may remember from the days of old. Let's face it: Salespeople do not want you to be wasting their time any more than you want them to be wasting your time. If they peg you off the bat as a person who is just sitting through their presentation in order to enjoy a free vacation—who really has neither the money nor the inclination to buy a timeshare in the first place—then they really have no reason to bombard you with high-pressure tactics. They realize they would be smarter to focus on other people in the room who are more likely to be potential clients.

Even better, if you are a qualified buyer who is genuinely interested in learning more about the timeshare units for sale, you can learn a great deal of information during these sales pitches—and even buy from developers at what are sometimes substantially discounted rates.

═FAST FACT

It is estimated that as many as 300,000 people purchase timeshare units either during or immediately following sales presentations at resorts every year.

Some people who own multiple timeshares make a practice of attending as many as a half-dozen sales presentations each year, just so they can keep tabs on what the different resorts and exchange companies are offering in comparison to one another. They find that the sales presentations offer a unique opportunity to ask pointed questions of timeshare salespeople, as well as the chance to inspect properties firsthand and compare them with others they might choose instead from other resorts.

What you need to develop, as a timeshare sales presentation rookie, is the same level of inquisitiveness that these veterans have honed while maintaining your own personal level of comfort in terms of what you do, or do not, want to buy. In other words, you need to do as much preparation as possible before you sit down to listen to the sales pitch—and you need to have a game plan for what you will have left in your pockets when you stand up to leave.

What Happens When You Get There

Ideally, what happens when your airplane touches down is that the sun is shining, the temperature is soothing, and you immediately feel a smile creeping across your lips. After all, you are supposed to be on vacation, right? The place should at least look and feel like paradise, whether it is on a Caribbean beach or in the Swiss Alps.

Assuming round-trip airport transfers were part of your all-expenses-paid promotional deal, you should be met at the airport by a representative from the timeshare resort who will help you collect your luggage and take you to a courtesy shuttle or van. Then, after what hopefully is not too long of a drive, you should find yourself being welcomed to the timeshare resort.

Checking in, finding your room, and getting to know the grounds should be about the same for you at the timeshare resort as it has been at various other resorts and hotels during your previous vacations. The marketing company's goal is to get you nice and relaxed—and, hopefully, to have you grow quite fond of the resort—before they sit you down for their sales pitch, so you should have at least a half a day to settle in and look around before you have to attend the presentation.

E-ALERT

It's perfectly acceptable for you to have as much fun as possible at the timeshare resort before and after you attend the sales presentation. However, you would be wise not to drink alcohol before walking into the pitch room. You will want all of your faculties fully functional when it comes time to speak with the salesperson.

Eventually, of course, the time will come for you to join the other prospective timeshare owners in the sales pitch conference room. Do not think you can skate by and enjoy your free vacation without attending! If you fail to sign in and attend the sales presentation (you usually will be asked to show a form of personal identification, such as a driver's license), you will be charged for your entire stay at the timeshare resort, regardless of what the promotion promised.

Remember, your attendance at the sales pitch is a *requirement* that goes along with accepting the free vacation. Whether you attend the presentation is not a personal decision, unless you are willing to foot the bill for your whole trip—sometimes at higher-than-usual rates—after the fact.

Getting to Know You

When you arrive at the sales presentation, the mood should be decidedly upbeat. Most of these pitch sessions are a good hour to two hours long, and the salespeople want you going into them relaxed with a good attitude. They should welcome you, introduce themselves, and ask you a few questions about benign things like who you are and where you are from. Do not worry about answering these questions. Smile and introduce yourself. In most cases, the salespeople are just being polite and trying to set a good tone.

After everyone has shaken hands, grabbed a complimentary cookie, and the like, you will be asked to sit down so that the sales presentation can begin. Usually, the salesman will start by telling everyone a little bit about himself and the timeshare resort, perhaps with a video, PowerPoint, or slide presentation. There may be accompanying music, as well as handouts passed around of newspaper or magazine articles that have been written about the timeshare resort. The salesman's job is to help you to understand what you can expect during the rest of his presentation, and to ensure that you understand exactly what product he is selling.

The last thing that is likely to happen before you get into the nuts and bolts of the timeshare purchase details is a segment of the presentation during which the salesman will try to get to know you—and your vacationing habits—better. Again, you can feel free to answer these questions politely, but know that the salesperson, at this point, is beginning to accumulate information that he hopes he can use later to close a deal with you. If you really aren't interested in buying a timeshare, it is best to say so at this point—perhaps by telling the salesperson that you never really go on vacations and that this is your first one in years.

On the other hand, if you are interested in buying a timeshare, now is the time to be perfectly frank. Tell the salesperson exactly what you expect to get out of a vacation, and make him work hard to respond with detailed information about precisely why his timeshare opportunity is the one you should be considering. The more information you give him, the better able he will be able to explain how his product might meet your needs.

TRAVEL TIP

If, for whatever reason, you are uncomfortable with the salesperson who is asking you questions during the timeshare presentation, it is entirely within your rights to ask to speak with someone else. Do not feel pressured to work with someone you do not like. There are plenty of other salespeople waiting in the wings.

The Presentation

At some point, the salesman will begin going directly into his pitch. This should include some combination of information about the developer who is building the timeshare resort, the company that is going to be managing it (if different from the developer), and the types of units that he has available for sale that day. You are likely, again, to be shown pictures, either in the form of slides, a movie, or glossy brochures. Room layouts, resort layouts, even topographical maps may be handed to you for consideration.

If you are at a resort managed by a well-known company, such as Marriott or Hilton, you also are likely to be given additional information about the company's history, financial strength, worldwide reach, and the like. The salesperson, of course, wants you to understand that the timeshare units he is selling come with the full backing of a powerful brand name that you may already know well.

Do not be surprised if the salesperson talks quite a bit about how important a timeshare purchase can be in strengthening your family. Phrases like "investing in memories" are certain to be lobbed about, with the goal being to keep you thinking more about your family— and feeling heartwarming emotions—than digging analytically into every single word of the sales pitch.

 **E-QUESTION**

Is it all right to interrupt a timeshare salesperson's presentation if you want a point to be clarified?
Absolutely yes! If there is anything you do not understand, at any time during the presentation, feel free to speak up. The whole point of your being there is to leave with a better understanding of the timeshare product.

If the salesman can get you to feel all warm and fuzzy about spending more time with your kids, for instance, you are far less likely to question his math when he begins to explain exactly how much of your savings he wants to collect that very afternoon. Be sure to keep your wits about you, especially when the dollars and cents portion of the program swings into effect.

Money Matters

One of the most powerful portions of the salesperson's timeshare presentation is likely to be the segment about how much money you stand to save during the next twenty or thirty years if you simply invest in a timeshare today. This part of the pitch can certainly be true—and it is therefore worth considering very carefully. The trick, of course, is to make sure you are being given all the numbers you need to make a realistic assessment of your own long-term financial picture.

For starters, make sure that the price you are being given for the timeshare unit is the lowest price available. Many salespeople inflate the price of the unit for sale, just to gauge your reaction, and then lower it later on as if they are giving you a really good deal. Your smart move—no matter what the asking price—is to haggle. Odds are, you will be able to lower the asking price by at least several thousand dollars.

As you read in Chapter 2 of this book, there is a compelling case to be made for the long-term financial savings that can come with buying a timeshare at the right price. If you are willing to accept—and this is definitely an *if*—that vacation accommodations such as hotel rooms are going to see inflationary rises in the neighborhood of 5 percent, per year, for the rest of your vacationing lifetime, then it is difficult to deny the financial advantages that can come with purchasing a timeshare.

Remember the timeshare-versus-hotel examples from Chapter 2? According to the Marriott Vacation Club calculator, if you spend $150 per night on hotel rooms this year, you can anticipate spending $251.32 per night in ten years, $409.37 per night in twenty years, and $666.81 per night in thirty years (based on a 5 percent, per year, inflation model). By taking one week's worth of vacation each year for the next thirty years, at those rates, the calculator shows that you will have spent $75,341.65 on hotel rooms.

■ TRAVEL TIP

When speaking with a timeshare salesman, imagine that you are speaking with a new-car salesman. Haggling should be part of the conversation, and it could save you thousands of dollars.

That is, of course, far less than you will have spent if you plunk down $25,000 for a timeshare unit at today's prices—and therein lies the sales pitch. What you need to remember is that your $25,000 purchase price is far from the only fee you will be paying during the next few decades.

Hidden Extra Costs

A good salesman will break down the entire financial picture for you, instead of simply comparing a timeshare unit's price against the cost of thirty years' worth of hotel rooms. Additional financial considerations that you must take into account include:

- Annual resort maintenance fees ($200 to $600 per year)
- Special assessment fees (possibly hundreds of dollars every few years)
- Exchange fees (in the neighborhood of $125 per exchange request)
- Mortgage interest payments (possibly many thousands of dollars, depending on your financing)

When you roll all of these costs into one bundle, and only *then* compare that total number against the total cost of hotel rooms, will you be dealing with an apples-to-apples comparison.

Any time you are asked to compare simply the timeshare's purchase price against the cost of hotel rooms, you are being given an apples-to-oranges set of figures that cannot be trusted.

E-ALERT

If your timeshare salesman insists that a unit's purchase price is the only fee you will ever have to pay throughout the duration of timeshare ownership, you are being duped. Demand to see, in writing, the resort and exchange company's list of other fees. If the salesman cannot produce one, the odds are that he is a crook.

Also keep in mind that you are under no obligation to answer any questions during this part of the discussion about your income, savings, or any other personal financial information. You are there to listen to the salesman discuss *his* financial offer, not to share *your* financial status with him or anyone else in the room.

Timeshare Tour

After the salesman has given his presentation and allowed plenty of time for a question-and-answer session, you and the other potential timeshare buyers will be taken for a tour of one or more of the units being sold. If you are already at the resort, you will not have to go far, but if you are far from the location of the available units, you should be provided with transportation such as a golf cart or courtesy shuttle.

Ask as many questions as you like during the model tour. Remember: This is your opportunity to examine the timeshare product with all five of your senses. Examine the timeshare unit as you would any other real estate property, looking for, among other things:

- Evidence of water leaks on the ceiling
- Evidence of poor construction, such as crumbling grout in the bathroom
- Evidence of cheap construction, such as peeling countertops in the kitchen
- Reputable brand names on appliances such as washers, dryers, and refrigerators
- Evidence of maintenance around terraces or balconies

The odds are, as this is a model unit meant to wow you, that none of these things will be a problem during the tour. The timeshare unit should be in pristine condition, leaving you drooling instead of dreading. In fact, a model timeshare that is in less than five-star condition is a sure sign that the resort may have some sort of problems. This is just common sense: If the resort can't take care of the one unit it is showing off frequently to potential customers, imagine how little it is doing to maintain other units and amenities that existing customers see only once a year.

The Unit-for-Unit Question

One of the most important questions you can ask during the tour is whether the model that you are being shown is identical to the model you will be offered for purchase.

Do not assume that just because you are being shown a spotless two-bedroom timeshare with a gorgeous view of the stunning Caribbean Sea that this particular unit is the same size as—or even on the same side of the resort as—the unit you will be offered for purchase. Far too many people have taken tours of top-level timeshares only to find out later that what they in fact went on to purchase were units with excellent views of the resort's garbage cans.

If you are serious about signing a timeshare contract that day, *insist* on being shown the exact unit you would own after the deal goes through. Again, this is common sense: You wouldn't buy a house or a car back home without seeing it at least once, would you? The same rule applies to a major purchase in paradise.

If Your Unit Isn't Built Yet

As the popularity of timeshare vacations continues to grow, developers are building more and more resorts—and sometimes offering units for sale before a single shovelful of dirt has been moved on the site. In this case, you of course cannot be shown an actual timeshare unit, as none yet exist. You will be asked to rely on the reputation of the developer, resort, and exchange company when making your purchase.

TRAVEL TIP

Your best bet, always, is to buy a timeshare unit that you can walk into and inspect before signing on the dotted line. If that is not an option because the resort is still pre-construction, you will have to make your choice depending on your own comfort level with accepting the intangibles of the future.

This can be a reasonable request, and it is not necessarily a bad move to purchase a timeshare unit before it is built. However, you must go into such a purchase with the full knowledge that problems might occur along the way. Construction permits could be denied, underground problems could be discovered on the site, unforeseen issues may force unit floor plans to change—the list goes on and on.

The Moment of Truth

Okay: You've been greeted, fed, pitched, toured, questioned, answered, and then some. At this point in the timeshare salesman's program, you will be asked to buy—at least a few times, and likely by at least a few people. The salesman in the room, like all salesmen everywhere, is trying to get you to purchase his product. He wants you to buy it that day, and he will do everything in his power to make the deal happen.

Do not be surprised if you are offered a one-day-only substantial discount, such as a 10 percent knockdown on the purchase price, or a one-day-only hefty incentive, such as additional points to be used at a points-based resort. This sales tool is commonly used during timeshare presentations to give you and everyone else in the room a reason to sign on that day. It is no more a scam than, say, an on-the-spot discount offered by a replacement window salesman in your home. It is simply a way to entice you into spending your money on that particular day.

Of course, it doesn't feel that way when you're sitting in the chair being told that if you don't commit right at that very moment, your potential discount or bonus points will be lost forever. In fact, it can feel almost threatening, as if you are being told you are an idiot if you fail to purchase at that precise second.

Simply knowing in advance that this type of offer is likely to be made is one way of buffering the psychological blow. Knowledge, as they say, is power, and if you know going in what you can expect, you will be less disturbed by it when it actually happens.

The multiple-salesman pitch is another sometimes off-putting sales tool that will seem less abrasive to you if you know it is likely to come your way. This is a method of sales in which the original salesman, seeing that you are not moving in the direction he wants, will bring in another salesman or supervisor to talk with you. Again, this is commonplace in timeshare sales, and it can feel very high-pressure to you during the actual sales process.

Just remember that you are under no obligation to buy anything, from anyone, no matter how many different salespeople are sent your way. Be honest, be straightforward, and do not feel pressured to deviate from your desires whether they are to buy or not to buy.

≡FAST FACT

Many timeshare resorts offer buy-today discounts or incentives as a matter of course. However, some are willing to offer those discounts after the day of the sales pitch, too. If you are interested in buying but want to do research for a few more days before signing the contract, ask if the promotional offer can be extended. Sometimes, the answer will be yes.

The odds are that you will see no more than three salespeople during the course of any presentation; it doesn't make sense for the resort to waste any more employees' time at that point—so keep in mind that there is an end coming soon if you find yourself being double- or triple-teamed.

How to Protect Yourself in Advance

You've already done a great deal to protect yourself in advance simply by buying and reading this book. Knowledge is the biggest asset you can have when it comes to making any major purchase, and if you have read this far, you already know 99 percent more about timeshares than about 99 percent of the other people out there.

There are, of course, also specific things you can do to ensure that you will be financially protected.

Don't Go

For starters, you might just stay home. It seems like basic advice, but the easiest way to prevent yourself from getting roped into a deal you cannot afford is simply to keep yourself out of the salesman's pitch room in the first place. As much as 90 percent of the people who accept free or reduced-price timeshare vacations in exchange for agreeing to listen to a sales pitch have absolutely, positively no intention of purchasing a timeshare unit. If you are among that whopping majority, it would behoove you to seriously reconsider whether to accept the vacation in the first place.

There are many last-minute travel deals out there—to resorts, aboard cruise ships, and beyond—and you can find many of them with nothing more than a quick search of the World Wide Web. Why waste your time—and the salesman's time—sitting in a room listening to a sales pitch when you can be relaxing on the beach somewhere else that's just as beautiful, and just as cost-efficient for your vacation budget?

Follow the Rules

If you do decide to take advantage of the vacation offer, be sure that you stick to every condition that the resort or timeshare developer places upon you. Be sure you meet the age requirement, for example. If you are married and required to bring your spouse along, make sure that you do so. Have proof that you meet the minimum income requirement that most likely is spelled out in tiny little type on one of the many pieces of paper the company will have sent you before your trip begins. Also be sure you have booked your trip for the days of the week that the offer spells out. Your failure to meet any of these predetermined conditions can result in your being forced to foot the bill for the entire trip, regardless of what was promised to you in the initial offer.

Compile Your Questions

One of the easiest things you can do to help you stay on track during the sales presentation is to have your questions spelled out, in writing, before you even get to the resort. With a list that you can follow, you will be less apt to get distracted by a sales pitch that tugs at your emotional heartstrings. Instead, you can fill in the salesperson's responses to your important questions, checking them off one by one as you get the answers you need. Some examples of important questions you should ask include:

- Is this timeshare a deeded or right-to-use property?
- Am I buying into a weeks-based or points-based system?
- Is this a fixed or floating week?
- If this is a fixed week, what season is it within?
- If this is a floating week, is it within a specific season?
- What are the current maintenance, exchange, special assessment, and mortgage interest fees?
- What is the history of those fees during the past few years?

Of course, your list can be as short or as long as you like. If you want to know everything down to whether the resort will charge you an extra fee to have a "starter set" of sundries in the timeshare upon your arrival each year, you should add that question to your list. If you want to delve into the matters of who votes on maintenance issues—the resort alone, or a homeowners' association—you should make it a point to ask. If you are on a restricted diet and want to see menus from the restaurants at the timeshare resort, make a notation on your list. If you need a blender in the timeshare unit to make your low-carb milkshakes, or if you need an electric can opener because you have arthritis, or if you prefer a DVD player to a VCR, you should add the item to your list of questions about what, exactly, your timeshare unit will include.

The devil, as the saying goes, is so often in the details. Thinking them through with a clear head, before you arrive at the sales presentation, is the surest way for you to keep all of them straight while you consider making such a major purchase. And remember: Whenever possible, get the salesman's answers in writing. His signature will be far more important than yours should a problem arise down the line.

Know Your Rights

Perhaps the most important thing you can do before attending a timeshare presentation is make a point of learning your rights—as they exist in the state or nation where the timeshare is located. Sometimes, the resort itself will provide you with a copy of the U.S. state or foreign nation's timeshare laws (if you ask in advance). Other times, you will have to go directly to the state or nation's Real Estate Commission and get the written law on your own.

 **E-QUESTION**

How do I locate the Real Estate Commission in the state where I want to buy a timeshare?
The fastest way is to use an Internet search engine, such as Google. Type in "Real Estate Commission" along with the name of the state where you plan to buy a timeshare unit. The link should show up on the first page of search results.

Among the things you want to learn when looking through the state or nation's timeshare laws is whether you are entitled to a rescission period (also known as a "cooling-off" period). In the United States, you—the buyer—are almost always entitled to cancel a contract of this nature without penalty for several days after signing it (as you learned in Chapter 7). Remember: That is not always the case in some foreign countries, where if you buy it, you own it, case closed.

One of your goals in finding the timeshare laws for the resort where you may buy a unit is to find out just how long that state's rescission period is, and what steps you must take to cancel a contract should doing so become necessary. If there are forms that need to be filed, for instance, see if you can download them from the state's Web site before you even leave for your trip.

Knowing in advance how to undo anything that you might do will give you great peace of mind, especially if you decide to take advantage of a discount and buy a timeshare unit the day of the sales presentation. After all, knowing that you have two days or even a week to cancel the deal when you get back home—and knowing exactly what you must do to make that happen—can take away much of the stress of the buying process itself.

How to Protect Yourself During the Sales Pitch

Simply having purchased this book can be a boon to you in this department, as well. Salespeople know that some potential customers are better-informed than others. As such, it is a smart move for you to bring your copy of this book with you to the timeshare sales presentation. Simply having the book in front of you, in the salesman's line of sight, will tell him or her that you have done your homework and are no easy mark when it comes to closing a quick deal.

Aside from that, the best way to protect yourself during the sales pitch is to stick with the plan you made when you and your spouse arrived. Make sure all of the questions on your checklist have been answered. Make sure you have done your homework about the state's timeshare laws in advance. Make sure you have learned enough not just about the resort or developer, but about your specific timeshare unit, as well. Make sure you have haggled the price down to the very lowest that the salesman will go.

If, after all of that, you decide you simply do not want to purchase a timeshare unit that day, you will likely find yourself in a verbal battle that could leave William Shakespeare himself tongue-tied for days. Timeshare salespeople have been trained to memorize retorts for virtually every excuse you can give them. You say you can't make a decision today, and they launch into an oft-used speech about why waiting will only make your decision harder. You say you need to talk with a parent, accountant, attorney, or friend, and they question your adulthood and ability to make decisions for yourselves. The list, just like their predetermined responses, goes on and on and on.

Should you find yourself in a battle of verbiage with a timeshare unit salesperson, stick to the basic "no, thank you" and try not to engage him in conversation at all. Even if he asks you a question such as, "Why are you so hesitant to buy today?" you can respond by crossing your arms and saying, "No, thank you." He will get the message after a few of those.

≡ FAST FACT

Body language can be as strong, if not stronger, than words when trying to help a salesman understand that you simply do not want to buy. Crossing your arms, looking away, and scowling are all good tactics if the salesman simply will not take no for an answer.

And, if all else fails, some couples have reported success by telling the timeshare salesman that they recently became pregnant. Think about it: You tell him you are having a child in less than a year and need to spend your savings on a cradle and diapers. How in the world could a salesman argue with that?

If You Want to Buy

There is, of course, the chance that you will find yourself among the one in ten people who actually do want to purchase a timeshare unit at the end of the presentation—and perhaps with very good reason. Sometimes, the financial picture makes sense. Other times, you just want the peace of mind of knowing that your personal villa will be waiting for you during the same week every year. Still other times, you will feel comforted by the notion that you will have a network of rated resorts from which to choose for your vacation each year, instead of having to research every single vacation on your own for many years to come. Sometimes, you will simply fall in love with a resort and want nothing more than to return there, year after year, for many years to come.

Whatever your reason for buying on that day, rest assured that your salesperson will do everything in his or her power to make the process as easy for you as it can be. You likely will be taken into a separate office, so that your personal transaction will not become part of the conversation among the rest of the people who hear the sales presentation. Once you are in that separate office, your experience will be much the same as it is when making any other major purchase, such as a car or a home. You will have a good deal of paperwork to sign, a down-payment check to write, and literature to collect. And, hopefully, a big smile on your face, to boot.

CHAPTER 9

Buying from a Developer

THE MAJORITY OF PEOPLE WHO BUY timeshares nowadays are purchasing them direct from developers. Sometimes the units are part of a brand-new complex, sometimes they are the last remaining units in a sold-out resort, and sometimes they are nothing more than a yet-to-be-built vision in the developer's mind. Buying from a developer, instead of on the resale market, certainly has its advantages, but there are also drawbacks that you should keep in mind before you sign on the dotted line.

What's a Developer?

A developer is a person, company, or corporation that buys a piece of land with the intention of building upon it. For your purposes in understanding how timeshares work, the developer is the person or company that is building and selling the units that you are considering for purchase.

The developer also tends to own at least a share in the restaurants, shops, spas, golf courses, and other money-making services that are built alongside the timeshares on the resort properties, which means that the developer has a stake in making sure the resort runs well even after all of the timeshare units are sold. Developers also earn profits on the high interest rates you and other timeshare buyers pay should you choose to finance your purchase over a five- to ten-year period.

Developers come in all shapes and sizes, from single, wealthy individuals to massive worldwide conglomerates such as Marriott, Hilton, and Disney. By some estimates, timeshare development divisions account for as much as 10 percent of profits at some major global companies—meaning it is as important to those companies as it is to you that timeshares are developed properly. They do not want to see a major portion of their revenue curtailed by bad timeshare developments any more than you want to see your money put into a lousy resort project.

≡FAST FACT

Timeshare developers—after surviving an initial few years with negative cash flow—can see anywhere from a 20 percent to a 50 percent profit on their investments, depending on their overhead, marketing, and other costs, according to one industry research firm.

For companies whose brand names you know, customer loyalty is also a huge factor in their decision to become timeshare developers. Once you are, for instance, a member of the Hyatt Vacation Club, you will likely be entitled to discounts and services at Hyatt hotels, as well. This means the company not only is getting a timeshare customer for the next decade or more, but also a more reliable hotel customer.

Timeshare developers have to follow the laws of the state or nation in which they are developing their resort. A good place to start when researching the developer of your timeshare unit, no matter where it is located, is the American Resort Development Association. ARDA is a Washington, D.C.-based trade association that has existed since 1969. Its primary purpose is to represent the vacation ownership and resort development industries.

📼 TRAVEL TIP

Before purchasing a timeshare unit, check to see if its developer is a member of the American Resort Development Association. The group's Web site, *www.arda.org*, includes an alphabetical listing of its more than 1,000 members. Each is required to adhere to the group's Code of Standards and Ethics.

No matter how big your developer is or where its timeshare resort is being built, you—the buyer—will face a specific set of pros and cons when choosing to buy direct instead of on the resale market. Here is a look at some of the most important factors that you should keep in mind when buying a timeshare unit straight from the developer.

The Pros

Buying direct from the developer does have its benefits, not the least of which is the lack of hassle you might encounter when trying to buy a timeshare unit on the resale market. As with used cars, used furniture, or used anything, there are good sellers and bad sellers out there in the world with top-notch products and hideous lemons alike. Timeshares are no different. When you are making what very well may be a purchase worth $10,000 or even more, you want to know that there will be no hidden problems that suddenly materialize after your paperwork is signed and you have taken ownership rights.

Other benefits of buying direct from the developer also tend to fall into the peace of mind category—which is important when considering a purchase that you will use for the next decade or longer. Legal rights are certainly a major factor, as are timeshare unit condition and customer support services.

Rescission Period

Your legal right to a rescission period, or a cooling-off period, is perhaps the greatest incentive you have for purchasing a timeshare unit directly from the developer. Rescission periods, to put it in basic terms, allow you at least a few days to change your mind and get all of your money back after signing a contract. The length of rescission periods varies from state to state, but they are usually at least three days long. When buying a timeshare unit on the resale market, you will not always be entitled to a cooling-off period. Sometimes, yes—if you are working with a reputable resale broker, for instance, who provides one *himself*—but when buying directly from a developer in the United States, you almost always will have a *state law* on your side.

E-ALERT

> While rescission periods vary from state to state, you almost always are entitled to them when buying a timeshare unit from a developer within the United States. However, when buying a unit overseas, the law may not allow you time to change your mind. Some Caribbean islands, for instance, offer no legal protections at all for cooling-off time.

Before you purchase your unit, determine what the rescission rights are in the state where the resort is located (details on that can be found in Chapter 7). You want to know not just how many days you have to change your mind, but what steps you must take and what paperwork you must fill out within that time period.

If possible, download rescission forms from the Web site of the real estate commission that governs the property where your timeshare unit is located. Having the forms organized and ready to go in case a problem is discovered will be key to your exercising this important right.

Also check with your credit-card company. Some Visa and

MasterCard users are entitled to ten-day cooling-off periods after purchasing a timeshare unit—a nice benefit, especially if you are buying in a place where there is no legal rescission period.

New Construction

If you are among the people who prefer new cars to used ones, new homes to lived-in dwellings, and the like, then for you another important benefit of buying a timeshare straight from the developer is the fact that you can often get a unit that is part of a new construction phase.

There is no doubt about it: Buying straight from the developer can greatly increase your chance of getting a timeshare unit that is in sparkling new condition—and that is sometimes one of the last remaining units at the timeshare resort of your choice. Often, this is because the units are not even yet built during the initial sales period (more on that later in this chapter). Sometimes, you can literally be the first person ever to stay in a timeshare unit, meaning everything will be as crisp and clean as it can possibly be. At the very least, your first week of usage can come during the unit's first year of existence, when wear and tear will be minimal.

The other benefit to buying a new-construction unit from a developer is that it is sometimes the only way to get the week you want for your timeshare use. Plenty of resale units may be available, say, for the low seasons when demand is minimal, but you may need to vacation each year during a peak week, such as between Christmas and New Year's Day. Often, buying directly from the developer is the only way to ensure you get the actual week you want, if you have limited flexibility in that area.

Brand-Name Backup

Developers such as Disney, Hilton, Hyatt, Marriott, and Starwood are backed by something very important: a name and reputation that you already know. You don't often hear anyone refer to these conglomerates as fly-by-night-operations, which is important considering that your timeshare purchase is a long-term investment that you are going to want to rely on for the next decade or more. Brand-name developers come with backup in the form of financial stability, ingrained service standards, and more. Those are things you will not always find if you buy a timeshare on the resale market instead of from a developer.

 **E-QUESTION**

Does buying a timeshare from a brand-name developer entitle me to special loyalty rewards programs?
Yes—almost always. Developers such as Disney, Hilton, Hyatt, and Marriott typically allow their timeshare owners to take advantage of special deals at their hotels and with their loyalty program partner companies.

Another benefit of buying your timeshare directly from a brand-name developer is that you often will be entitled to full use of the developer's loyalty program. With Marriott Vacation Ownership, for instance, you can trade your weeks in for points that can then be used in the Marriott Rewards system. Some of the things you can get with those points include hotel room bookings, hotel room upgrades, airline tickets, cruise-ship vacations, golf lessons, spa certificates, theater tickets, theme park admission tickets, shopping vouchers, and more.

The Hyatt Vacation Club, too, allows you to convert the timeshare unit of your choice into Hyatt Vacation Club points that are good for stays at other Hyatt timeshare destinations, hotel room bookings, and more. In addition, your membership in the Hyatt Vacation Club allows you access to members-only rates on airfares, car rentals, and cruise-ship vacations. You also will be automatically enrolled in Hyatt's Gold Passport program, which rewards frequent guests with complimentary benefits.

Hilton Grand Vacation Club timeshare owners also get similar benefits, including the ability to exchange timeshare use for Hilton HHonors points. Those HHonors points are good for things such as hotel stays, getaways to additional Hilton timeshare resorts, airline and train tickets, car rentals, cruise-ship vacations, theme-park admission tickets, gift certificates to stores such as Sharper Image, and more. You can also use the HHonors Reward Exchange program to convert frequent-flyer points from airlines such as American and Virgin Atlantic into additional HHonors points should you come up a bit short for the reward you are hoping to receive.

Timeshare owners in the Starwood Vacation Ownership program receive similar benefits as those explained in the previous few paragraphs, including the ability to use timeshare points for hotel stays at participating Westin, Sheraton, Four Points by Sheraton, St. Regis, The Luxury Collection, and W Hotels. Points also can be used for rewards such as car rentals, airline tickets, and the like.

E-ALERT

You can use the resale market to try to get a better price for a brand-name timeshare unit, but that price rarely includes access to the developer's loyalty programs and other benefits. Buying directly from a brand-name developer will ensure you receive all the benefits that come from doing business with a brand-name company.

Disney Vacation Club members receive many of the same benefits as explained in the previous few paragraphs. With Disney, though, members also are entitled to loyalty program benefits in keeping with Mickey Mouse style, such as discounts on annual passes to the Walt Disney World and Disneyland theme parks, exclusive events such as theme-park attraction previews and private Disney Cruise Line sailings, and member publications that show you behind-the-scenes goings-on at the Disney theme parks and resorts.

Possible Bonus Time

Sometimes when you buy a timeshare from the developer, you will be entitled to purchase bonus time later on at your home resort, or at another resort that is specified by the exchange company. Bonus time does not affect the timeshare unit usage that you already own; instead, it allows you to purchase additional vacation time—often at a substantially reduced rate. You can get bonus time when buying on the resale market, depending on your resort and exchange company, but when you buy from a developer, your chances tend to be greater.

How does bonus time work? The general public may be paying upward of $150 per night for a one-bedroom unit that you, with your bonus time option, can get for less than $50. You sometimes will have to commit to a full weekend, or two nights, but that is still a pretty great deal if you want to make a long-weekend getaway. If your timeshare resort is close to your home, you can even use bonus time as additional housing for out-of-town guests.

≡FAST FACT

Bonus time is not a standard part of timeshare-unit purchase agreements, and therefore may not be offered with the unit you are buying. Be sure to ask about this option if you think you may want to use it, and get the associated fees and wait-list rules in writing from your resort or exchange company before you sign anything.

If bonus time is offered with your timeshare unit, you should not have to pay for the bonus time in advance. Instead, it should be available on a first-come, first-served basis throughout the year.

Possible Bargains

While it is true that buying a timeshare unit on the resale market, instead of directly from a developer, will often help you to get a better price, there are some deals to be had from developers if you are willing to be patient and look around.

Timeshare resorts that are nearly sold out, for instance, will have a handful of units left that the developer's salesmen are trying to push. They may not be peak units—don't think beachfront; think parking-lot view—but that does not always matter. If, for instance, you are trying to buy a unit during a sought-after week in a top-dollar timeshare resort simply so that you can trade it away year after year to take full advantage of its value, you likely will not care what the view is from the living room balcony (or whether there is a balcony at all). These kinds of direct-from-the-developer purchases can be hugely beneficial, as you can sometimes get a bargain while still gaining access to things like the developer's loyalty points programs.

Owner Referral Programs

Sometimes, if you have bought a timeshare directly from a resort developer, you will be eligible for an owner referral program. These are incentive programs through which you receive certain benefits if you give the developer the names and contact information of relatives and friends who are also interested in buying a timeshare unit in the same resort.

Owner referral program benefits can include everything from free points or long-weekend stays to upgraded unit usage and discounted bonus time. These benefits are *not* available from every resort developer, but you should ask about them before signing on to make sure that you receive them if they are an option in your case.

The Cons

Of course, if you are one of those people whose grandmothers convinced them that buying retail is never the right way to go, you will not be surprised to learn that there are just as many cons to buying from a developer as there are pros. As with any major investment that you choose to buy directly from a manufacturer—such as a new car—buying a timeshare unit directly from a developer will come with things like higher unit cost, long-term financing and interest, and, in some cases, the requirement that you buy before actually seeing the product.

Of course, the one con this list does not include is the possibility of buying a lemon—something that you very well might encounter should you choose to buy off the resale market instead of directly from the developer. That's not to say that every purchase you make from a developer will be as good as the next, but thanks to legal rescission periods, you are far less likely to walk away owning a unit that is worthless when you buy from a developer than you might be should you buy off the resale market.

Having said that, there are significant drawbacks to buying your timeshare unit directly from a developer. Here is a look at some of the most important ones.

Higher Unit Cost

There is a well-known term for the higher costs that are normally associated with making a major purchase directly from a manufacturer: sticker shock. Just as when you buy an automobile from a dealership instead of from a used-car lot, you will encounter top-dollar pricing when buying a timeshare unit directly from a developer instead of on the resale market And just as you lose value in that new car the minute you drive it off the lot, you will lose value in your new timeshare purchase the minute you take over ownership.

 **E-QUESTION**

How much higher are the developer's prices?
Developer's prices can be sometimes hundreds of dollars, sometimes thousands of dollars—sometimes as much as 50 percent more than used timeshares in the same resort are selling for elsewhere. There have been cases where a $12,000 or $15,000 unit that could be purchased directly from a developer has shown up on a Web site such as eBay for pennies on the dollar.

Of course, the time and patience required for ferreting out bargains is sometimes the very thing that may drive you to buy directly from the developer in the first place. Just keep in mind that you are paying for the convenience of making your timeshare-unit purchase when you want it and how you want it, just as you pay for the convenience of taking a shiny new car home from a dealership instead of buying one at a reduced price after months of looking through the classified ads in your local newspaper.

Expensive Long-Term Financing

In addition to the higher timeshare unit price you will likely pay if you decide to buy directly from the developer, you also are likely to face high interest rates associated with your long-term financing. Remember, developers are often the "bank," so to speak, when it comes to financing a timeshare purchase. They set the interest rates—and they usually set them much, much higher than your real bank has when you have made real-estate purchases in the past.

A typical interest rate for a timeshare-unit purchase in late 2005 was in the neighborhood of 15 percent. Those interest payments can add up to thousands of dollars over the years of your timeshare-unit financing. Let's say they add up to a smaller amount, like $1,700 on an asking price of $12,500—bringing your total cost to $14,200 over the long term. If you take one week of vacation in that timeshare unit each year for seven years, you will be paying—not including maintenance fees and special assessments—about $2,025 per week (as compared with the $1,785 per week that would be advertised alongside the $12,500 asking price). That's a significant difference, which is why it is among the noteworthy drawbacks to buying directly from the timeshare developer.

Preconstruction Pitches

One of the major downsides to buying your timeshare unit directly from the developer is that sometimes the resort itself will not yet have been built. In this situation, you will be shown oodles of colorful charts, maps, diagrams, and brochures, all designed to entice you to buy a piece of a project that is still in its initial phases. There is an inherent danger here, of course, in that should anything go wrong with the developer's plans, you will have bought into the idea of a resort that may never come to exist in reality.

Some of the potential problems that developers have faced in the past include a lack of sufficient funding to complete their plan, denied permits that are key to major construction, and delays forced by multiple factors that lead to years worth of waiting before timeshare owners can actually use their vacation units. Developers who have limited backing or who are getting into timeshares for the first time are most likely to run into such problems.

E-ALERT

If you are interested in buying a preconstruction timeshare unit, your safest bet is to purchase from a developer with a long history and strong pedigree. Brand names like Disney, Hyatt, Marriott, and Hilton are far less likely to come up short in the long run when compared with first-time developers building a single resort.

Some experts warn against buying preconstruction timeshares altogether, since you cannot walk around in them, see the quality of the craftsmanship, and so forth. This is less of a concern with second-phase developments—timeshare units being added on to an existing resort by the same developer—but it is wise, no matter where you are thinking about buying, to at least see a sample of the developer's work before signing on the dotted line.

Those Dreaded Sales Presentations

If you find yourself buying a timeshare unit directly from a developer, the odds are you will have just finished sitting through a sales presentation. This, in and of itself, is considered a drawback by many people because a fair number of timeshare sales presentations are high-pressure and uncomfortable for the buyer.

There is, however, a little-known fact that can help you overcome this problem when buying a timeshare unit directly from the developer. Instead of accepting an invitation for a free weekend trip that includes the dreaded sales presentation, simply call the resort that interests you and ask to arrange a private meeting with a salesman.

There is no rule that states you must sit through a high-pressure presentation before purchasing a timeshare unit from a developer. You can arrange a meeting one-on-one with the salesperson of your choice, just as you might arrange a loan meeting at your local bank.

The downside to this approach, of course, is that you will be footing the bill for your trip to and from the resort, and for everything you do while you are in town checking the place out. But if you truly dread the idea of sitting through the sales presentation, and if you are honestly interested in buying a timeshare unit, the extra money you will have to spend up front might be worth it in terms of saving you headaches and aggravation later on. Heck, if you tell the reservations desk that you are interested in buying a timeshare, you may even get a discounted rate.

How to Find Units

The easiest timeshare units to buy directly from the developer are those that are part of brand-name resorts. Companies like Disney, Hilton, Hyatt, Marriott, and Starwood have well-designed Web sites that you can use as a starting place for exploring your options within those particular companies. In some cases, the Web sites even promote new resorts that are under development at any given moment—giving you the option of a preconstruction purchase. You can find links to the Web sites of the major brand-name timeshare developers in Appendix A.

After you take some time to look through the materials on these companies' Web sites, you can click on the "Learn More" or "Contact Us" button. From there, you will find a phone number that you can call, or you will be asked to provide your contact information so that a sales representative can contact you in the near future.

If you are interested in looking for a timeshare development that is not necessarily part of the brand-name conglomerates—but you want to do some research on your own, in privacy, without handing over your home telephone number and address—a good place to look is the Web site maintained by Resort Condominiums International, *www .rci.com*. It allows you to search through all of the exchange company's resorts worldwide, with basic information provided for each. In some cases, you will be able to learn everything from the types of units offered to the distance of the resort from the airport.

≡FAST FACT

Before buying any timeshare unit from a developer, you can go to the Web site of the industry's leading professional group, the American Resort Development Association. The group's site, *www .arda.org*, includes a search engine that lets you type in the name of a developer and find out instantly whether it is a member of the group—which promotes a Code of Ethics for timeshare sales.

Remember, though, that Resort Condominiums International is a timeshare-unit exchange company, not a developer of timeshare resorts. If you find a resort on the company's Web site that interests you, you will have to contact the resort developer or its homeowners' association directly. You can do this either by researching the resort further on your own (simply finding its telephone number and calling will suffice), or by contacting Resort Condominiums International and requesting contact information for the resort's sales department.

The main competitor to Resort Condominiums International, called Interval International, does not allow nonmembers to view similar information on its Web site, *www.intervalworld.com*. However, Interval International does post contact information for several of its offices and departments, including customer service/customer relations, so you might start there if you are interested in buying a unit inside a resort that is part of the Interval International exchange network.

CHAPTER 10

Buying a Resale Timeshare

THE GOOD NEWS ABOUT THE timeshare resale market is that supply is far greater than demand. There are some real bargains to be found, sometimes for 50 percent or less than you would pay a developer for a new unit in the very same resort. The bad news is that mixed in with those great bargains are countless scams, lousy units, and unsavory businesspeople trying to make a quick buck. Settle in and take notes, because there is plenty to learn before you enter the timeshare resale marketplace.

Buying New Versus Buying Used

For many people, the question of whether to buy new or buy used already has an ingrained answer. Countless people refuse to even set foot on a used-car lot, for instance, because they cannot imagine owning an automobile that someone else has driven—or because they want the newest model available in exactly the color and styling of their choice. Still other people refuse to even look at existing homes in the same neighborhoods where new housing developments are being built. They just do not like the idea of living in a place where other people have lived, especially when a sparkling new option is available just around the corner on a yet-to-be-built-out lot where they can choose everything from the color of the walls to the brand names on the appliances.

For other people, though, the thought of buying a car, home, or virtually anything else from its manufacturer or developer is simply ludicrous. Why pay more, they reason, when a bit of extra elbow grease can often turn up fabulous prices on major purchases that are in excellent condition? These people know that they often will have to spend far more time researching and examining their purchase before actually making it—because they often are not shielded by the same consumer-protection laws that go along with buying new— but they are willing to invest that time and effort in exchange for the financial benefits that can come in the long run. Sure, they may have to settle for a different color or model than they would have purchased if they had gotten their first choice, but what they end up with, to their thinking, is still better than what the vast majority of other shoppers ever find.

═ FAST FACT

People who buy only new things do pay a premium for their choices— sometimes a hefty premium when compared with the cost of buying a gently used car or year-old home. But they feel it is worth it, because they know exactly what they are getting, and they usually have lemon laws on their side should anything go wrong after the signing of the contracts.

If you count yourself among the latter group, then perhaps buying a timeshare unit on the resale market is for you. There are thousands of timeshare units available at any given time, and many of them are indeed excellent bargains. People decide to sell their timeshare units for perfectly valid reasons every day. Some of these reasons include:

- The realization that they just don't have the time to use their unit as expected

- The death of a spouse and resulting change in vacation accommodation needs
- The birth of a child and resulting change in vacation accommodation needs
- Personal financial problems that force an owner to sell
- The realization that timeshare ownership simply is not for them

As a buyer, you of course stand to benefit from any of these reasons, as some timeshare-unit owners will be more eager to sell than others—and thus more willing to give you a good deal on their unit in exchange for a fast agreement.

You also, though, stand to lose big-time if you mistakenly choose to do business with someone who is selling their timeshare for another reason, such as "dumping off" a lousy unit or quietly "handing off" what could be thousands of dollars in unpaid maintenance and special assessment fees. By the same token, many timeshare resale brokers are good people just out to earn an honest living, but others have been sued for scamming buyers and sellers alike out of hundreds, if not thousands, of dollars at a time.

When considering buying a timeshare unit on the resale market, then, it is imperative that you understand all of the pros and cons. Here is a look at the key factors you need to keep in mind.

The Pros

Of course, the number-one reason for buying a timeshare unit on the resale market is price. In some cases, you can find perfectly great units for sale at 50 percent or less than the developer's asking price on new units in the exact same timeshare resorts. There are, however, other reasons to consider buying on the resale market, not the least of which are being able to walk through, thoroughly examine, and perhaps even determine the historical exchange value of the exact unit you are buying.

Better Prices

Without a doubt, you stand to save a great deal of money if you choose to buy a timeshare unit on the resale market instead of from a developer. In fact, many timeshare owners who purchase second, third, and even fourth timeshare units do so *only* on the resale market—after they have had a chance to learn about their needs and how to make the most of the worldwide exchange system.

How much money can you save? Most experts agree that 50 percent or more is standard. The key is learning that there really is no benchmark for timeshare resale prices. Since supply is so much greater than demand, the best price a seller can get is simply equal to the highest price the overcrowded market will bear. If you are a buyer, this of course works beautifully in your favor.

 **E-QUESTION**

If I see a timeshare unit for sale at what seems like an incredibly low price—say, $500—does that automatically mean it is a scam?
Not necessarily. People sell timeshares for all different reasons, including personal financial difficulties that require them to sell quickly. Research the property thoroughly, but do not write it off simply because it sounds too good to be true.

Another way you stand to save when buying on the resale market is through financing. Remember, when you buy a new timeshare and need financing, you almost always have to get it from the resort developer—sometimes at long-term interest rates of 15 percent or higher. When buying on the resale market, you are free to finance the purchase however you wish. You can pay cash and avoid interest payments altogether, you can get a loan from your local bank at a more favorable rate, or you can use a home equity line of credit and (in many cases) turn the interest you will pay into an annual tax write-off.

Simply avoiding the resort developer's financing terms, then, can save you hundreds if not thousands of dollars in interest payments during the length of your timeshare agreement. When you combine those savings with the half-price or better cost of the unit in the first place, you begin to see why so many people are willing to do the extra legwork that buying on the resale market requires.

Existing Properties

As you read in Chapter 9, sometimes when you buy a new timeshare directly from the developer you are asked to make the purchase on a preconstruction basis—meaning your particular unit has not yet been built. There can be serious ramifications to this, such as construction snafus and last-minute changes that may leave you with a property that ends up being less than you bargained for when you made the original deal.

You do not run this risk when buying on the resale market. By simple definition, a property that someone else already owns is likely to exist in bricks and mortar, and that means that you will have the opportunity to set foot in it and examine it thoroughly before agreeing to any deal.

E-ALERT

If you have the opportunity to actually tour a resale timeshare unit before purchasing it, do not pass up the chance. Even a tour as short as twenty minutes will give you a good feel for the amenities at the unit and at the resort, and you just may bump into some other unit owners who can give you details about their ownership experiences.

Of just as great importance is that, with a resale unit, you also will be able to tour the resort and learn about its history of maintenance, fees, problems, and the like. You can meet other unit owners and ask their opinions about the place, and you can learn about the history of timeshare construction in the area—to protect yourself against buying in a soon-to-be-built-out region.

Proven Track Records

If you are planning to buy a timeshare unit simply so that you can exchange it annually on the worldwide market, then buying resale makes some sense because you may be able to determine your particular unit's track record for garnering exchanges at the kinds of properties that interest you.

Some experts recommend that when buying for the sheer purpose of exchange, you should purchase only a top-level week at a resort of highest demand. This is a good bit of advice in many cases, but if you know there are only two resorts that you ever hope to visit—and neither is a high-demand place or at a high-demand time of travel—then a lower-end resale unit might be exactly what you need (saving you even more money in the long run).

You can check with the unit's current owner about his or her history of exchanges, or you can try contacting the owner's exchange company directly. You will not always be able to get such personal information from an exchange company without the current owner's permission, but taking the extra step may prove very valuable to you during the length of your timeshare ownership.

Rent Before You Own

Many people who are hoping to sell their timeshare units put them up for rent while looking for potential buyers. This gives you, as a potential buyer, a great opportunity to actually experience at least a minivacation in the unit of choice before agreeing to a long-term ownership commitment.

On a broader scale, the fact that there are so many more timeshare sellers out there than there are buyers means that you can rent several units during the course of a few months or even a year, just to test out different types of resorts during high- and low-demand seasons. Doing this may cost you a bit of cash up-front in rental fees, but it will give you a wealth of timeshare-use experience to help you make a smarter long-term purchase when you finally decide to buy your own unit.

▣ TRAVEL TIP

If you already know which timeshare resort interests you most, call its front desk and ask if any unit owners are looking for renters while they wait to sell. In some cases, you will be able to work directly with the resort or unit owner in arranging a pre-purchase minivacation on a rental basis.

No Dreaded Sales Presentations

While it is true that you do not have to sit through a sales presentation before buying a timeshare unit directly from a developer, most people do—and most people dislike them. With a resale market timeshare, the only sales presentation you will need to endure is the one from the unit owner or the resale broker, and in many cases, he will be a regular person just like you.

You do need to be careful to verify anything and everything that a timeshare owner or resale broker tells you. (After all, he *is* trying to get you to buy something he wants to sell.) But in many cases, most of the pertinent information will be listed on the classified or Internet ad that gets your attention in the first place, and all you will need to do is ask a few pertinent questions. These can include:

- Why are you selling the timeshare unit?
- Are all maintenance and other fees paid in full?
- How will the title transfer, money transfer, and closing contracts be handled?

If there are questions that you feel the current owner is not answering in full, you can contact the timeshare resort or exchange company to try to get more information. If you are working with a resale broker (which you will learn more about later in this chapter), she can also sometimes be of great help in filling in information gaps.

The Cons

While there is a lot that you stand to gain when buying on the resale market, there are also pitfalls that await you as a buyer, whether you are a novice or an expert. Some of these cons—such as limited access to timeshare developer loyalty programs—are more important to some people than they are to others, but there are legal and financial missteps that can affect everyone equally. Pay close attention to the fine print when purchasing a timeshare unit from an existing owner, and you will have a much better chance of avoiding many of the problems that other resale market buyers have encountered.

Savvy Competition

One of the biggest problems with the resale market—and one that you will never hear a developer mention when selling a brand-new unit—is that there are people who have actually made careers out of prospecting for the best resale unit bargains. These people are savvy competitors to anyone looking to buy a resale unit, many of them having owned multiple timeshares in the past and learned all the ins and outs of working with various exchange companies and brand-name developers. These people scan classified and Internet ads all day long, eagerly snapping up the very best bargains almost immediately after they appear. This makes it much harder for you to find the top-notch deals, especially if you are new to the game, and it also means that you will be left paying at least a little bit more than you otherwise might for any given timeshare unit.

There is not much you can do about competing with these savvy timeshare buyers beyond educating yourself about the market and being patient while you look for the best deal that you can find. The fact that it costs less than $25 to join the major timeshare users' organizations makes those memberships well-spent money in terms of research. You can use the members-only chat rooms as your own personal question-and-answer gold mines, in addition to making use of all the resale market advice the groups already offer.

≡ FAST FACT

If you want to learn from other timeshare owners' mistakes, you can join the Timeshare User's Group at *www.tug2.net*. This Web site includes sections on regional supply and demand, as well as recent resale prices. You also can subscribe to TimeSharing Today, a magazine whose Web site, *www.tstoday.com*, includes a resale value tracker. And the magazine *Hiatus* (*www.gohiatus.com*) offers a timeshare buyer's guide.

Limited Historical Data

When you bought your home, you probably worked with a Realtor to look up historical data about the sale prices of similar homes in your neighborhood. It is much, much harder to get this kind of information where timeshares are concerned, especially if you are buying a points-based unit instead of a deeded unit (as points-based units usually do not involve land-ownership records).

In the great majority of cases, you simply will lack access to historical data of any kind—a real drawback when trying to determine the true value of a resale timeshare unit. You can try using timeshare users' organization chat rooms and Web sites to determine the sale prices of timeshare units that are similar to the one you are considering, and in some cases, you may be able to find timeshare-unit auction results through TRI West Real Estate (*www.triwest-timeshare.com*), a California-based company that oversees timeshare auctions.

Of course, the particular timeshare unit or resort that you are considering may not pop up in any of these resources, which again leaves you looking to the unit's current owner for whatever historical data you can find. It is certainly not an ideal situation, so caveat emptor is the wisest advice.

No Rescission Period—Usually

Some states have instituted lemon laws that protect you for at least a few days when buying a used car, the same way rescission periods often protect you when buying a new timeshare unit. But when you buy a timeshare unit on the resale market, you are not always entitled to a rescission period. In many cases if you sign the contracts and hand over the cash, then you own the unit—no unforeseen problems withstanding.

Now, if you have found a perfectly great unit for $1,000 in a resort where new units are running closer to $10,000, this lack of cooling-off time may not trouble you too deeply. A thousand dollars is certainly a good amount of money, but it likely is not so much money that you will not be able to recoup it should you choose to resell your resale unit in the future, especially with new units in the same resort costing so much more.

Sometimes you actually will be entitled to a cooling-off period—if you are working with a resale broker who offers one through his company. This is, of course, different than having a state law to back up your claim should something go wrong, but there are reputable resale brokers out there who give both parties a few days or even a week after signing the papers to ensure that everyone is happy with the deal.

▐█▌ TRAVEL TIP

If you decide to work with a resale broker, be sure to ask up front whether the broker's company offers a rescission period, or cooling-off time. Also check with your credit-card company. Visa and MasterCard users sometimes are entitled to a ten-day cooling-off period after purchasing a timeshare.

The point is that you must be darn sure about the fact that you want to purchase a particular resale unit before you go ahead and do so. If there are any lingering questions or doubts in your mind about a given unit or its current owner, your best bet is to walk away from the deal and wait for a better one to come along. Remember: Timeshare resale is a buyer's market. There almost *always* will be a better deal, or at least one that is just as good, out there in the future.

Possible Unpaid Fees

A top-notch unit in a high-demand resort during a prime week of the year can look like a pretty good deal when you find a deeply discounted price—until you factor in the payment of years' worth of unpaid maintenance, special assessments, and other fees. This is a classic trap into which many first-time resale market buyers fall, and it is one that you can avoid simply by doing your homework in advance and making sure that the unit's current owner has met his financial obligations to date.

E-ALERT

Unpaid maintenance fees can add hundreds or even thousands of dollars to the cost of a timeshare unit that you buy on the resale market. It is imperative that you confirm with your resort of choice that the timeshare unit's current owner has kept his payments up to date.

If the timeshare owner is offering to transfer anything else into your name along with the sale of the unit—such as exchange-company membership or loyalty program access—be sure that you check with the companies offering those programs to ensure that such transfers are allowed. Again, these could be marketing add-ons that will not really exist after you take ownership, and their absence will, in effect, add to the cost you are paying solely for the timeshare unit itself.

Limited Access to Loyalty Programs

As explained in Chapter 9, when you purchase a timeshare unit directly from the resort's developer—particularly from a brand-name resort's developer—you often are automatically granted access to that developer's loyalty programs. Such memberships can get you things like discounted stays at same-brand-name hotels, deals on rental cars, and the like.

When you buy a unit at the very same resort through the resale market, you usually are *not* entitled to any of the loyalty program benefits. If your only reason for buying the timeshare unit is to return to it year after year on vacation, this lack of loyalty-program access may make no difference to you. On the other hand, if you are a person who travels frequently and would save a good deal of money over the years through all of these discounts, you might want to reconsider and look into buying a unit in the same resort directly from the developer.

Well-Used Units

Buying a resale unit means that you are buying a used piece of property, and as you likely already know, the term used has many meanings. There is nothing wrong, of course, with gently used properties whose maintenance oversight has been stellar over the years, but you do not want to fall into the trap of buying a timeshare unit that is falling apart in a failing resort with no hope of repair.

The underlying fact of timeshare resale is that you have to choose your unit from among those that other people are selling—meaning that you will not always be able to get the exact unit you want in a precise location in a given resort. You will have to take the best that you can get, so to speak. As with other drawbacks to buying resale, this matters more to some people than to others. Just make sure you are going to be satisfied with your unit before you sign on the dotted line.

Legal Legwork

If you and the seller are not using a resale broker (you will learn more about that later in this chapter), you will have to do all the legal legwork of your resale unit's purchase. This can include getting title insurance for deeded properties, arranging the title transfer, negotiating payment of the transfer fee (which is set by the developer for the transfer of a unit from one person to another), setting up an escrow account for the exchange of money, ensuring that the contract is written as necessary to comply with property transfer laws in the state where you are buying, arranging for the receipt of any unused timeshare weeks or points, and ensuring that all maintenance and other fees are fully paid to date.

═FAST FACT

The TimeSharing Today Web site, *www.tstoday.com*, offers resale document kits to members for $30. The kits include fill-in-the-blanks timeshare contract forms, model letters for every step in the closing process, promissory note forms with payment schedules, exchange company transfer forms, and more.

These can be time-consuming items if you are new to the timeshare resale game, and a misstep at any point can suddenly turn your deal of the century into the lemon of a lifetime. If you are at all concerned that these tasks are beyond your current knowledge, consider using a resale broker or buying a unit from someone who has already signed on with a resale broker.

If you want to go ahead and give the purchasing process a try on your own, you can get some good advice about protecting yourself by searching through the timeshare user organizations' Web sites, and by asking pointed questions in the members-only chat rooms. Sometimes, if you simply ask, you will even be able to procure a sample contract that has worked for another resale buyer in the past.

How to Find Resale Units

Once you start to look around—even if you never before knew that the timeshare resale market existed—you may feel as though there are countless choices from all over the world that are so overwhelming in number, you are not sure where to start. There is a lot of truth to that notion, as there are far more properties for sale than there are buyers looking to purchase them. Again, this is to your financial advantage, but it will require you to weed through a fair number of advertisements on your way to finding the timeshare unit that will suit you best for many years to come.

There are a lot of places that you can look to find resale units, and none is better than the next. Using these resources is all a matter of how you want to conduct your search, whether on the Internet, in print, by telephone, or by using a combination of all these options.

Timeshare-Specific Web Sites

If you took the advice given earlier in this chapter and joined the Timeshare User's Group, the *TimeSharing Today* magazine membership, or both, you have a built-in place to start when looking for resale units. Both organizations list units for sale on their Web sites, *www .tug2.net* and *www.tstoday.com*, with search engines that will allow you to at least get a handle on some of the choices that await you. Because these groups also provide some historical data about resale prices, you may also get lucky and have your background information at your fingertips, as well.

▐▄▌ TRAVEL TIP

If you have the chance to go to your resort of choice and walk around in the exact unit that will be yours, take the opportunity. This is the only real way to verify that you are not getting a well-worn unit at a resort that is crumbling all around it.

There are countless other Web sites out there that claim to be experts in buying and selling on the timeshare resale market. If you choose to work with one of these, be sure to ask if the resale broker is licensed to do business in the state where you are hoping to purchase a timeshare unit. This is one of the only customer-protection tools you have when trying to ferret out the real brokers from the scam artists (more on that later in this chapter).

eBay

Believe it or not, you can buy a timeshare on eBay. Why not, right? If you can buy an 1890s Victrola from Oshkosh or a high-fashion full-length gown from Paris, why not a vacation unit anywhere in the world of your choosing?

There are absolutely, positively many great timeshare deals to be found on eBay. The trick is to do the same due diligence you would when buying a resale timeshare unit anywhere else: Ask the important follow-up questions about maintenance fees and the like, be sure the sale will follow all legal rules and restrictions, and by all means go see the property if the opportunity presents itself.

Resale Brokers

If you know that you want to buy a resale timeshare, but you do not want to do any of the legwork yourself, your best bet is to work with a resale broker. These are people who perhaps charge the seller a specified amount of money for advertising a timeshare, and then get paid a commission on the sale—just like a regular Realtor on a house.

Resale timeshare brokers are supposed to be licensed, just as Realtors are supposed to be licensed. Where can you find a good resale broker? Again, a good place to start looking is in those timeshare users' organizations, the Timeshare User's Group and *TimeSharing Today* magazine. You might even get personal recommendations by asking for leads in the members-only chat rooms.

If you are not a member of those groups, you can start by calling the Better Business Bureau that services the area where you hope to buy a timeshare. Log on to *www.bbb.org,* and you will be able to search for the appropriate regional office. From there, you can ask for references on good resale brokers—and tips on the people who have been the subject of complaints. To help get you started, a list of resale brokers is included in Appendix A.

E-ALERT

Any guy with a cellular phone and a business card can call himself a timeshare resale broker. Be sure to ask whether the resale broker you are working with is indeed licensed to do business.

Classified Ads

Good old-fashioned newspapers are a great spot to locate resale timeshare units. The classified ads in even your smallest local rag are bound to contain at least one local seller looking to make a deal, while the real-estate and travel sections of major metropolitan newspapers are usually brimming with ads from all over the country, especially on Sundays, when newspaper circulations are greatest.

Some newspapers now put their classified sections on the World Wide Web for easier searching. You may have to pay a fee to access these ads, but if you know that you want to buy a timeshare unit in, say, San Jose, California, it might be worth the Internet search fee to become a registered user of the *San Jose Mercury News* Web site—just so you can search its classifieds for local timeshares that are up for sale.

Timeshare Resorts Themselves

If you know which timeshare resort you like the most, sometimes your best bet is to go straight to it when looking for a resale unit.

Owners sometimes post flyers on bulletin boards seeking resale buyers for their units. A simple call to the resort's front desk will often result in your being given the names and telephone numbers on those homemade advertisements—saving you tons of research time elsewhere. Also, timeshare unit owners sometimes try to rent their units while they are looking for a buyer, and those same front-desk workers should be able to tell you whether that is an option for you, as well.

If you are looking to purchase a unit in a region where there are multiple timeshare resorts, this method of information-gathering can also be useful in scouting out the competition—and in giving you a clue as to how your unit's value might hold up over time in the midst of a crowded marketplace.

Timeshare Homeowners' Associations

Just as the timeshare resorts keep track of which units are for sale, so do timeshare homeowners' associations, which also keep track of which units are being foreclosed upon or rented, as well. In some cases, if you call the homeowners' association directly, you can find out about a great deal that is not being marketed elsewhere and also about the reasons why the property went into foreclosure in the first place. If there is a problem with the owner, for instance, and not with the unit, you just may get even more than you hoped for even less than you dreamed of paying. The front desk at the resort of your choice should be able to put you in touch with the homeowners' association.

CHAPTER 11

Maintenance and Ownership Issues

ONE OF THE MAIN REASONS you may decide to buy a timeshare unit is that you do not want to do any hands-on maintenance, as you would if you bought a vacation home outright. Still, you likely will want to know where your annual fees are going, and you will certainly want an insider's perspective on what major capital improvements might be planned down the road. Therefore, it is important that you understand the structure of your homeowners' association and your resort's system for making improvements and repairs.

Developers and Management Companies

If you buy a timeshare unit from a new-resort developer, the chances are good that you will have minimal, if any, maintenance or other responsibilities beyond paying your annual fees—at least for the first few years of your ownership experience. Heck, that is one of the reasons you bought a timeshare, right? Hands-off ownership without a blade of grass to mow, ever!

In many cases, developers will oversee everything from maintenance to capital improvements during the first year or two of a resort's existence, often even subsidizing annual maintenance fees to make them appear lower to you and other would-be buyers. Their goal, of course, is to make timeshare ownership as attractive to you as possible—and that means taking on the majority of headaches and hassles themselves.

Some of the things the developer may look after during your initial period of new-resort unit ownership could include:

- Maintenance fee collection
- Property tax collection
- Insurance premium payments
- Reserve account balance
- Resort repairs

As with all good things, though, this initial period is bound to come to an end. Your timeshare paperwork will often specify exactly what percentage of a resort's units need to be sold before this happens, but rest assured that eventually, when most or all of the timeshare units are taken, the developer will turn over the day-to-day management of the resort to a body called a Resort Property Owners' Association, a Homeowners' Association, or a Condominium Owners' Association.

 **E-QUESTION**

Are timeshare management companies similar to condominium management companies?
Yes, they are similar in that they oversee the duties that a homeowners' association might otherwise handle. These include the collection of annual maintenance fees, capital expenditures, insurance policy premiums, and the like. Sometimes, the timeshare groups are even called Condominium Owners' Associations.

This is when your responsibilities as a timeshare owner will begin to take shape, either in the form of helping to elect officers or by running for a seat on the board of directors yourself. In some cases, you and the other homeowners' association officers will be responsible for everything from the resort's expenses and upkeep to its future viability and infrastructure improvements (more on that later in this chapter). In the vast majority of cases, though, you will simply cast a vote aimed at selecting a management company to oversee those homeowners' association duties and more.

With many brand-name resorts, such as Marriott, your association will generally contract with the development company to continue providing oversight and services of everything from the planting of flowerbeds to the services provided by the front desk. And why not, as long as the price is competitive? Their management system was good enough in your mind to buy the timeshare in the first place, so why not just let them keep running it in the same manner?

Other resorts, though, look to outside management companies such as Utah-based Owners' Resorts & Exchange and South Carolina–based Defender Resorts, which manage more than a dozen timeshare homeownership associations apiece at various resorts all over the United States. Owners' Resorts & Exchange, for instance, prides itself on adding two new homeowner associations—or approximately one thousand timeshare units—to its stable of customers each year. These companies' fees, of course, are rolled into the annual maintenance premium paid by you and the rest of your fellow homeowners' association members. The fees vary based on the services provided, and they typically will make up a relatively small percentage of your overall maintenance fee payment each year.

Whether your homeowners' association contracts with a brand-name developer or other management company, it will be that hired hand's job to ensure that you and all of the other members of your homeowners' association get everything that you need and want.

If your association decides to forgo a management company's fees and take the do-it-yourself approach, you will have to be much more conscious about the details that are involved with homeowner association responsibilities—if only to make sure that yours are being met, to keep your timeshare unit's value as high as possible.

Homeowners' Associations

In timeshare resorts, homeowners' associations do a lot of the things that you would expect them to do, from auditing the books to collecting delinquent maintenance fee payments to ensuring that you are paying the lowest possible premiums for insurance coverage. In many cases, homeowners' associations also keep track of things such as unit foreclosures, resales, and rentals—working to promote them when necessary or to clamp down on timeshare unit owners who try to skirt the rules of the resort. The list of responsibilities is long even when it is standard, to be sure.

Sometimes, though, timeshare homeowners' associations have to deal with extraordinary things that you might not anticipate based on your previous experience owning, say, a condominium. For instance, in 2004, an estimated 25 percent of timeshare resorts in the United States—most of them in Florida—were battered by Hurricanes Charley, Frances, Ivan, and Jeanne. The losses ranged from power outages to complete destruction, with at least thirty timeshare resorts having to stay closed well into 2005, according to a report in the *Wall Street Journal's Real Estate Journal.*

As you may have surmised, the challenge for homeowners' associations was multifold at these timeshare communities and far beyond the traditional scope of day-to-day management responsibilities. For starters, the homeowners' associations were tasked with:

- Keeping owners apprised of when repairs would be made, and when units would again be available for use
- Dealing with insurance companies to ensure coverage was provided
- Assessing any needed repairs that were not covered by insurance
- Finding local contractors at reasonable prices to make those uninsured repairs
- Using reserve funds responsibly, or levying special assessments, to pay for additional repairs

Other timeshare resorts have faced other unique challenges. For instance, back when timeshares first began to be developed in the United States, they did not typically include things like restaurants, spas, and other amenities that are in high demand today. Homeowners' associations were in the business of simply managing the business of the resort's units, such as taxes and property maintenance. They did not have to be experts in everything else under the sun, from pricing a hamburger competitively to hiring qualified massage therapists.

Today, of course, a resort without a restaurant is not likely to get a whole lot of attention from timeshare vacation-goers, and spas continue to be all the rage—which means that homeowners' associations sometimes need to take on the burden of managing an ever more complex series of services. In these types of situations, expertise is required on many levels. That type of specific knowledge base can be hard to find, especially when the homeowners' association members are scattered all over the country and, perhaps, the world.

TRAVEL TIP

When deciding whether you want to sit on your homeowners' association's board of directors, be sure to ask exactly what the association oversees. In some cases, the developer will retain ownership and management of restaurants, shops, and other ancillary amenities, while in other cases, your group will have responsibility for the oversight of these widely varied and potentially complex businesses.

It is for this reason, in part, that the American Resort Development Association offers assistance to do-it-yourself homeowners' associations by holding regional meetings full of tips and advice. Their experts fly around the country providing firsthand experience with things such as contracts, legal maneuvers, and other specialized information that homeowners' associations might need to know. You can learn more about the services that the American Resort Development Association provides at the group's Web site, *www.arda.org.*

The American Resort Development Association also works to generate support for ARDA-ROC, its grass-roots political action committee. The committee's mission is to fight any and all legislation that it feels is written in a way that could hurt timeshare owners financially or otherwise. Its efforts are usually at the state and federal levels, and they are important as the timeshare industry continues to evolve.

Some of the would-be laws that ARDA-ROC has fought against include attempts to limit the second home mortgage deduction, to impose state sales taxes on timeshares, and to tax timeshare owners as transient occupants, just as hotel guests are taxed in many states. If you end up sitting on your homeowners' association board of directors, these may be some of the issues that you will end up facing in addition to day-to-day management concerns.

In general, though, your homeowners' association's primary responsibilities will include holding any contracted companies—including management firms and maintenance workers—responsible for doing their jobs, setting the annual maintenance fees, and calling for special assessments. What do the maintenance and special assessment fees constitute? Read on.

Maintenance Fees

Annual maintenance fees will be set by either your resort's developer or your homeowners' association, whichever is in control of the property at the time that you purchase your unit. As mentioned earlier in this chapter, the maintenance fees may be subsidized by the developer early in the life of the resort, but they will eventually, without fail, become the obligation solely of the homeowners' association members. This means that the association will do everything from setting the rate to ensuring that it gets collected on time, or with late penalties attached.

Basically, maintenance fees are composed of three things: hard costs, property taxes, and escrow accounts. If there is anything else rolled into your annual maintenance fee payment, it should be spelled out either in your purchase contract or in your association rules documents (as you learned in Chapter 7).

 **E-ALERT**

When you purchase your timeshare unit, ask whether the resort developer is subsidizing any percentage of the annual maintenance fee. If you do not ask—and if the developer is indeed footing part of the bill to make the fees look more attractive to you during the sale—you may be in for a huge increase a few years down the road when the developer hands off his responsibilities to the homeowners' association.

Hard Costs

Hard costs are the fixed expenses that your resort must sustain simply to continue running properly. These can include landscaping charges for maintaining gardens and waterfalls, indoor and outdoor swimming pool maintenance fees, unit-by-unit telephone and cable service bills, snow removal from streets and sidewalks in colder climates, and a bevy of similar outlays that are usually anticipated and negotiated with the service providers in advance. That is why they are called hard costs: They tend to be rigid and unchanging, at least for the duration of the service contracts that have been negotiated for any given year of timeshare ownership.

Hard costs can also include any fees that your homeowners' association agrees to pay a management company for services such as collecting dues, distributing a newsletter, monitoring on-site operations, and the like. These management company fees are not likely to be spelled out on your yearly bill, but you should be able to look at your association's annual audit to see exactly what percentage of your money is being used for this type of expense.

Property Taxes

Property taxes, while unfortunately nonnegotiable (darn that Uncle Sam!), are also a fixed expense—albeit one that tends to go up from year to year, just as the taxes on your primary residence typically increase annually. They can be very high or relatively low depending on the location of your resort and the size of your unit.

≡FAST FACT

Property taxes are often included in your annual maintenance fee. However, with some resorts, they are a separate levy for which you will receive a separate bill each year. Be sure to ask up front whether your resort's annual maintenance fee includes all state and local property taxes, and be sure the answer is in writing in your contract.

Property taxes are typically controlled by the state government, although local taxes may also be a factor in some states. As with everything else in the world of timeshares, it is your duty to ask what your responsibilities will be before you sign anything.

Escrow Accounts

Escrow accounts are reserve funds that homeowners' associations keep set aside for things like preventive maintenance, ongoing upkeep, and the scheduled replacement of everything from decorative outdoor cactus plants to wall-to-wall carpeting inside the actual timeshare units. Usually, these types of refurbishments are scheduled well in advance of their actually occurring, so that the escrow account will have enough time to build up and compound with interest before payment actually becomes due.

In some cases, escrow accounts can also be used to pay for unexpected one-time expenses such as natural disaster cleanup, replacement of damaged lounge chairs, or the purchase of a new painting to hang in the resort's lobby. But in most cases, these kinds of above-and-beyond expenses will take the form of special assessments.

Unit by Unit

As you learned a few chapters ago, all maintenance fees are not created equal. Timeshare unit owners who spend their vacations in the exact same resort will often pay greatly varying fees, sometimes with hundreds of dollars of difference between them.

Why? For the most part, the total amount you are charged in annual maintenance fees depends on two things: the size of your timeshare unit and the number of weeks of use that you own. If you buy the right to use a three-bedroom timeshare unit for three weeks out of every year, you are—rightly so—going to pay a heck of a lot more in maintenance fees than someone who bought one week's worth of timeshare use in a studio unit that sleeps only two people. You will have more people using the resort's facilities and services, and you should pay for that usage.

E-ALERT

For the purpose of determining maintenance fees, every two-bedroom timeshare unit in a resort is exactly the same. You will be charged in accordance with how many people your unit sleeps, not whether it has an oceanfront or garden view. The latter unit may have been less expensive to purchase, but it will have the same annual maintenance fees as the more-expensive, same-size unit overlooking the beach.

It is important to keep in mind that, more often than not, there are no other purchasing factors that will affect your annual maintenance fees. Whether you buy one week's worth of two-bedroom timeshare use during a low-demand season or one week's worth of two-bedroom timeshare use during a high-demand season, you are going to pay the same amount in annual maintenance fees. After all, the resort needs to be staffed, cleaned, and overseen no matter what time of year you decide to visit it. Hence the fact that seasonal concerns—oh so important when considering exchange value—are not taken into account at all when maintenance fees are determined.

Special Assessments

A special assessment is any charge that your homeowners' association or management company passes on to you and the rest of the timeshare unit owners, in addition to your regularly scheduled annual maintenance fees.

═══FAST FACT

A management company usually can pass on only fixed-expense increases, such as rising insurance premiums, to timeshare owners as a special assessment charge. A homeowners' association, on the other hand, can pass on any expenses it chooses as special assessments, from planting new rosebushes to building a swimming pool complex.

In some cases, a special assessment will be needed to pay for an unforeseen and unavoidable expense. This was the case after the terrorist attacks of September 11, 2001, when insurance companies all across the United States decided to raise the premiums they charged on everything from automobiles to vacation property by as much as 30 to 40 percent. Most timeshare resort homeowners' associations did not have enough money in their escrow accounts to cover this big of an increased cost, so they had to levy special assessments to pass the newfound expense on to individual timeshare owners.

In other cases, though, a special assessment will be levied upon you and your fellow timeshare-unit owners to pay for something that the homeowners' association either wants or needs—above and beyond what is already budgeted for in the escrow account planning process. These types of special assessments can be as small as $1 per unit owner, to cover the cost of a new leather couch in a resort's lobby area, to $100 or more per unit owner, to pay for a more substantial purchase such as tennis court lights or a new ski lift motor.

When a special assessment is charged, you should expect to receive not only a notice of it, but also an explanation of why it is occurring. In the previously cited example of rising insurance premiums, for example, you should have received a letter from either your homeowners' association or your management company explaining not only the fact that rates had gone up, but also detailing what steps had been taken to negotiate better pricing—either from your resort's existing insurance provider or from that company's competitors. You also should have received an explanation of how the higher rates were scheduled to be paid for in future years, whether by way of increased annual maintenance fees or additional special assessments.

E-ALERT

If you feel you have been hit with a special assessment without being given a clear explanation as to why it is necessary, you are perfectly within your rights to demand more information from your homeowners' association or management company.

Similarly, in the case of a homeowners' association deciding to levy a special assessment for the purchase of a new leather couch in a resort's lobby, you should receive an explanation as to why the association deems the couch necessary in the first place. You also should be given information about what kinds of bargain-hunting the home owners' association did when shopping for the couch that it decided to buy, along with a projection of exactly how the association feels this new couch will improve the value of the property in which you and your fellow unit owners have invested your vacation dollars.

In the end, the point to remember is that as a timeshare owner, it is in many ways your responsibility to make sure that your unit and resort are being taken care of in a way that will maintain your investment's value. Just because you don't have to mow the lawn with your own riding tractor doesn't mean that you should just let it grow out of control. Being active in—or at least aware of—your homeowners' association is a right and responsibility that you should keep at the top of your mind for many years to come.

CHAPTER 12

Your Home Resort Unit

ONCE YOU FIND AND BUY the unit of your dreams, it is important that you know how to get the most out of it—whether that means returning to it for a week of relaxation year after year, exchanging it for vacations abroad at new and exciting resorts, or even taking advantage of the additional perks and benefits that your exchange company might offer along with your membership. Read on to ensure you get every penny's worth out of your timeshare ownership.

Using Your Timeshare

Perhaps your dream timeshare unit is a two-bedroom, two-bathroom villa on a sparkling white beach overlooking a turquoise sea. You are not alone in this idea; the large majority of timeshare owners choose beachfront timeshares as their home resorts for the simple purpose of returning to them year after year. The lapping surf, the warm sunshine, the endless array of water sports, the steel-drum music at the tiki bar, the freshly cracked conch chowder on the resort's restaurant menu—it all combines to make for a family vacation that many timeshare owners want to experience again and again.

If you are among this large (and ever-growing) group of timeshare owners, you will want to get right to the task of making the most of every minute that you own at your home resort unit. Whether you have purchased a fixed week, a floating week, or enough points to buy a week at the beachfront resort of your choice each year, there are things you will need to do if you want to be sure your timeshare vacation is as stress-free as possible.

Register Early—for Everything

Whether you own a fixed week, a floating week, or points-based rights to a timeshare unit, you almost always will have to register well in advance of your vacation to ensure that your unit will be available to you during a given week of the year. With floating weeks and points-based systems, you do run the risk of not getting into the resort of your choice during the exact week of your choice, but registering as early as possible will greatly enhance your odds. Sometimes, you can register as much as a year in advance according to resort policy—and sometimes, you will *need* to register that early or even earlier if you want to get a prime unit during a high-demand week of the year.

If you own timeshare-usage points, you usually can check into your timeshare resort on any given day of the week. On the other hand, if you own a fixed or floating week, you likely will have to stick to checking in on a Friday, Saturday, or Sunday, depending on which weeks schedule your resort uses. Check out the calendars in Appendix B to see which weeks fall on which dates for the next several years.

≡FAST FACT

Even if you have purchased a fixed week of timeshare use, you will usually have to contact your home resort in advance to say that you actually intend to use your unit. The amount of lead time required differs from resort to resort, but sometimes, you will need to reaffirm your usage rights several months or even a year in advance.

In addition to registering early for use of the timeshare itself, you also should consider registering early for things like boat and Jet Ski rentals, spa treatments, golf tee times, restaurant tables, and children's activities. As timeshare resorts are vacation properties, these amenities should be available to you even if you do not preregister—and sometimes, you will not be allowed to register before checking into your unit for the week—but if the option for early registration exists, take it. You certainly will be happy you spent a few extra minutes on the telephone back in January when you arrive at your timeshare resort in September and already have reservations for the best golf lesson times, the restaurant tables with the best views, and the Swedish massages given by your favorite in-demand masseur.

Make Specific Room Requests for Handicapped Travelers

If you are traveling with someone who is physically challenged, you should make a specific request for a room that is outfitted to meet that person's needs—and you should make that request as early as possible, just as you do with every other request that is important to ensuring your vacation goes smoothly.

Thanks to the Americans with Disabilities Act, which took effect in July 1992, pretty much every newer resort in the United States has at least a few rooms with specially outfitted bathrooms, wider doorways, and furniture layouts that are meant to make life easier for people who use wheelchairs. Your best bet is to find out exactly which units these are—712A, for example, versus knowing simply that there's one on the seventh floor—and make sure the unit number is written into your timeshare contract with a clause explaining that you are demanding that unit specifically because you have a fellow traveler who requires the special design features inside. Carry a copy of that written contract with you during your reservation and check-in processes, just in case there are any questions or problems.

Resorts built before the 1990s—and many resorts overseas, no matter their age—have no such rooms, or have one or two rooms that are called handicapped accessible but that really are just retrofitted regular rooms that lack the kinds of amenities you might require. Again, asking questions before making your reservation is key to getting the right room for your needs—and reserving that room early is paramount, especially if there are only one or two in the entire resort that you can use.

The Interval International resort directory, for instance, defines resorts as wheelchair-accessible if they have at least *one* unit that can access an elevator or ramp, has wide entryways, and has bathroom handrails. Imagine the demand for that single unit during peak travel times for grandparents! Reserve early, for sure.

⚡ E-ALERT

Do not assume that overseas resorts will have rooms with special equipment and furniture layouts to accommodate people who use wheelchairs. If you are traveling with a person who is physically challenged, be sure to ask before confirming your reservation whether a handicapped-accessible timeshare unit is available.

Check the Checklist

Most timeshare units have some sort of kitchen facility, be it a small kitchenette or a full-on gourmet galley. This is usually the place where you will find the inventory checklist for everything in the timeshare unit, from towels to dinner plates to DVD remote controls. Items will usually be listed by quantity (three rolls of toilet paper, one bottle of dishwashing detergent, etc.), and they usually will be categorized room by room if you have a two- or three-bedroom unit.

One of the first things you should do upon arriving at your timeshare unit is to find this checklist and make sure that everything listed on it is, in fact, inside your unit. If you find something listed that is not really there—such as a set of bed sheets or two or three steak knives—you must immediately report the missing items to the resort's front desk. If you wait until checkout time, you may be forced to pay for the missing items, which the resort can assume that you lost or even stole during your vacation stay. These can include anything from inexpensive hair dryers to top-of-the-line DVD recorders—none of which you want added to your bill at the resort's discretion.

📼 TRAVEL TIP

If you cannot find the inventory checklist inside your timeshare unit, call the front desk and ask where it is—and demand to have one delivered if there is none. Going item by item through the checklist is the only way you can ensure you are getting everything to which you are entitled, and to prevent charges for lost items at checkout time.

If your original timeshare contract lists items that will be inside your unit upon your arrival, bring a copy of that document with you, as well, and use it as a secondary checklist when going through the items the resort has provided. Again, if you find any discrepancies, call the front desk immediately and have the problems remedied right away. Then, you can get to the important business of unpacking and beginning to enjoy your vacation stay.

Pack Wisely

Packing for vacation, to most people, is an exercise that builds both the imagination and the muscles. First, you try to envision every possible outfit you might need, and then you try to jam pretty much every piece of clothing you own into a suitcase that is meant to hold about half as many items. Nine times out of ten, you end up lugging along a bunch of clothes that you do not wear at all during your vacation, and your aching arms remind you that you will once again want to try a bit harder to pare down the load the next time around.

When packing for a vacation in a timeshare unit, you will face the added responsibility of having to supply items that you might want to use in your home-away-from-home, things that you would not be likely to pack for a cruise-ship or regular hotel vacation. Some of these items may include:

- DVDs and CDs that you can use in your timeshare unit's players
- Favorite spices for cooking in your kitchen or kitchenette
- Laundry detergent and fabric softener for use in your private laundry area
- Juice boxes, snack packs, and other kids' foods for your refrigerator
- Wines and liquors to store in your unit's entertaining area

The trick to saving yourself from lugging an entire grocery cart's worth of items along on your vacation is to determine what you absolutely, positively must bring from home—versus what you can get from the resort's store or a nearby shopping center after you arrive and settle in.

For instance, while you are likely to need laundry detergent during your vacation, you certainly do not want to lug a five-pound or larger bottle of the stuff from your home laundry room all the way down to your beachfront paradise. If you want to save money by buying in bulk at home, try buying small cardboard boxes full of detergent (they are the same size as individual cereal boxes and often come in family-size packs). These weigh far less and are therefore easier to transport, and you can even break down the family packs to carry just enough for the three or four loads of wash you anticipate doing during your vacation.

TRAVEL TIP

Be sure, when making your resort reservation, to ask what kind of starter pack will be available in your unit when you arrive. Usually, there will already be a small amount of laundry detergent, dishwashing liquid, paper towels, and breakfast drinks like coffee and tea. There may be enough to get you by for the first day or two of your stay, until you can find the time to go to the local grocery store and stock up on anything else you might need.

Be Friendly, but Firm

Sometimes, you will encounter problems caused by other time-share owners or users. This is an inevitable part of any vacation, right? There is always a jerk lurking around, and he tends to pop into your world just when you are settling in and starting to relax.

If you have a dispute that you need to resolve with someone else in the resort, you can of course first try to take it up with that person directly. Say your neighbor is throwing rowdy, late-night parties in the room adjacent to the one where your youngest daughter is trying to sleep. A simple knock on the door, or a room-to-room telephone call, may be all you need to fix this problem. Heck, the rowdiness may be the fault of some teenagers whose parents are unaware of what is going on. Your complaint, phrased politely, may even make you some new friends.

On the other hand, you may find yourself in a situation where resolution of a dispute requires third-party intervention. In this case, your first call should be to the timeshare resort's front desk. Simply making this telephone call puts the burden of solving the problem onto the shoulders of the resort, which can call for in-house security or even local police if necessary.

Should you require further, long-term dispute resolution, you can also work with your resort's homeowners' association (in which you may have become an automatic member when you bought your timeshare unit). Most homeowners' associations have grievance procedures for handling a variety of complaints, everything from usage concerns to maintenance issues. Check with your resort if you do not know how to contact your homeowners' association, and keep the number handy in case future problems arise.

Making an Exchange

All of the advice so far in this chapter is good for when you're using your home resort, and much of it applies when you use a timeshare unit at another resort, as well. Having said that, there are other, specific concerns you will have to address when you decide to exchange your home resort unit for a timeshare unit elsewhere.

For the most part, you will be at the mercy of your exchange company when trying to trade your unit for another one. Yet understanding your exchange company's system—along with all the other services you may be able to use—will enhance your chances of getting the exchange you want, plus every other perk to which you might be entitled.

Every exchange company is different. Some of the organizations listed offer direct, owner-to-owner timeshare exchanges, but the vast majority of timeshare owners choose to use an exchange company for their timeshare trades. That is what the following sections of this chapter focus on: how to make the most of your exchange company services to get the timeshare trade you want.

≡FAST FACT

A key phrase in the vocabulary of timeshare businesses is space bank. This is the available inventory of timeshare weeks in any given exchange company's system. The space bank is made up of weeks that other timeshare owners have deposited, along with any unsold weeks that developers have contributed to entice people into their resorts during the initial timeshare sales period.

There are important differences among timeshare exchange companies, specifically in the way that exchanges themselves are made and in the way that the exchange company controls its space bank. Understanding your exchange company's system can be key to making a successful trade. You have to understand your exchange company's lingo and policies at least as well as your fellow timeshare owners do, since you are essentially competing with them to get the trades that you want.

Internal Versus External

It is a common misperception that an internal exchange is one that is made within an exchange company's resort network, while an external exchange is one that is made outside the company's network. This confusion, perhaps, comes from many years of health-care coverage that forces you to stay in-network to receive the most benefits compared with services you receive out-of-network. With health care, doctors who are internal to your system of coverage are different than doctors who are external to your system of care. Hence the perception that timeshares are similar, with internal resorts inside an exchange network and external resorts outside of the network.

In fact, though, an internal timeshare exchange refers to trading your home resort unit for another unit in that very same resort. It has nothing to do with your exchange company's broader network of resorts, all of which are considered external exchanges no matter where they are in the world.

 **E-QUESTION**

Why would I want to make an internal exchange for a timeshare unit in my own home resort?
You might want to exchange because you have additional friends or family traveling with you, and you need more space, or maybe because you are injured and want to be closer to the elevators, or perhaps because you want to be adjacent to amenities such as the golf shop or scuba rental area for early-morning reservations.

Making an internal exchange, as far as the exchange companies go, is often no different than making an external exchange. The exchange fee itself may be lower, but the timing is no different in terms of the exchange system—filing your request as early as possible can be the key to getting what you want. In some cases, as an owner in the same timeshare resort, you will have priority when requesting a room through an internal exchange. Be sure to check with your exchange company and your resort if you think this is a service you may want to use often.

Domestic Versus International

A domestic exchange is usually one that occurs within the forty-eight contiguous United States, while an international exchange is one that you request outside of the United States borders, or in Hawaii or Alaska. With some exchange companies, Hawaii and Alaska (along with the United States territory of Puerto Rico) are considered domestic exchanges, but occasionally you will find these locations listed on the international exchange roster in your company's resort directory.

Why is this important? Because international exchanges almost always cost more than domestic exchanges, no matter which exchange company you use. Sometimes the difference in fees is less than twenty dollars, while with other companies, it can be as much as fifty dollars. Hawaii is one of the most sought-after timeshare resort destinations in the world, and if you plan to exchange your home resort unit for time there, you need to understand in advance that you will be paying a premium to do so.

▐▌ TRAVEL TIP

If you intend to make a lot of international exchanges throughout the course of your timeshare ownership, be sure to work with an exchange company that charges lower international exchange fees. By doing this, you can save yourself hundreds, if not thousands, of dollars during the long-term use of your timeshare—especially if you travel to overseas resorts several times a year.

The request forms you will have to fill out for domestic and international exchanges are usually quite similar, if not identical, within each exchange company's system. Deadlines for making domestic and international exchanges are also usually the same, though with the most popular resorts, you of course must be sure to make your exchange request as early as possible. This rule applies to domestic and international timeshare resorts alike.

Deposit-First Systems

Some exchange companies require that you put your time-share unit into their space bank before you can request—or even search their inventory for—an exchange timeshare unit. Resort Condominiums International is one of these companies, meaning that you have to give up the timeshare week that you own before you can begin the process of finding and making your exchange. Interval International also has a deposit-first option, though with that company, you can also do a request-first trade, which you will read about later in this chapter.

Who does this deposit-first system benefit most? Timeshare users who are absolutely certain that they want to leave their home resort and try someplace new. Usually, once you deposit your week, you have the right to exchange it for a given time period before or after the date of the week you have exchanged. With Interval International, for instance, you can deposit your week as much as two years early and then exchange it for another week that occurs as much as one year before, or as long as two years after, the first day of your exchanged week.

In most cases, you can deposit your week as much as two years before you decide to make an exchange—a process for which you will be rewarded by getting extra value assigned to your unit. Why? Because the exchange company wants as many weeks as possible in its space bank, so that it can make more exchanges and charge more fees. With Resort Condominiums International, for instance, if you deposit two years in advance, your timeshare week is rated higher in terms of exchange power than someone who deposits the exact same unit in the exact same resort a few months after yours gets put into the exchange system. If you and that other person then both request the same exchange at another resort, you will be entitled to it first—all because you deposited your identical week earlier. Check with your resort before buying your unit to make sure you will have the most trading power possible in terms of exchange-deposit timing.

With deposit-first systems, it is key that you understand that you are being forced to trade away what you own without the guarantee that you will get the exchange you want in return. If that makes you uncomfortable, you will likely feel better about making exchanges through a request-first system.

E-ALERT

Some resorts allow you to deposit your timeshare week for exchange just ten months in advance, as compared with the two years' lead time that most other resorts and exchange companies allow. This is an important distinction, because the earlier you put your week into a deposit-first exchange system, the more trading power your week will have.

Request-First Systems

Request-first exchange systems are just what they sound like: You get to request the exchange you want *before* you agree to give up the timeshare week that you already own at your home resort. The benefit of this type of system is that you can confirm an exchange that makes you happy before you agree to relinquish the time you already own at your home resort—or you can decide to keep your home resort time if you are unable to get an exchange that suits your needs.

As with deposit-first systems, you often can use your exchanged week in a request-first system even before your week has occurred. Interval International, for instance, has an Early Request system that lets you place a vacation request and travel from two years *before* the week you offer in exchange up until the dates of that week. Not all resorts participate in this Early Request program, though, so be sure to check with yours if you think this might be the right exchange program for you.

If you want to have the easiest access to a searchable database of resorts for your request-first deposit options, be sure to work with an exchange company that has all of its resorts online. That way, you can scroll through and compare different resorts at the click of a mouse—and sometimes even make an exchange online—as opposed to having to read through resort catalogs and then make a time-consuming telephone call to an exchange company operator.

≡FAST FACT

Whether you are using a deposit-first or a request-first system, you almost always will have to select several different resorts and travel dates that you are willing to accept in exchange for your home resort week. This gives the exchange company a better chance of fulfilling your request overall.

Other Exchange Company Services

In addition to facilitating internal, external, domestic, international, deposit-first, and request-first timeshare unit trades, exchange companies now offer many additional services that are designed to make your entire vacation-planning experience an easy, one-stop-shopping effort—and to put more profit into the exchange company's coffers instead of having you work with another company on things such as airline tickets and travel insurance.

A lot of these services are similar to the ones offered by major cruise-ship companies nowadays. If you are among the tens of thousands of people who have ever booked an extended cruise package that includes airfare, hotel transfers, and travel insurance, then you have experienced the kind of service that timeshare exchange companies are now offering to their clients, as well.

Travel Planning and Discounts

Resort Condominiums International, Interval International, and even some of the smaller exchange companies that you learned about in Chapter 1 offer travel-agent style vacation planning services, as well as discounts that you cannot always find when shopping à la carte for items such as airfare, hotel transfers, and rental cars. In some cases, these services include everything from complete cruise-ship vacations to weeklong theme-park itineraries to spa vacations with entire days full of discounted treatment packages.

In some cases, your membership with an exchange company will include access to many of these discounts and services. In other cases, you can augment your membership benefits by purchasing an upgraded membership package. Interval International, for instance, offers a basic Interval Travel service agency as well as an Interval Gold package that gives you more year-round discounts, services, and options.

 **E-QUESTION**

Is it worth it to pay for an upgraded exchange company membership?
It can be—if you think you will take advantage of the services it includes throughout the duration of your timeshare ownership. Simply buying access to discounts is not financially smart, but buying access to discounts that you will actually use can save you hundreds or even thousands of dollars during a lifetime of timeshare vacations.

To give you an idea about the level of services available, the basic Interval Travel membership includes travel packages, travel insurance, car rental and airline discounts, entertainment and theme park coupons, and pre-purchase ticket options (for everything from Ticketmaster shows to Universal Studios attractions). With Interval Gold, you get all of that plus discounts on weekend timeshare getaways, buy-one-get-one-free coupons for restaurants and attractions, 50-percent-off discounts at participating hotels, 20-percent-off discounts at participating restaurants and merchants, complimentary memberships with car-rental companies, and concierge service for help with everything from sightseeing suggestions to dinner reservations, and cash-back deals on cruises, golf, and spa packages.

Resort Condominiums International, as well as some of the smaller exchange companies, offer similar travel services and discounts—which can be important to you if you travel frequently in general, or frequently at the last minute. If you think these services might be useful to you, be sure to do business with an exchange company that offers them.

Last-Minute Getaways

Both Resort Condominiums International and Interval International—as well as some smaller exchange companies—offer last-minute getaways that you can purchase in addition to your regular week of timeshare use (or in addition to the timeshare-usage points that you already own).

The Resort Condominiums International options include extra vacations that last from one night to one week long, as well as "Last Call" travel options for vacations that are going to start within the next forty-five days. Last Call options, if your personal schedule allows you the flexibility to use them, can be real money-savers. Studio timeshare units are just $99 during Last Call vacations, while one-bedroom units are $149 and two-bedroom units are $199—and those prices are for the entire week of timeshare use, not per-night fees.

Interval International calls its additional vacation time Getaways. Many are available up to a year before the date you want to travel, while some can be purchased as little as twenty-four hours before you head out of town. The prices change from resort to resort, and from Getaway to Getaway, but the rates are usually lower than you will find at hotels in the same area—and you will have the benefits of a timeshare unit, perhaps including a kitchen and larger living area.

Discount Programs

Some timeshare exchange companies and resorts offer programs that give you discounts on everything from golf lessons to spa treatments. The Disney Vacation Club is an easy example to cite in this area, offering discounted theme-park tickets at the Magic Kingdom, Epcot, and more to its timeshare unit owners.

Resort Condominiums International has a program called RCI Activities that not only gives you discounts on certain things, but also lets you search a database to see which activities other members of the exchange company have enjoyed at or near specific resorts. By using the company's Web site, *www.rci.com*, you can search for discounted activities by continent, country, region, or city, as well as by activity—with choices ranging from airport parking to wine tasting. Some of the discounts being promoted as of this printing include deals on a cooking course in Florence, Italy; a tour of the Country Music Hall of Fame and Museum in Nashville, Tennessee; tickets to National Football League games played by the Jacksonville Jaguars in Florida; a whale-watching expedition in San Diego, California; and a bicycling tour of Paris, France.

Interval International's Web site, *www.intervalworld.com*, is similar in that it lists hundreds of sightseeing tours and activities in more than forty countries that you can browse through and even book online. In many cases, you can prepurchase tickets for everything from theme parks to boat rentals in advance, so that you can avoid long lines and sold-out attractions during your timeshare vacation. In addition, Interval International has a Golf Resort Program at some of its affiliated resorts that gives the exchange club's members access to discounted greens fees, discounted lessons, advance tee times, and more. You can search for resorts that have this program on the Interval Web site, or look for the Golf Resort Program logo in your resort directory.

Additional Exchange Options

Sometimes, you will want to do more than make a straight one-week-for-one-week timeshare exchange—and again, your exchange company will be at the ready, often charging you additional fees for the privilege of getting done whatever it is that you would like to do with your timeshare unit.

Banking Your Weeks or Points

Most exchange companies allow you to bank your timeshare weeks or points for future use. Say you own one week of timeshare use each year, but you want to take a special two-week vacation for your twenty-fifth wedding anniversary in a few years. In most cases, you will be allowed to bank your timeshare week for the next two years—taking no timeshare vacation at all during those years—and then use both weeks back-to-back for your longer anniversary trip.

The same is usually true for points-based programs, which may allow you to bank points so that you can save up for bigger purchases including extended timeshare stays or more-expensive cruise-ship vacations.

Splitting Your Lock-Off Unit's Value

If you own a lock-off timeshare unit, your exchange company can work with you to split its value. Sometimes, this can give you even more vacation options than the single week you own, without costing you much extra in exchange company fees. For instance, let's say you own a two-bedroom lock-off unit. You can split this unit in half by locking off half of it, and then using your resulting pair of single, locked-off units to trade for two separate, smaller timeshare unit vacations at other resorts. You may get two studio units during two different weeks, for instance, in exchange for the value of the single week you own of two-bedroom unit use.

You will, in many cases, have to pay two separate exchange fees if you want to take two different vacations after locking off your unit and splitting its value—but this is still likely to cost you far less than you would have paid for two separate vacations' worth of hotel accommodations.

🧳 TRAVEL TIP

If you intend to use your timeshare unit's lock-off capacity when making an exchange, be sure to confirm the move with your exchange company in writing. You must specify that this is something that you want to do, and you can lose your unit's lock-off value if you fail to make your intentions clear when making your exchange.

Unit Upgrades

Whether you own a points-based or weeks-based timeshare unit, you almost always can pay an additional fee to upgrade your home resort unit. In points-based systems, you can often purchase such upgrades with any extra points you have accumulated, while in weeks-based systems, you usually need to pay an additional fee in order to accomplish the upgraded exchange.

Upgraded units can mean anything from larger timeshares to timeshares with better locations in your home resort. For instance, your two-bedroom timeshare overlooking a resort's gardens may be identical in layout to one with an oceanfront balcony, but in some cases, using the latter unit would be considered an upgrade. The fees for upgrades tend to be lower than the fees for exchanges to other weeks or other resorts, so if you are looking for a change of scenery—but not necessarily a change of resort—an upgrade might be an economical solution for you.

Bonus Time

Bonus time is any additional timeshare usage period that is beyond what you own in terms of weeks or points. Bonus time can be added to an existing week of timeshare vacation, or it can be purchased separately for things like weekend getaways or one-night stays in city resorts. You usually buy bonus time directly through your resort, but in some cases, your exchange company will be able to help you facilitate the purchase.

In many cases, bonus time comes at a fraction of the cost of regular timeshare uses—or even nightly hotel stays. Some timeshare owners have been able to get bonus nights at first-class resorts for less than $50 per night, and at the last minute, to boot. Walk-ins are even accepted for bonus time at some timeshare resorts, so be sure to keep your timeshare identification cards in your wallet if you are traveling on the spur of the moment.

E-ALERT

Not all resorts offer bonus time. If you think this additional service might be important to you, be sure to ask about it—and get its terms in writing—before purchasing a timeshare unit at any given resort.

Guest Certificates

If you want to let someone else—a relative, a colleague, a friend—use your timeshare unit, you will need to purchase a guest certificate from your exchange company. Typically, these cost somewhere in the $25 to $50 range, and they will be required for presentation upon check-in for anyone other than you during your reserved week of timeshare use. In some cases, the person using the guest certificate must be at least twenty-one years old.

Do not think that you can forgo the guest certificate purchase and simply hope that the resort won't notice the person in your unit is someone other than you. Your name is on file, and anyone checking in will be required to show identification—which will prove that they are not you. A guest certificate purchase is mandatory *before* check-in time, and if you skip the process, you may be responsible for paying additional fines to your resort in the future.

≡FAST FACT

Guest certificates are not necessary for guests staying with you in your timeshare unit. They are required only if you want to give your timeshare usage to another person, be it for a few days, a week, or whatever amount of time you have reserved at a timeshare resort—and they can make great gifts.

Transferring Weeks

Some exchange companies, including Resort Condominiums International, will let you transfer your timeshare points or weeks to another member of your exchange company. You will have to fill out a form, and the person you are giving your timeshare use to will need to have documentation when she checks in at the resort. As you may have already guessed, with some exchange companies a fee will apply to this transaction.

The ability to transfer weeks can be a handy service if, say, you and your spouse each own a separate week of timeshare use and you want to give a two-week honeymoon vacation to your children. Or, perhaps you have made good friends at your timeshare resort, and each of you wants to take a two-week vacation without purchasing an additional week of time. You could transfer your week to your friends one year, and they can transfer their week back to you another year.

Informational Breakfasts

At some point during your exchange or resort check-in process, you likely will be asked if you want to attend an informational breakfast or some other type of meeting that will be described to you as a way to keep informed on all the updates at your resort.

Resorts and exchange companies may consider this an additional service, but you should be aware that usually these types of meetings are actually sales presentations. The companies figure that as long as you are enjoying the resort, they may as well try to get you to purchase another week of timeshare use there.

If you might be interested, by all means attend—you may even get some bonus points or other promotional freebies out of the deal. But if you are happy with the timeshare unit you already own and do not want anything more, stay away from these update meetings.

Working Without the Exchange Company

If you are willing to do a little bit of extra leg work, you often can find and arrange a timeshare exchange without paying any extra fees to a third party like Resort Condominiums International or Interval International.

How? By using the direct owner-to-owner swap services that are part of your membership fees with the Timeshare User's Group and *TimeSharing Today* magazine. Each group's Web site has a link that you can follow to either a chat area or a searchable database full of other owners who are looking to make exchanges, as well.

 **E-QUESTION**

Is it difficult to make a direct owner-to-owner timeshare exchange?
It's not difficult logistically speaking. All you really need to do is fill out guest certificates for each other, if you are working with someone you believe you can trust.

Your options when making a direct owner-to-owner exchange will be far more limited than if you were working with the entire resort catalog of a major exchange company, but you just might see a trade that you think would be fair and fun. You also will get the chance to know other timeshare owners, who can put you in touch with people they have done successful direct exchanges with in the past.

Potential Pitfalls

When working within any timeshare exchange system, you have to be cautious about falling into traps that can not only hurt your timeshare use during a particular year, but that can blacklist you for the life of your timeshare ownership.

Honest mistakes happen, of course, but watch out for the following problems that have befallen other timeshare owners in the past. They can put a real damper on your vacation time for many years to come.

You Can't Get Your Desired Exchange

This is a common complaint that is voiced by owners of all kinds of timeshares working with all kinds of resorts and exchange companies. The exchange companies make clear that when requesting a timeshare trade, you will have to consider multiple resorts and different times of the year, but still many timeshare owners say they have difficulty getting the exchanges of their choice. In some cases, with points-based resorts, timeshare owners have even had problems getting a week of their choice at their home resort.

Why are you having trouble getting the timeshare exchange you want? Some of the reasons include poor exchange power, ineffective trading on your part, or scenarios by which the resorts do business with nonowners who potentially get in your way.

Low Exchange Power

In some cases, your timeshare unit simply is not valuable enough to garner the type of trade you want. Even if the resort developer told you that you were buying a first-class unit in a high-demand resort during a peak season for exchanging, you still may not have enough trading power to get the kind of exchange you are seeking.

Your unit's exchange power is determined by several factors, including its number of bedrooms and the demand level of the season in which you own. But if you continually get turned down for the exchanges you are requesting—and that you believe to be fair trades—you would be wise to contact your exchange company and ask them exactly what about your unit is holding you back. Sometimes, you will be able to affect the problem, while at other times, you may simply be out of luck with a bad purchase.

Late Deposits

In many cases, the key to getting the exchange you want is banking your timeshare week or points into the exchange company's space bank as early as possible. Remember, the space bank is the place where exchanged weeks and points are held until another exchange company member agrees to trade for them. You want to have your unit in the space bank and waiting when this happens, lest you miss out on your opportunity for a great trade. Depositing your week close to the time that it begins is a surefire way to fail at getting the exchange you want.

The rule in exchanges is simple: Deposit early for the best odds of getting the exchange you want.

▐█▌ TRAVEL TIP

Resort Condominiums International assigns a point value to every week of exchanged timeshare use. Some of the points are based on how early your week was put into the RCI space bank—meaning that if your unit and an identical unit are both in the space bank requesting similar trades, the person who deposited her week first will be most likely to succeed.

Bulk Space Banking

Bulk space banking occurs when a resort gathers up all the timeshare weeks that went unused during the same time of year during the previous few years—in other words, its historically lowest-demand weeks—and then gives those weeks, in bulk, to an exchange company's space bank. The resort's idea is that the more weeks it has available, the more people might exchange for them and go to the resort.

The problem this can pose for timeshare owners—particularly people who own floating weeks—is that when you call your home resort to get a week assigned for you to deposit in an exchange company's space bank, your resort may tell you that it has already bulk space banked all of the available weeks. It will then assign one of the previously banked weeks to you, so that you can facilitate an exchange.

You do get credit for having deposited your week early, which is good in terms of trading power, but on the other hand, you are being given a week of timeshare use that is not historically high in demand— thus negatively affecting your trading power. Some people who own floating weeks have complained that this practice has made it all but impossible for them to get any exchanges of decent value, since they are always being forced to deposit weeks of timeshare use that occur during off-peak seasons.

≡FAST FACT

Not all resorts practice bulk space banking with exchange companies. If you are buying a floating week of timeshare use and intend to exchange it year after year, ask your home resort if it does bulk space banking. Should the answer be yes, you might consider buying through a different resort so that you can have access to the floating week of your choice—and thereby enhance your timeshare exchange value.

Another problem that floating-week timeshare owners have reported in terms of bulk space banking is that once they accept a previously banked unit as the one they are depositing for exchange, they need to take their timeshare vacation within a year or two of the date when the week was banked—not the date when they requested the exchange. In some cases, this means a mere few months' window for travel—and in some cases, it also means an additional maintenance-fee payment. If, for instance, you requested an exchange in November—but because of early bulk space banking, you have to take your vacation by February of the upcoming year—you may be forced to pay the upcoming year's maintenance payment in advance, even if you just paid your current year's maintenance payment and weren't expecting another bill for the next twelve months.

Bulk space banking has its complexities, but if you want to learn more, there is a terrific consumer-led discussion about the issue posted at the Timeshare User's Group Web site, *www.tug2.net*. If you are considering purchasing a floating timeshare week for exchange purchases, you might want to read this discussion—and perhaps contact some of the TUG members involved—before signing your contracts.

Renters

There have been complaints by some timeshare owners that resorts are allowing renters (or short-term vacationers) to take over so many timeshare units that there are not enough left for perfectly legitimate timeshare exchanges. In some cases, points-based time-share owners have complained that they cannot even get a float-ing week of choice at their home resorts because the resorts have allowed too many units to be booked by non-timeshare owners who have simply called and asked for an available room.

It is virtually impossible to say whether this is true or not, unless of course you work in the resort's reservations department. But it is a prac-tice to watch out for, and one that has drawn the attention of at least one class-action lawsuit (that was yet to be settled as of this printing).

Renting Out a Week You Exchanged For

Some people get the nifty idea that if they exchange their time-share week for another one at a ritzier resort, they can then rent out that traded week to make a fast buck. This is a no-no—one that the exchange companies and resorts take so seriously, they often keep a list of perpetrators on file and refuse them further exchanges for life.

If you get caught renting out a timeshare week that you have exchanged for, you also may be subject to fines from both the resort and the exchange company. Truth be told, it's simply not worth taking the chance if you want to make the most of your timeshare ownership for many years to come.

Double- or Triple-Booking Your Unit

If you try to work with more than one exchange company at a time—by requesting exchanges in several places and seeing which ones you can confirm first—you run the risk of double- or triple-booking the timeshare unit you own.

Say you request three different resorts through three different exchange companies. By a stroke of good luck, you get one of the requests you were after—but you fail to rescind the requests you have placed with the other two companies. Eventually, they come through as well, meaning that you have now promised the one week of timeshare use you own to three different exchange companies.

You will face penalties for this kind of double- or triple-booking, and you could end up listed as a problem exchanger in the companies' computers. Again, it's simply not worth taking the chance if you want to make the most of your timeshare ownership for many years to come.

Lost Home Resort Week

There have been cases reported in which some timeshare owners deposited their week into a deposit-first exchange system, only to be told that the week had been lost in the computer when it came time to confirm a requested exchange.

A simple solution to this problem is to get—and keep—a written confirmation of your timeshare week deposit. It should clear up any questions with the exchange company immediately, or, at worst, it will serve as valuable evidence for your attorney.

Travel Insurance

Travel insurance is not specific to the timeshare industry, and people have been debating for years about whether it is a wise thing to buy. A good rule to remember is that if the insurance is low-cost and high-benefit, it may come in handy—especially if you are traveling to or from a snowy city, or if you have children or elderly grandparents who might get sick and force you to stay home at the last minute, after your full-refund cancellation options have expired.

The Resort Condominiums International Vacation Protection Plan, for instance, is offered in partnership with BerkleyCare, which is part of The Berkley Group—a company that provides insurance specifically for the travel industry. You cannot buy these policies on your own (though you may find similar policies through your travel agent). The RCI/BerkleyCare policy covers protection against some vacation cancellations, lost or stolen baggage, and injury, sickness, or accident during your vacation. If you are traveling within the United States or Canada, you can sometimes get roadside assistance for your rental car, as well.

TRAVEL TIP

If you plan to purchase travel insurance, be sure to shop around. Sometimes, your exchange company will offer you the best coverage for the least amount of money, but other times, you may be able to find better deals by working through a travel agency that is outside of the exchange company network.

Interval International's travel insurance plan is provided by Travel Guard, which reportedly is the largest travel insurance provider in the United States. The policy costs $59 per week, or less than $9 a day, and will cover the value of your forfeited vacation accommodations up to $1,000 if you have to cancel or postpone your trip because of a death in your immediate family, severe weather, jury duty, or some other unforeseeable circumstances. You must buy the travel insurance within twenty-one days of confirming your timeshare exchange.

No matter what kind of travel insurance you purchase—or where you find it—you should look for clauses that cover as many hazards as possible. Some terrorism clauses, for instance, are useless unless the United States Department of State declares a travel warning for your resort's area. Some policies do not cover natural disasters, such as hurricanes and tornadoes, if major airline companies are still offering flights into the affected areas—even if your resort is flattened just a mile away from the landing strip. And remember: You usually have to buy travel insurance within about two weeks of buying your vacation itself. You cannot wait for your vacation week's weather report before making a decision.

If you choose to forgo travel insurance, you still may have some coverage if you booked your timeshare vacation with a high-end credit card, or if your homeowner's insurance policy has clauses covering loss and theft while traveling.

CHAPTER 13

Renting Out Your Timeshare

THERE MAY BE SOME YEARS when—because of work scheduling, family obligations, or a simple lack of time in general—you cannot use your week of timeshare. If this is a rare occurrence for you, it will not be so financially off-putting that you will want to sell your time-share altogether. Still, though, why just let your unit sit there unused? Sometimes, you can make back a little bit of the money you have already spent by finding a renter to take your week's worth of usage off your hands.

Market Demand

Now that you know a bit more about the wide world of timeshares that exists out there, you may find it hard to believe that there is no great demand for rental units. After all, most people would prefer to spend their family vacations in two- or three-bedroom villas than in sardine-can hotel rooms where they don't even have a separate bathroom from the kids. That, plus the fact that timeshare rentals can cost the renters significantly less than a hotel room in the same city, would make you think that everybody and their brother's cousin would be scouring the newspaper classified ads and World Wide Web sites for timeshare rental units.

So why aren't more people clamoring to get in on timeshare rentals? The main reason seems to be that the majority of the vacationing public simply does not know that they are an option. Think about it: Less than 10 percent of vacationing Americans own a timeshare unit. The other 90 percent is composed of people who either do not want to buy a timeshare, or who do not realize that they even exist.

E-ALERT

As with timeshare resales, the timeshare rental marketplace is buyer-driven. There are far more people trying to rent their timeshare units than there are people out there looking to use them—which means that the going rate will usually be better for the renter than it is for the timeshare owner.

In either case, the majority of people out there planning vacations are predisposed not to think about timeshares at all. They either do not like them as investment properties or do not know about them in the slightest. Why on earth, then, would they ever think of renting a timeshare unit? A hotel or motel is likely to be the only place they look when deciding where their vacation accommodations will be— and popular reservation Web sites such as *www.hotels.com*, *www.expedia.com*, and *www.orbitz.com* do not even offer timeshare rentals as an option.

Still, there is a bevy of timeshare units available for rental at any given time during the calendar year. On a single day in late 2005, for instance, the Timeshare User's Group Web site, *www.tug2.net*, had about 1,265 classified ads that had been posted by members looking to find renters for their timeshare units. The available timeshares were all over the world, including popular locations such as Hawaii, Orlando, the U.S. Virgin Islands, and Las Vegas.

On the very same day, the *TimeSharing Today* magazine site, *www.tstoday.com*, had more than 130 classified ads that had been posted by subscribers looking to find renters for their timeshare units. And again, they were all over the world, including the hot spots mentioned above as well as in Mexico, Colorado, and New York City.

The problems with these figures, though, are twofold if you are a timeshare owner. For starters, there is far more supply than there is demand, and you may have a hard time making any decent money by adding your unit to these lists. The other concern is that these popular venues for timeshare rental listings are frequented mostly by fellow timeshare owners—who aren't as likely as non-owners to be in the market to rent a timeshare in the first place.

There are other places that timeshare rentals can be listed, including the popular auction Web site eBay, where you are more likely to find non-owners looking for bargains on vacation accommodations. On that same day that there were close to 1,500 total listings posted on the Web sites of the Timeshare User's Group and *TimeSharing Today* magazine, for instance, eBay had about eighty-five timeshare units listed for rent in many of the same destinations.

So, with market demand far less than supply in the timeshare rental arena, what can you do to increase your odds of finding someone to take your week of vacation off your hands? As with the timeshare resale market, the key typically lies with savvy pricing and smart advertising. And the best way to figure out how to beat your competitors is to look at exactly what they are already out there doing.

Setting Your Price

Pricing your timeshare unit for the rental market can be an exercise in frustration. If you are like most people, you will not realize that you cannot use your timeshare week until it is literally a month or two away. This, then, will lead you to make a last-minute advertising push with a rock-bottom price intended to grab somebody's— anybody's—attention while they are planning their own last-minute vacation. And since the vacationer will know that you need him far more than he needs you at that point, he will shop around to ensure that he is paying the absolute minimum that he can for a timeshare-unit rental in his city of choice.

E-QUESTION

What is the easiest way to see what other people are charging for rentals of timeshares that are similar to your unit?
Check the three Web sites with the most classified-type listings: *www .tug2.net, www.tstoday.com*, and *www.ebay.com*.

The one good thing about this scenario is the fact that it is the most common one out there. This, in and of itself, gives you an easy way to see what other, similar timeshare units are listing for—even those available in your very same resort during the exact same week. Armed with this market information, you can price your unit just a hair lower than other people have priced theirs, making yourself the most likely candidate to get that last-minute vacation shopper's business. To help you understand this point, take a look at the following breakdowns of popular vacation destination timeshares that were posted for rent about a month before Christmas in 2005.

Orlando, Florida

If you had done about ten minutes' worth of searching on the World Wide Web in early December 2005, you would have found no fewer than 130 timeshare units available for rent in the Orlando area alone.

- On the Timeshare User's Group Web site, the ads ranged in price from $275 for a one-bedroom unit that sleeps two people to $850 for a two-bedroom unit that sleeps six people.
- On the TimeSharing Today Web site, the ads ranged in price from $575 for a one-bedroom unit that sleeps four people to $1,400 for a three-bedroom unit that sleeps as many as ten people.

- On the eBay Web site, the ads ranged in price from $225 for a three-bedroom unit that sleeps eight people to $1,495 for a two-bedroom unit that sleeps six people.

What do these numbers tell you in terms of setting a market value for your own timeshare rental? For starters, they tell you that prices are literally all over the map in Orlando—and that they often are deeply discounted by owners who desperately need to find a renter for a timeshare week that is coming up quickly (such as the case of the $225 three-bedroom unit, which was available the very next week).

These numbers also tell you, though, that if you own a one-bedroom unit, you would be in the ballpark of general pricing if you listed it at $300 to $600 for the week's worth of use. Plus, you could further narrow that number down by searching through the ads for other units listed at, or near, your home resort. If one-bedrooms in your resort are listing at $500, you could probably increase your odds of finding a renter by lowering your price only slightly, to $450 or $475.

Take a look at the figures for Las Vegas and Hawaii, below, and you will begin to understand how searching for prices in this manner can help you to set yours in a way that will make a rental deal more or less likely to actually happen.

Las Vegas, Nevada

That same ten minutes' worth of searching on the World Wide Web in early December 2005 would have led you to about twenty timeshare units available for rent in the Las Vegas area:

- On the Timeshare User's Group Web site, the ads ranged in price from $300 for a one-bedroom unit that sleeps four people to $750 for a one-bedroom unit that sleeps four people.
- On the TimeSharing Today Web site, the ads ranged in price from $500 for a one-bedroom unit that sleeps four people to $1,000 for a two-bedroom unit that sleeps as many as six people.

- On the eBay Web site, the ads ranged in price from $300 for a studio unit that sleeps two people to $1,000 for a two-bedroom unit that sleeps as many as six people.

As with the Orlando units, the time of year affects the pricing greatly—with Christmas and New Year's units priced the lowest, since the holidays were merely a month away. But you would have been able to deduce from these numbers that your own one-bedroom timeshare unit might be considered a relative bargain had you priced it between $300 and $500.

Hawaii

Again, had you spent your ten minutes' worth of time searching on the World Wide Web in early December 2005, you would have come across about 150 timeshare units available for rent in Hawaii:

- On the Timeshare User's Group Web site, the ads ranged in price from $499 for a one-bedroom unit in Waikiki that sleeps four people to $1,100 for a two-bedroom unit on Kauai that sleeps as many as six people.
- On the TimeSharing Today Web site, the ads ranged in price from $650 for a one-bedroom unit on Molokai that sleeps as many as four people to $2,700 for a two-bedroom unit on the Big Island of Hawaii that sleeps as many as six people.
- On the eBay Web site, the ads ranged in price from $399 for a two-bedroom unit on Kauai that sleeps as many as eight people to $1,700 for a one-bedroom unit on Kauai that sleeps up to four people.

As with the examples in Orlando and Las Vegas, these Hawaii numbers show you that prices are literally all over the map—and often are dependent on how close to the timeshare usage date the ad is placed, more so than the actual unit or number of people that it sleeps.

Your one-bedroom timeshare unit, in this Hawaii rental marketplace, would have been reasonably priced anywhere from $400 to $1,000, depending on how many people it sleeps. That's a very wide range, one that you could use to your advantage if you wanted to undercut your competition by pricing your unit at the lower end of the scale.

TRAVEL TIP

If you are not yet a timeshare owner and want to experience a slice of the timeshare lifestyle at a discounted price—and without the pressure of a sales presentation—consider renting a timeshare unit for your next family vacation. You often will get not just a good bargain, but also plenty of firsthand insight into whether timesharing in general might be right for you.

What the Numbers Mean

The most important thing to remember, based on all three of the previous examples, is that the timeshare rental market is literally all over the map in every destination—and that it is continuing to adjust itself every day. As more and more people search through these popular Web sites to see what other timeshare owners are charging for similar rentals, more and more prices will be set toward the bottom of the financial curve (at least by people who really do want to find a renter).

If you want to make sure that you have the best chance of finding bargain-hunters online to rent your timeshare unit, you will have to not only set your rental fee competitively, but also check back daily on each of the Web sites where you list it to ensure that you have not been under-priced by somebody else. You also will have to mount an eye-catching advertising campaign so that your unit stands out among the rest.

Advertising

The World Wide Web is the best place to get the most eyeballs on your timeshare rental ad. The Web sites already discussed throughout this chapter are places where Internet shoppers are being trained to look for timeshare rental options, and thus places where your advertisement should be if you want to ensure that it is seen by serious shoppers.

Every one of these Web sites has a format in which it lists basic information about the timeshare unit for rent. The fields in the databases typically include:

- City, state, and/or nation where your timeshare is located
- Your resort's name
- The number of bedrooms in your unit
- The total number of people your unit can sleep
- The week during which your unit is available
- The price you are asking for the rental

Beyond these details, it will be up to you to use a bit of marketing savvy to catch the attention of shoppers surfing for a good timeshare rental deal. Every one of these Web sites also allows you a space where you can talk about your unit's amenities, explain why you believe your resort is better than others out there on the rental market, and even offer advice to would-be renters so that they can envision themselves experiencing their vacation in your unit.

One very effective advertisement that was posted on eBay, for example, was written not in marketing buzz words such as "great deal!" and "act now!" but in the straight talk of what appeared to be an honest timeshare owner who simply could not use his unit during this particular year: "This resort is located only one block from the Strip (directly behind the Imperial Palace—we always walk through the casino to get to the Strip) . . . I also have four Nascar Nextel Cup three-day weekend package tickets on auction . . . so you can go to the races and use this timeshare rental at the same time!"

Simply reading this ad, a potential renter could envision not just how he would get to and from the popular Strip, but also what else he could do for fun during his time in the city. In other words, the owner of the timeshare unit managed to convey what he loves about using the place—and made it possible for rental shoppers to put themselves in his shoes, at least in their imaginations. This is the key to effective selling.

═FAST FACT

The most honest sales pitches are usually the most effective. Help potential renters to see themselves living in your unit—in your vacation city—for a week. If you are comfortable explaining why you cannot use the unit yourself, that can be helpful too. It makes the potential renter feel like they are getting something that you enjoy, but simply can't use this one year out of many.

Of course, you can also advertise your timeshare for rental offline, in places like newspaper classified ads and resort bulletin boards. These can be just as effective, assuming that you have done your online research regarding the going rates. You also can choose to work with a broker, usually one who works in an office that specializes in timeshare resales. Many people forgo this option because the commission eats too much into the already minimal amount of income that you can expect. However, if you think a broker may be right for you, then you can learn more about them—including how to find reputable ones—in Chapter 14.

Rental Agreements

Should you be lucky enough to find a renter for your timeshare week, you will need to work out the details of the paperwork. In some cases, your resort or timeshare exchange company will provide you with everything you need—and they should be the first places you ask when trying to make sure that you are covering all your legal bases.

If you decide that you want (or need) to work outside of these formal systems, you can use the rental document kit that is available for a $10 fee at the *TimeSharing Today* magazine Web site. It includes fill-in-the-blanks worksheets along with detailed instructions and model letters that you can use as examples when corresponding with your renter.

A rental broker, if you decide to hire one, will be able to handle all of the paperwork for you. Do not pay any extra paperwork fees if you have hired a broker; doing the contracts is part of the job for which the broker earns her commission.

Potential Pitfalls

The most obvious pitfall that you face when trying to rent out your timeshare week is failing to find a taker. Advertising on Web sites and in newspaper classified sections can easily cost you $100 or more, and that will be money that you lose in addition to the lost time on your unit, for which you will already have paid in mortgage and maintenance fees.

It can be worth the gamble if you do your homework and price your unit competitively, but you must be prepared to eat the marketing costs should you end up advertising for renters during a peak time when the market is even more crowded than usual. There is no way of knowing when these peak times might be, so you will simply be at the mercy of the marketplace.

⚡ E-ALERT

Before you place any advertisements for renting your timeshare unit, set a marketing budget that is no more than 10 percent of the total price you hope to get from a renter. Spending $300 to market a timeshare unit that will rent for only $350 is probably not worth your time.

Another pitfall to watch out for is trying to rent out a week for which you have exchanged. In other words, if you own a week's worth of timeshare use at a resort in Orlando, and you trade it for a week's worth of timeshare use at a resort in Phoenix—and then try to rent out that week in Phoenix—your exchange company can ban you from *all future exchanges* for the rest of your timeshare ownership. Would you always get caught? Not necessarily. But do you want to take the risk and put the entirety of your timeshare ownership on the line? Most definitely not.

CHAPTER 14

Selling Your Timeshare

YOU MAY DECIDE—perhaps right away, or maybe after many years of vacations—that timeshare ownership is no longer right for you. You will be in good company: There are far more timeshares listed on the resale market than there are people looking to buy them. This means you will have to do everything in your power to ensure that your unit is presented in the best possible light, be realistic about what price you can expect to garner, and understand how long it may take you to close the deal.

When to Sell

People sell their timeshare units for a wide variety of reasons every day. Sometimes, it is simply because their vacation needs have changed. Other times, they may need to divest their units in order to free up some spending money. At still other times, they might have found new and exciting timeshare opportunities that they want to take advantage of in place of the timeshare unit they currently own.

It really does not matter why you decide to sell your timeshare as long as you have a strong understanding of your reasons. Knowing that you simply are not using it as much as you thought you would have, for instance, might mean that you can afford to sell it at a leisurely pace and wait for your target price. That is in contrast to knowing that you need a few thousand dollars to pay an unexpected debt or bill right away, and that time—more so than money—is going to be the driving factor in your sale process. Some of the reasons that you might consider selling your timeshare are outlined below, along with how those reasons might affect your decision making in terms of pricing as you try to sell.

You're Not Using It

It's pretty basic, really: If you buy something and don't use it, the money is not particularly well spent. This is true with everything from all-too-trendy sweaters that live out their lives in the backs of closets to perishable vegetables that languish in the corners of refrigerators until they turn to mushy rot. Timeshares—which hopefully don't literally rot—are no good if they are neglected in this way, either. They represent a sizable amount of money, including annual maintenance fees, that you could be spending on other things that you might enjoy more.

 **E-QUESTION**

If I use my timeshare only half of the time I am allowed to use it, is it still a good investment?
Usually not. In order to reap a financial benefit from a timeshare (as opposed to renting hotel rooms), you usually need to use your timeshare unit annually for at least five years—and sometimes longer.

Sometimes, you will have happily used your timeshare with your family and friends for many years when a change occurs that alters your needs. A spouse who favored the resort may die, young children may go off to college and leave you without the need for such a big unit, or your work schedule may have increased your time constraints and left you unable to travel during your traditional annual week of vacation.

Simply maintaining your ownership rights without actually using your timeshare is not a good option in any of these cases, as you will be paying mortgage and maintenance fees for a property that is, at its essence, worthless to you. If you forgo using your timeshare for two or more years in a row, the odds are that it is time to start thinking about selling.

You Need Money

While selling your timeshare is not a good way to make a profit on an investment, it can be a good way of freeing up several thousand dollars in cash—along with eliminating monthly maintenance fees and annual exchange company charges that also are nibbling away at your pocketbook.

If a need for cash is the main reason that you are considering selling your timeshare, you may have to move quickly, thus making it likely that you will settle for a price lower than what the market might otherwise bear. On the other hand, you may be able to hold out for a higher price while renting your timeshare unit, thus at least earning back a little bit of the money you have already laid out in mortgage and maintenance fees. You will learn more about pricing and profit later in this chapter. For now, suffice to say that a need for funds is certainly a valid reason for selling your timeshare unit.

You're Trading Up

When you bought your first car—say, a 1962 powder-blue Dodge Dart—you probably thought it was just the coolest thing ever, a car that you would want to keep until the day you died. Today, as you sit comfortably behind the wheel of your new Audi TT convertible, that old Dart has a nostalgic quality you're fond of but it lacks a certain cachet to which you've now become accustomed.

The same thing can happen to you when buying timeshares. That first studio unit you and your spouse decided to buy in southern Florida has served you well for six or seven years, but your vacation tastes have graduated to the coast of Maui, in Hawaii, and you want to trade up to a two-bedroom unit so that you can vacation with other friends who are doing just as well as you are in terms of vacation spending.

If exchanges just won't get you there, and if you can't afford to own two units at once, you will need to sell what you have in order to get what you want in the future.

You're Unhappy with the Resort's Direction

Resorts are properties with owners. As with anything in the business world, owners can change. The one you had on the day you bought your timeshare unit may not necessarily be the one you have now—and the new guy may have ideas about going in a direction that does not jibe with your annual vacation plans.

TRAVEL TIP

Should you find yourself dealing with a new resort owner whose vision is drastically different than the one that you bought into, sometimes the only way to keep your sanity is to sell your timeshare unit and find another one in a place that better suits your original needs.

What could this mean? It could be heavy-duty special assessments to build a golf course, restaurant, or other new amenity. It could be the opposite: a lowering of expectations and service in terms of maintenance throughout the resort property. It could be a switch from one exchange company affiliation to another that leaves you less than satisfied with your new options.

Exchange Company Woes

As you learned in Chapter 1, there are two major exchange companies in the timeshare industry along with a dozen or so smaller exchange companies that are working hard to make inroads into the business of the big guys.

Resort Condominiums International and Interval International have tens of thousands of longtime members who are happy with the services they receive, but there also are people who prefer one company over the other. For whatever reason, these people feel that one company offers superior service, better resort selection, or some other distinction that makes them unwilling to work with the other company.

You may be one of these people, and yet your resort may not be affiliated with the exchange company that you prefer (or it may change affiliations after you buy your unit, forcing you to change along with it). If this is the case—and you want to put the exchange company before the resort in terms of your customer loyalty—you will have no choice but to sell and buy a new timeshare unit at a resort that works with the exchange company of your choice.

Realistic Versus Unrealistic Expectations

Make no mistake: Selling your timeshare unit is likely to involve an even longer, more drawn-out process than you endured when you bought it in the first place with wide eyes and big hopes for the future. The long-haul experience is likely to be your reality no matter where your unit is, no matter how nice of a resort it is part of, and no matter what season of the year you have the right to use it.

≡**FAST FACT**

On a typical weekday at the end of 2005, there were 879 timeshare units posted for sale on eBay alone—ranging in price from $1 to $28,000. On the exact same day, the Timeshare User's Group's online service listed 416 classified ads for timeshares just in the city of Orlando, Florida, with another 1,637 units for sale in other destinations in the United States and around the world.

The simple fact is that timeshare resale has been a buyer's market pretty much since the market came into existence nearly forty years ago. Far, far more people are out there trying to sell their units than you may imagine, and there are easily a dozen or more resale time-share owners for every single person who is looking to buy a unit.

Once you start to look for places to advertise your timeshare, you will realize that your competition is literally everywhere: in the Sunday newspaper classified ads, on the television, on the radio, in real-estate office brochures, on consumer group Web sites, in time-share magazines, in telemarketing phone calls, and, of course, posted in multiple places on the World Wide Web.

It is important that you understand from the outset that your expectations should not be to make a $10,000 or $20,000 profit on a sale that occurs the same day you post your first timeshare advertisement. You may have gotten lucky and made deals like this in the primary housing market during the recent boom, but they are virtually unheard of in the world of timeshares. Disabusing yourself of the idea immediately will save you a lot of angst and heartache in the long run.

What can you realistically expect in terms of time and money? Usually, the answer is just the opposite of what you are hoping to hear: You'll tend to spend a lot *more* time, and make a lot *less* money, before actually closing a deal.

Length of Process

Some timeshares sell within a couple of weeks, some timeshares sell within a couple of months, some timeshares sell within a couple of years, and some timeshares never sell at all. It is impossible to say which one of these categories your unit will fit into, but you would be wise to prepare yourself for a longer process rather than a shorter one.

E-ALERT

There is no average amount of selling time for timeshare units on the resale market. Many factors contribute to the amount of time a sale takes, including price, location, competition, and the seller's willingness to adjust his or her expectations when the market grows especially soft.

A simple look at any classified section, whether in print or online, will open your eyes to timeshare units that have been on the market for anywhere from five days to five years. Unfortunately, the only resale factor that you truly have any control over when it comes to speeding up the sale process is price—which means that you may have to ask for a much lower amount than you intended if you need to move your timeshare unit off the market quickly.

Profit and Loss

When you get into the nitty-gritty of trying to figure out how much money you can get for your timeshare unit, your best bet is to set your expectations at no more than 50 percent of the price you originally paid.

Only a handful of people ever make more than half of their original purchase price back—and even fewer people are so lucky as to see the smallest of profits. A reasonable assumption is that the price you end up taking will be between 30 percent and 50 percent of your original purchase price, and not a penny more.

If you own your timeshare unit only a year or two before you decide to sell it, your financial loss will likely be far greater than that of someone who owned the very same timeshare for five or ten years—and at least got some value for the money she spent before having to sell at a loss.

How to Set Your Price

Keeping in mind that you can expect to make back no more than 30 percent to 50 percent of your timeshare's original price, there are some other factors that may help you to move that number upward a bit—or at least to walk away with closer to the 50 percent mark after spending as little time as possible on the resale market.

Doing your homework is going to be key when it comes to setting a price that will get the attention of worldwide buyers. You also can learn from the mistakes that other people have made when selling their timeshares, be it in the same region, the same city, or even the very same wing of your resort.

Worldwide and Local Trends

One broad indicator that it would help for you to keep in mind is what is happening with worldwide and local economies in general. Setting your price high during a period of recession, for instance, is sure to do nothing but drive away the vast majority of potential buyers. During a recession, you are likely to have only bargain-hunters looking at your advertisements, and they will pass you by because they will know that you need them more than they need you.

Another indicator that it pays to watch is the trend in new timeshare sales. A slowing in the city where you own a unit, for instance, could indicate that that city has reached its capacity—and that you are going to have to charge far less than the new resorts if you want to get your unit off the resale market.

 **E-QUESTION**

Where can I find out the latest data on timeshare sales and trends?
Start by checking with the American Resort Development Association at *www.arda.org*. It posts the most recent studies available. Also check with your resort's local Chamber of Commerce, and even with a local Realtor if you know one.

Still another indicator that will affect the way you set your price is whatever is happening in the city where you own your resort. Many owners along the Gulf Coast and Southern Florida, for instance, either lost their timeshares altogether or had to give them away for pennies on the dollar after the 2005 hurricane season, which included the devastating Katrina, Rita, and Wilma. These are factors that will be beyond your control, unfortunately, but they will play a major role in helping to determine how high a price you can hope to set.

Historical Data

Barring any destructive acts of nature that substantially change your region's outlook in terms of overall vacation travel, you can sometimes find historical data about previous timeshare unit sales not just in your city, but in your very own resort.

Historical sales data are a good map to follow when determining what your final selling price might be, but they are not to be taken as gospel. Just because somebody else got $24,000 for a unit identical to yours when the market was at its peak does not mean that you will be able to do the same. You may, in fact, end up with substantially less.

E-ALERT

Timeshare units are unlike primary residences when it comes to seeking out historical sales data. Sometimes, you will not even be able to find out what any other owners sold their units for in your very own resort.

Where should you look to find historical sales data? If you are working with a resale broker, she should be able to help you. If you are working on your own, go back to your tried-and-true standbys: the Timeshare User's Group and *TimeSharing Today* magazine. All the historical data their members have agreed to share are posted on the groups' Web sites.

Resale Broker Tips

A qualified resale broker—one who is licensed and who deals with timeshare resales on a regular basis—should be able to give you valuable tips about pricing your timeshare unit. If you are working with a resale broker who seems fuzzy on what kind of price you should set, walk away and find another person to help you. Better resale brokers understand the market and should lead the way for you, not the other way around.

A good resale broker may know, for example, that the resort where your unit is located recently finished selling the last of its new timeshare units—meaning the market may be ripe for a used unit like yours at a price just slightly lower than the new-unit buyers were paying. On the other hand, a good broker may be aware that the timeshare units in your resort have historically low selling prices because of factors you never dreamed of, and that you will have to stomach a far lower asking price than you had hoped if you want to sell at all in the near future.

Before signing on with any resale broker, ask how many time-share units she has sold altogether, in your resort's region, and in your resort itself. The more specific knowledge a given broker has about your unique marketplace, the better tips she will be able to give you about pricing your timeshare unit properly.

Other Owners' Advice

You may decide, as many timeshare owners do, to forgo hiring the resale broker (and paying her commission) and simply set the price for your timeshare resale yourself. There is nothing at all wrong with this approach, and in some cases, you will be able to make as much money as you would have had you gone with a broker at all.

Being out on your own, though, does not mean you should turn away the advice of people who may be able to help you. Specifically, you should talk with any friends you have met at your timeshare resort, as well as with your homeowner's association, to find out what prices similar timeshare units have garnered in recent resales.

If you are dealing with a particularly friendly fellow owner, you might also ask what helped the highest-price units get more money than the lower-priced ones. It could be a matter of simply positioning yourself in the marketplace in a certain way—such as writing a classified ad with specific catch phrases or advertising in a certain geographic location. You don't have to pass up this kind of insider information simply because you are choosing to work without a resale broker.

Appraisals

There are companies out there that specialize in timeshare appraisals, and you can get one done with a single phone call if you think it will be worthwhile in terms of setting your price. Any local Realtor or resale agency can put you in touch with a reputable appraiser, or you can simply look under "appraisals" in your resort's local telephone directory.

Usually, though, it is the buyer who pays for the appraisal, not the seller, and even that is done only when there are other matters at hand, such as working with a trust or an estate. The vast majority of timeshare resales are handled without an appraisal for the simple reason that the appraisal itself can cost several hundred dollars—money that sellers usually do not want to spend when their entire sale may only be worth a few thousand dollars in the end.

≡FAST FACT

Most people who have sold their timeshares in the past agree that paying for an appraisal is not worth the money. It is a simple matter of math: If your unit is for sale for $4,000 and an appraisal will cost you $400, you will have lost 10 percent of your profit—a far bigger percentage than, say, an appraisal on a $500,000 primary residence.

If you truly do not know where to start in setting the price for your timeshare unit, then investing in an appraisal might be worth that sort of payout to you. But usually, you can find information about similar sales either online or by working with a resale broker, either of which will save you the cost of the appraisal in the long run.

Advertising

Now that you have decided to sell your timeshare, researched all the historical sales data you can find, and set a price that you believe is likely to get a deal done according to your timetable, you will have to get the word out that your timeshare unit is for sale. This is where advertising comes in.

Advertising your resale timeshare can be as simple as posting a flyer on your resort's bulletin board or as complex as designing different classified ads with language specifically tailored to the markets where they will appear. What will work best for you? Often, you won't know until you undergo a process of trial and error. Different people shop in different ways, and you are trying to find that lone person out there who wants the property that you are selling. You really have no way of knowing what his advertising preferences are.

📰 TRAVEL TIP

Instead of trying to figure out which form of advertising will be most effective for your timeshare resale, you might instead set a firm budget on what you want to spend in terms of advertising—and then simply use how many ever kinds of advertisements you can without breaking the bank.

No matter which form of advertising you choose, it is smart to look through examples of other timeshare owners' advertisements to see which ones you find the most compelling. Try to figure out what makes one advertisement "pop" or stand out when compared with the others around it. Copy its language, its style, its look, or all three. Learn from other people's successes, and turn them into your own.

Classified Ads

Newspaper classified sections, despite the general trend toward lower newspaper circulations, still remain a powerful tool for advertising personal property. You can often spend no more than $10 and get a full-size classified ad in your local shopper, with the rates going up as you try to buy space in higher-circulation regional and statewide newspapers. Sometimes, that money can buy incredible reach: *The New York Times* alone, for instance, has more than a million readers a day.

One important thing to do when advertising in any newspaper is to ask—or, if possible, see for yourself—what headings timeshares tend to fall under. Sometimes, the heading is "timeshares," but other times, the majority of units may be listed for sale under headings such as "vacation properties" or "second homes" or "Florida getaways." The readers of every newspaper are trained to look in the same place every week for timeshare information, and you want to make sure that your unit is positioned properly for maximum exposure.

World Wide Web

The World Wide Web has become a shopping mega-marketplace unto itself, featuring everything from searchable newspaper classified ads to product-specific sites where you can search not just for timeshares, but for the lowest-priced timeshare at a specific resort. If you plan to advertise in cyberspace, there are plenty of options out there.

People who already own one week of timeshare use are often good candidates to buy another week, which is why advertising with *TimeSharing Today* magazine or the Timeshare User's Group can be an effective choice. You also can advertise on sites such as *www.ebay.com*, which encompass far more than timeshares alone, but where people can type in the word "timeshares" and come up with a list of properties for sale.

E-ALERT

When evaluating the reach that different Web sites have, ask how many unique users each site counts in its daily hits. This is different from the total number of hits any Web site might receive daily, because a lot of people log on to the same sites more than one time a day. You want your ad to reach as many unique eyeballs as possible, not just to keep popping up in front of the same shoppers.

How much should you pay for advertising on the Web? It all depends on how many people your advertisement will reach. Some sites will let you post for as little as $15, while others will charge you upward of $150. If you are working with a resale broker, the online advertising fee should be part of his overall commission; do not be suckered into paying any online advertising fees up front if you have an agent under contract.

Resale Agencies

Resale agencies should include advertising in the cost of their broker's commission. The advertising can include everything from newspaper classified ads to online ads to networking done with timeshare buyers who contact the agency itself.

E-ALERT

Do not pay extra up-front fees for advertising if you are working with a timeshare resale broker. If you want to augment the marketing effort that the broker is making on your behalf, you can purchase additional advertising directly, by yourself, after you see how the broker's initial ads work out.

Your Resort Itself

Sometimes, the best place to advertise your timeshare unit is in the lobby of the resort itself. Many of the other people who stay there will enjoy themselves, and some of them may be renters or guests of owners who decide on the spot that they want to buy into the property. What better place to have your advertisement waiting?

Most timeshare resorts have a homeowners' association area, such as a bulletin board, where you can post for-sale flyers that you either bring to the resort yourself or mail with a request to have them pinned up in a good spot. If you decide to go this route, make sure your flyer includes the following details:

- A real description of your unit (remember, the people reading this flyer are staying at the resort; they will spot phony information)
- The annual week or number of points you own
- Your asking price
- Your contact information (telephone and e-mail are best)
- Any other information that may help your chances, such as successful trades you have gotten with the unit in the past

You can use this information as the basis for classified and World Wide Web advertisements, as well.

Other Owners in Your Resort

A nifty resale trick that experienced timeshare owners sometimes try is to contact their resort and find out who owns the weeks immediately before and after theirs. This makes a great deal of sense, as a person who owns one week may want to stretch their ownership to two back-to-back weeks—something they can do far less expensively by working with you than they otherwise could if shopping for a straight two-week timeshare deal.

Your resort should not give you the name and phone number of the other owners directly, for privacy reasons, but you usually can leave your name and telephone number and ask the front desk to pass them along to the owners who own the weeks on either calendar side of yours.

Rental Markets

The rental market is not just a great place to find potential resale buyers, but to make a little money while doing so. More and more people are getting hip to the fact that timeshare owners sometimes rent out their units—which can be less expensive and more comfortable than hotels in the same cities. This is a potentially lucrative base from which to work when trying to identify new buyers of timeshares. If you can get somebody to rent your timeshare, they just might have such a good time that they will want to go ahead and buy it. You may not only win over a buyer, but you will get to pocket their rental fee in the process

Finding potential renters is a lot like finding potential buyers. You can work with timeshare consumer groups, rental agencies, Web sites, and newspaper classified sections. When creating your ad with renters in mind, though, be sure to include the word vacation in addition to the word timeshare. That way, if someone is searching online for a vacation resort, your ad will pop up even if they don't know that timeshares exist.

E-QUESTION

Is there anything I can do to tempt my timeshare renter into buying my unit outright?
Yes—tell them that if they choose to buy your unit within six months of renting it, you will consider their rental fee a deposit on the sale. They will feel like they are getting a discount, and you can consider the rental fee an advertising expense.

Little Extras

As with anything, it is the little details that often make the biggest difference. You need to think hard about what makes your timeshare unit special in a sea of competition, and then articulate those things in your advertising so that you will get the most bang for your buck.

For starters, think about what made you want to buy the timeshare unit in the first place. Do not think about why you bought *a* timeshare; think about why you bought *your* timeshare. Does it have the best view in the whole resort? Is it close to the elevators for handicapped access? Does it have a bigger master bedroom than most others in the city? Can the concierge get discounted tickets to local theme parks and theaters?

All of these little extras will help to make your timeshare unit seem just a hair better than others, even if they are identical units in the same resort, because their advertisements will not have those details listed.

Using a Resale Broker

Selling your timeshare on the resale market can be a real headache. This is how the timeshare resale brokerage business came into existence: Many people would simply rather pay a salesman's commission than do all the work of researching and advertising on their own.

There are good points and bad points when it comes to working with a resale broker. Make sure you understand what you are getting into before you sign any contracts with any agencies, no matter how good their reputation is.

The Pros

When it comes to working with a resale broker, the pros are similar to those you experience when working with a Realtor on the sale of a primary residence:

- You do less of the legwork
- You benefit from the broker's expertise
- You have a legal buffer between you and the buyer

These are all good reasons for choosing to work with an agency, though you will pay for every single one of them in the form of the broker's commission. If you are willing to fork over a share of your earnings—perhaps in exchange for saving time and aggravation— then using a resale broker might be the right move for you.

The Cons

The reasons people choose to sell their timeshare units on their own, without a resale broker, are also similar to those that you may experience when working with a primary residence real-estate agent:

- You have to pay a commission
- You may have to sign an exclusive contract with the broker
- You have to do things the broker's way, not yours

Paying that commission aside, the most significant con when working with a resale broker is that sometimes you will be asked to sign a contract that gives the broker the exclusive right to list the property for several months' time. Only after you sign on will you get to see whether the broker is doing a good job of marketing your timeshare unit, and the contract will prevent you from switching to a different agency in a timely manner if things are going wrong.

There is also the matter of being forced to do things the broker's way, which sometimes can be frustrating if she is a stickler for old-fashioned sales methods that you feel are simply outdated. If this is of concern to you, be sure to have the broker outline her plans in writing before you sign a deal with her agency.

Tips for Finding a Pro

If the good points about working with a broker outweigh the bad points for you, then your next bit of business will be finding a reputable agency to work with on your timeshare resale.

E-ALERT

Timeshare resales are a common focal point for scam artists looking to make a quick buck at your expense. Be sure you are working with a reputable resale agency before you sign even a single sheet of paper.

There are more than enough people in the timeshare industry who claim to be resale brokers, but you will want to work with one who is licensed and who has a good reputation for previous sales. You can check with other timeshare owners in consumer group chat rooms for recommendations, or look for agencies that advertise the seals of the Better Business Bureau, National Association of Realtors, or American Resort Development Association. To learn more about any of these groups, look in Chapter 19.

CHAPTER 15

Timeshare Scams

WHAT MOST PEOPLE DREAD when buying or selling a timeshare is falling victim to a scam—and losing hundreds, if not thousands, of dollars in the process. The fear is valid. There is a long history of less-than-reputable people floating around in the timeshare industry, and even today, scam artists are coming up with new and ever-more-clever ways of trying to separate you from your hard-earned vacation money. You need to know their game before they get you to play it—and know where to turn if you fall victim.

It Can Happen to You

There are no complete statistics to be found regarding the number of timeshare scams that have unfolded in recent years, nor throughout the decades-long history of the timeshare industry. Yet consumer group Web sites are littered with chat-room postings from people who have forked over tens of thousands of dollars (or the equivalent in pounds, pesos, and other foreign currencies) only to find that they had purchased a timeshare unit that was nothing like the one promised to them during the sales pitch—if the unit even existed at all.

There are also myriad postings by timeshare owners who have fallen victim to resale scams, which seem to be the field of growing enterprise for con men nowadays. More and more people are shying away from "free" timeshare vacations that turn out to be scams wrapped around high-pressure sales presentations, so the hornswog-glers are turning their attention to people who have already paid for their units. Simply because there are far more people trying to sell timeshares than there are people trying to buy them on the resale market, the owners-turned-sellers can become desperate—which is exactly the quality that draws sharks to a possible feeding frenzy in the first place.

TRAVEL TIP

Read the fine print on your timeshare purchase contract. It likely has a clause stating that the resort cannot be held liable for anything a salesman promised you, unless the details are in writing. That one-bedroom, one-bathroom, then, may in fact be without a toilet. It may be hard for you to believe, but it has happened.

In many cases, a healthy dose of common sense can save you from falling victim to many of these flimflam artists. In other cases, a little bit of knowledge about typical timeshare swindles can prevent you from being fleeced. There are classic danger signs to watch out for whether you are buying or selling, and they are often flashing bright red—just like the proverbial stoplight that you likely learned to heed so long ago.

Top 10 Danger Signs

It is interesting how the same schemes seem to pop up in mildly different variations over time. Bamboozlers truly are not all that creative; they simply look to take a tried-and-true hoax and then find a bunch of new saps upon which to play it. You can beat these bunco artists at their own game if you simply pay attention to the signals they are sending you. The following ten signs—in no particular order—are among the most common indications that you are being set up as part of a hoax.

Up-Front Fees

Would you give a used-car salesman $500 to advertise your 1987 Buick LeSabre without the promise of a sale? How about giving a travel agent $250 to try to find you a hotel interested in taking your reservation without the promise of actually finding one? What do you think about paying $100 for airline tickets to an out-of-state dinner where you may, or may not, meet someone interested in buying your primary residence?

The real question, of course, is this: Do you think that forking over a single penny without a promise of anything substantial in return is *ever* a good idea?

Of course it's not—and the lesson holds true in the world of timeshares, as well. Up-front fees are a dead giveaway that you are dealing with someone who is trying to bilk you, even if the amount of the fee is as little as $100. Think about the math: If the hustler can get just ten people a day to give him a hundred bucks apiece, he will be on track to earn $1,000 a day—or as much as $365,000 a year. Why make him rich when you can protect yourself by simply saying no?

The most common up-front fees that you will see from hucksters in the timeshare industry include advertising or listing fees for timeshare resales. Some nonlicensed, unprofessional "sales brokers" will tell you that you simply cannot get the advertising you will need unless they can pay for it up front, thanks to a generous donation from you. *Don't believe it.*

Would a licensed, honest, hard-working Realtor trying to sell your primary residence ask you for a cash advance so that she could market your house effectively? Heck no—that expense is built into the work she must do in order to earn her commission after the sale. Anyone who asks you for an up-front payment in order to sell your timeshare unit is likely to be a thief.

Free-ish Flights

There is a scam working its way through Europe that involves a telemarketer calling a timeshare owner and offering to put him up at a hotel in another city. At this hotel, the telemarketer explains, will be a pre-selected group of people who have indicated an interest in buying timeshare units, and who are financially qualified to make the purchases. All that you, the timeshare owner, have to do is pay a fee to cover your airfare to that other city, and you will finally be able to sell off your unit (which the telemarketer hopes has been languishing on the resale market for months, if not longer).

E-ALERT

Any timeshare resale broker who asks you for an advance payment to advertise your unit is a crook. Resale brokers earn their money on sales commissions, just like Realtors who work with primary residences. Advertising your timeshare unit is part of their job, not an expense you should bear in addition to paying their commission.

The "airline fee," of course, turns out to be a simple transfer of money from your savings account to the con artist's getaway fund. Again, it can sound realistic because the amount requested will be small—often in that $100 range—and some timeshare owners, facing a buyer's market, do become so desperate to sell that they will try anything.

With just a handful of takers each day in this game, as well, the "telemarketer" can make out like the bandit that he is. Your best bet? Simply hang up the telephone and go back to eating your dinner before it gets too cold.

Cold Calls

Speaking of cold, any time you receive a cold call offering to treat you to a free timeshare vacation or help you to find the timeshare buyer of your dreams, you are likely to be the unwitting target of a scam.

What is a cold call? Any call that you did not request from a business. Another word for cold calling is trolling, which is what some legitimate businesses do when looking to find new customers. It is under this cover of legitimacy that timeshare con men try to sting you. They call at the same time of day that other, well-intentioned businesses do, and they pattern their sales pitches after the dialogue that true telemarketers use.

There are several ways to protect yourself against cold calls. Some can be more fun than others, depending on your mood:

- Hang up the phone, simple and direct.
- Talk to the "telemarketer" for as long as you can. Really make her think she just might have you on the hook. And then, after an hour or so of leading her on, squish her grandest hopes like a gnat on a windshield.
- Tell the "telemarketer" that you are very interested in speaking with her, but that you need to finish changing your baby's diaper. Ask her to hold on, and then leave the room—not to return until long after she has gotten the message and hung up.
- Register your telephone number on the National Do Not Call Registry. Most timeshare cold-calling scams are not limited to a single state, so the federal registry—which is monitored by the Federal Trade Commission—will stop most of them from getting through. You can register online at *www.donotcall.gov*.

Unlicensed Brokers

One of the fastest, easiest ways to find out if you may be dealing with a scam artist in the resale market is to ask him or her to show you a Realtor's license. A person does not have to have a Realtor's license in order to sell resale timeshares, but anyone who *does* have a license is guaranteed to be among the most reputable people in the industry.

Unlicensed brokers—if they are, in fact, brokers at all—may whip out a litany of laminated cards at your request, proving their membership in everything from the local tourism bureau to the Howdy

Doody Club. But if they cannot show you proof that they are licensed Realtors, you would be wise to walk away. There are plenty of legitimate brokers out there who are eager to earn your business.

No Rescission Period—So They Say

This scam tends to crop up in Europe more so than in the United States right now, but anything that works with the masses—from the Beatles to the Mini Cooper—will eventually find its way across the pond. Take heed now, and save yourself in the future.

The hoax works like this: After sitting through a sales presentation for a new timeshare unit, you plunk down your deposit and head home for the weekend, confident that you have the law on your side in terms of a rescission, or cooling-off, period. You use this cooling-off time to check over every word of your contract, just as you are entitled to do. Something seems amiss in the fine print, and you immediately call the resort's salesperson to tell him that you want to cancel the deal.

"But there is no rescission period," he replies. You explain to him that rescission periods are mandated by law (which they are). He has a quick retort at the ready, telling you that unless you have the rescission period's length detailed in writing as part of your contract, you are not, in fact, covered by the national and state laws requiring the cooling-off time. Of course, as you fumble through your paperwork, there is no mention of a rescission period at all. You hang up the telephone in disgust.

 **E-QUESTION**

Will all of my legal rights as a consumer be spelled out in my timeshare contract?
Absolutely not. You often have far more leverage than scam artists want you to know about, much of it thanks to state and federal regulations. Know where you stand, and who has your back, before you sign anything.

The shyster is hoping, of course, that you will not take the additional step of actually contacting the federal or state oversight agency that governs timeshares wherever the resort is. If you did make the call, you would of course learn that you are indeed entitled to that rescission period and can cancel your contract immediately. By the time many people figure this out, though, the cooling-off period has ended. That's what the crook is banking on—and banking handsomely, at that.

Nonexistent Companies

Putting up a site on the World Wide Web has become so easy these days that children are doing it. It should come as no surprise to you, then, that some Web sites promising fabulous timeshare vacations are mere fabrications designed to get you to type in your credit card number—and leave you with nothing in return. Never, ever, *ever* do business over the Internet with any company promising you anything timeshare-related without first checking out that company's credentials. There are several places you can look for verification of proper business practices, including the American Resort Development Association's searchable database at *www.arda .org* and the Better Business Bureau's searchable database at *www .bbb.com*.

There are legitimate Web sites through which you can buy or sell timeshare units, of course, but due diligence will be your key to success. Just be sure you are dealing with a legitimate company instead of an empty shell with pretty graphics.

Maintenance Fee Shenanigans

Imagine that you go through the entire timeshare-buying process without so much as a glitch. You are happy with your unit, happy with your resort, and happy with your exchange company. You may have even taken several wonderful vacations already, and you are looking forward to using your timeshare again in the future—when you get a letter in the mail regarding your annual maintenance fees.

Your fees are paid up to date, of course, but as the letter explains, there are new owners of the resort. They are instituting a new policy: You and all the other timeshare owners must now pay a share of the maintenance fees for unsold timeshare units in the resort, or your timeshare unit will be repossessed. And you must pay the difference, perhaps as much as a thousand dollars, immediately. You cannot wait until your next annual maintenance payment comes due.

There are several cases of these and other maintenance fee she-nanigans explained on consumer group Web sites. Unfortunately, they are not as clear-cut as outright scams because if there is, indeed, a new owner of your resort, then it is his resort—to do with as he chooses. Can your unit be repossessed if you fail to cough up a chunk of change on such short notice? Possibly—but you, your home-owners' association, and your attorney may be able to stop the mad-ness. A lot will depend on the contract you signed, which means that, as with anything, it is important that you check the fine print upon buying to protect yourself later as a timeshare owner.

"You Can Sell It Back to Us"

Sometimes during the sales presentation for a new timeshare unit, the salesman will tell you that if you are unhappy at any time and for any reason with the purchase that you make on that day, you can sell your timeshare unit right back to his boss, the developer, for the same price you originally paid—even if that time comes a full ten years after your original deal. *Riiiiiiight.*

While it is true that some developers will buy back timeshare units, this is usually the case *only* at the precious few resorts whose units go up in value over the years. The incentive for the developer in this case is, of course, profit. He sold the unit to you once, probably collected your mortgage interest payments for a few years, and now is buying the unit back at its original or slightly less-than-original price. That price, he knows, is now several thousand dollars less than he can get for it on the open market when he puts it out there to the public again. So he will have an even bigger sale price and mortgagee in his future, and that timeshare owner will pay him even bigger mortgage interest payments than you did for the previous couple of years.

Is this necessarily a bad deal for you? No—but nine times out of ten, it's not the deal at all. As you have already learned, almost all timeshares go down, dramatically, in value after their initial purchase. Most people are lucky to get half of what they originally paid when it comes time to sell their units. Is a developer going to make good on a promise to take a unit back at full price when its value is far less? Of course not—which makes this a typical scam worth watching out for.

E-ALERT

More often than not, if you can get a developer to *take* back your timeshare unit—as opposed to *buying* it back—you will have to do so by forfeiting every penny you have paid (including your entire mortgage and all maintenance fees). You will learn more about this in Chapter 16.

No Exchanges Available

Some scams are more clear-cut than others. What one customer sees as a bad deal, a company may say is simply "the way things work." Such is the case with exchange companies and timeshare owners who say they just can't get a decent trade for the type of unit they own. Sometimes, as you have already learned, your inability to get a decent timeshare exchange may be a function of your unit's poor trading power—anything from a bad location to an off-peak season to a lack of the most sought-after number of bedrooms. But sometimes, more and more timeshare owners say, the lack of fair trades is being caused by unfair exchange company business practices.

One recent class-action lawsuit, for instance, states that a brand-name resort developer is going for the quick buck by allowing renters and regular hotel guests priority access to its resorts—thus taking up all the rooms that otherwise would be available to the people who bought timeshare points so that they could stay there. The points owners contend that, after several years of trying, they can't even get into a timeshare unit at their home resort because so many renters and overnight hotel guests are filling every bed. Their points are therefore worthless, as there is simply no more room at the inn.

There is really no way for timeshare owners to know whether a resort is playing such games with the available rooms (unless you can find a stool pigeon in the reservations department). But complaints of this nature posted on consumer Web sites by other timeshare owners are a good indication that there might be something amiss—perhaps not necessarily an outright scam, but definitely some shady dealings of which you will want to be wary.

≡FAST FACT

Legitimate timeshare exchange companies insist that they do everything within their power to ensure that timeshare owners get fair and timely trades for their home resort units. In some cases, your inability to get a trade is merely caused by the laws of supply and demand.

"Lost" Exchange Weeks

It is rare, but there have been cases where timeshare owners have reported depositing their weeks or points into an exchange company's space bank only to be told that those weeks or points have been "lost in the system" when it comes time to make the actual exchange. The simple solution to this problem is to make sure that you receive written confirmation after you deposit your points or weeks with any exchange company. The printout may not be enough to settle the immediate problem in time for your annual vacation, but it certainly will be a handy piece of evidence for your lawyer down the line.

Protecting Yourself

So, now that you know what kinds of conniving misanthropes are out there just waiting to take advantage of you in the world of timeshares, you undoubtedly are wondering what the best ways are to protect yourself from their schemes. Again, a healthy dose of common sense can often make all the difference in the world. As with any major purchase, you need to do your homework, take your time, and be absolutely sure that all of the details are covered.

Sleep on It

High-pressure sales tactics work only on people who go along with the notion that they absolutely, positively must make a decision on the spot. This is true whether you are buying a new or resale timeshare, or if you are trying to make a decision about whom to work with to sell a timeshare that you previously purchased.

Unless you are walking into a situation with all of your T's crossed and I's dotted, your best bet is to gather as much information as you can and then walk away to think things over. It is true that you may lose some day-of-sale-only incentives, such as extra timeshare usage discounts and the like, but getting a good night's sleep and taking another look through your paperwork in the light of a fresh morning can make all the difference in ferreting out inconsistencies and omissions that may cost you a great deal further down the road.

Ask for References

Whenever you can, get the names and telephone numbers of other timeshare owners who have worked on previous deals with your salesman, resort developer, or resale broker. Make good use of those telephone numbers, too, asking questions not just about whether the person is happy with the service she received, but also about whether she believes she got everything she was promised in the long run.

Be aware that any reference you get from the salesman, resort developer, or resale broker himself is likely to be someone who says glowing things about the person trying to gain your business. (After all, it is the salesman himself who is giving you the references.) Sometimes, you can get out of this entangled web by asking the reference to give you the names of other people he knows in the same timeshare resort who also have worked with the salesperson, developer, or broker. That way, you will be getting to a secondary source who might be a bit more impartial.

When you do get hold of an impartial reference, what should you ask? These questions are a good place to start, whether you are buying or selling a timeshare unit:

- What kinds of unexpected costs have you encountered?
- What, if anything, about the process left you feeling uncomfortable?
- Why would you work with this salesman/developer/resale broker again?
- How much of what you asked for were you given in writing?
- Is there anything else about your experience that you want to share?

These kinds of questions are open-ended, meaning that it would be darn near impossible for the reference to answer them with a simple yes or no. Asking open-ended questions makes it much more likely that the person answering them will talk for a longer amount of time, and thus divulge more information to you in the process.

Check Online Databases

Although they are not perfect, there are several reputable institutions that monitor business practices of all kinds of companies, including timeshare resort developers and resale brokers. In most cases, these groups have searchable online databases that you can comb through to find out whether the person you are dealing with has any complaints lodged against him, and if so, on what grounds. Some of the groups that are most likely to have timeshare-related information include:

- American Resort Development Association, *www.arda.org*
- Better Business Bureau, *www.bbb.com*
- National Association of Realtors, *www.realtor.org*
- National Chamber of Commerce, *www.uschamber.com*

Detailed information about each of these groups, including histories of how they began and who runs them today, appears in Chapter 19.

Join Consumers' Groups

All throughout this book, you have seen references to the two major United States–based timeshare consumer groups: *TimeSharing Today* magazine and the Timeshare User's Group. The services that these groups provide are invaluable when it comes to protecting yourself against timeshare scams.

📱 TRAVEL TIP

You do not have to pay a membership fee to make good use of a lot of the information offered online by TimeSharing Today and the Timeshare User's Group. The most detailed information is viewable by members only, but you can get a great start on educating yourself by logging on to their Web sites and simply browsing around.

Simply posting a message in one of the groups' online chat rooms can immediately yield a bounty of information that it otherwise may have taken you weeks to research on your own. You can be as specific as you want to be, as well, asking questions such as, "I am considering buying a two-bedroom unit at such-and-so resort in Las Vegas, Nevada. This is the price I have been offered. Can anyone tell me if this sounds like a reasonable deal?" Other timeshare owners will answer you—sometimes with information about their own experiences at the exact same resort. More information about *TimeSharing Today* and the Timeshare User's Group appears in Chapter 19.

Call Homeowners' Associations

Every timeshare resort that is no longer under a developer's control has a homeowners' association. You just may get lucky and find a member who lives in your state, or even your city, even if the time-share resort itself is thousands of miles away. Even if you have yet to buy a unit at the resort, other owners usually will be willing to talk with you about their experiences, either over the phone or in person if you live close by.

To get the contact information for your given resort's homeowners' association, simply call the resort's front desk and ask for it.

Get Everything in Writing

Getting things in writing is important with every contract, of course, but it is especially important when you are making a major purchase such as a timeshare unit. Thousands—possibly tens of thousands—of dollars are going to change hands, and you want to be sure that you have all the fine points covered in writing so that you will have an avenue of recourse should anything go wrong in the future.

E-QUESTION

What do I do if a timeshare salesman or resale broker refuses to put my business deal down on paper?
Walk away. Don't argue, just leave. There are plenty of reputable salespeople and resale brokers out there who will happily give you whatever you want in writing, without causing you any aggravation in the process.

So that you don't forget any important details, be sure that you check your contract for all of the important items explained in Chapter 7. If there is anything in the contract that you still do not understand, ask to have it clarified before you sign on the dotted line. And remember: Always ask the question, "Will you please show me where it says that in the contract?"

Visit the Resort

Whenever possible, your best bet for ensuring that you are buying exactly what you *think* you are buying is to make a trip to the resort property—and to your actual timeshare unit itself. It is all well and good for a timeshare contract to list resort features such as a fitness room and landscaped gardens, but only if you travel to the place and look around for yourself will be able to see whether those things are real amenities—or if they are, in fact, one stationary bicycle and a dying patch of flowers.

The same holds true for your timeshare unit. Walk inside. Look at the condition of the kitchen appliances. Make sure there is no evidence of water damage in the ceiling. Take a picture of the view from the balcony for your files. Do all of the due diligence that you can before signing on for the long run. That way, when it comes time to actually use your timeshare, you will face few, if any, surprises.

Stay Sober

As any young woman who has ever sat down on a barstool on a college campus can tell you, having a few drinks sure can cloud your judgment—and fast. Why on earth would you want to have a few martinis in you when it comes time to make a deal that will tie up thousands and thousands of your hard-earned vacation dollars?

E-ALERT

Any timeshare salesman who tries to ply you with alcohol is setting you up for a fall. Never, ever accept a drink if you intend to make a major purchase. You want your judgment to be as unclouded as possible so that you can pay attention to the details of the transaction.

Of course staying sober is the right course of action when buying a timeshare unit, be it new or on the resale market. After the deal is done, sure—go celebrate with a frozen margarita. But during the business deal itself, keep yourself as straight as a cocktail umbrella.

Be Educated

The fact that you have read this far into this book should give you the confidence that you know all of the basics, and then some. Education is power. Knowing your rights, your options, and your personally detailed needs are key to helping you protect yourself from swindlers of all sorts.

You can continue your education online, as previously explained in this chapter, and you also can gather a veritable library of information from timeshare developers themselves. They are eager to send you written information about their timeshare units if you simply give them a call. Get every piece of paper that you can and compare the details side by side. The truth is, you may know even more than the salesman—or the crook—by the time you get around to actually wanting to do business.

If You Think You're a Victim

Even the most steadfast students of timeshare rights, options, and companies sometimes fall victim to heinous injustices. If you find yourself in this situation, do not waste any time thinking about what could have or should have been. Immediately switch gears from self-pity to self-defense and get on with the business of trying to undo the damage as quickly as possible.

Explain your situation to other members of consumer organizations such as *TimeSharing Today* and the Timeshare User's Group. The odds are good that you are not the first victim of whatever problem you face, and those who have learned their lessons the hard way may have valuable advice that could help you.

Be careful when spreading the news about a timeshare developer or resale broker who you feel has shafted you. You do not want to be accused of slandering (with spoken words) or libeling (with written words) anyone in a way that they could later sue you over.

Simply leaving someone's name out of a general conversation is often enough to protect yourself from retribution.

E-QUESTION

How do I go about correcting the situation if I've become a victim of a timeshare scam?
Start by seeing if you are within a state- or federally mandated rescission period. If you are, you can quickly file any necessary paperwork to undo whatever contracts you signed in error. You should be out of trouble within a couple of weeks.

If the cooling-off period has already passed—or if you were in a foreign country without one to begin with—you may be stuck with your bad deal. In this case, there is no harm in reporting the con artist to the Better Business Bureau, the local Chamber of Commerce, the American Resort Development Association, and to anyone else who will listen, including consumer's groups and homeowners' associations.

While state Real Estate Commissions often are the highest-ranking body that regulates timeshare sales, the Federal Trade Commission does accept complaints about false advertising and marketing. Sometimes, you can use this to your advantage, and sometimes, not. To learn more, go to *www.ftc.gov*. At the very least, in contacting these organizations you may be saving someone else from suffering the same fate, and you may put the thief out of business for good.

CHAPTER 16

When You Just Can't Sell

EVEN IF YOU SET A FAIR PRICE, market your timeshare well, and work with upstanding resale brokers, you may end up being one of those unlucky people whose units simply do not sell. You may run out of time and need to get out of your contract, or you may own a unit in a resort that, for whatever reason, has become undesirable to other potential owners. But you still have options. This chapter will help you make the best of a not-so-great situation.

How Many Timeshares Are "Unsellable"?

As you have already learned in previous chapters, the timeshare resale market has forever been one in which the buyers are in control. There are far more people trying to sell their timeshares than there are would-be owners out there looking to pay for them, and the lack of balance in the marketplace can mean that, sometimes, a unit simply will not sell—no matter what.

It is impossible to say how many times this happens, but there are enough frustrated would-be sellers out there in timesharing chat rooms to assume that it happens more often than any resort developer will ever admit. Sometimes, a resort's management makes changes that nobody wants to live with at any price. Sometimes, Mother Nature unleashes a devastating tornado or hurricane that flattens an entire vacation region along with all of the timeshare units in it. Sometimes, there is simply a glut of supply in the marketplace, and your honestly fair price is just not low enough to compete with the bargain-basement deals that other people are willing to make.

≡FAST FACT

If you find yourself as one of the unlucky people whose timeshare simply will not sell, the problem may not be within your control. All of your pricing, marketing, and business associates may be perfectly legitimate while the marketplace itself may simply be overcrowded, as it often has been during the past few decades.

What can you do if you end up with a timeshare unit that you no longer want, but that you simply cannot sell? You can try to make one last-ditch attempt at unloading it on the resale market, or you can go other routes that will at least leave you with *something*—even if it is far less or far different than you ever envisioned.

Rethink Your Price

If you decide that you want to make one more kamikaze run at the resale market, your best bet is to try to undersell your competition. That's right: Look at what prices other units similar to yours, in your geographic region, are getting from resale buyers, and then price your unit just a hair lower than those final sale prices. You are almost certain to find a taker, even if it is a bargain-basement bottom feeder who trolls for unfortunate situations like yours all year round.

Of course, by taking this route you will likely be setting yourself up for a financial loss that is even greater than you had previously anticipated, but if time is the most important factor in your decision to sell— if you simply have to dump your timeshare and move on, for whatever reason—then for you, taking that loss may be worth the peace of mind that will come with signing the sale papers and moving on.

🧳 TRAVEL TIP

It is key, when you find yourself having to sell your timeshare at a rock-bottom price, to remember that you did not buy it as a real-estate investment in the first place. You may not have gotten all of the value out of it that you had hoped, but reminding yourself that you never intended to actually make money as an owner may help you to sleep a bit easier.

You may actually find yourself in a position where you have a paid-off timeshare unit from which you have gotten quite a good deal of value over the years. You may want to sell simply because you no longer want to pay the annual maintenance fees and occasional special assessments. In this case, you can list your timeshare for anywhere from $1 to $1,000, and you likely will find a taker quickly. The dollar amount may mean a break-even deal for you over the long haul, but that is nothing to sneeze at in the world of timeshare ownership. It's kind of like leaving an Atlantic City casino with the same $500 you had in your pocket the minute you walked in. You may not have won the jackpot, but at least you weren't among the countless big-time losers who walk away with nothing every single day.

If none of these options sounds right for you, there are others that you can consider, including auctions, charity donations, and permanent swaps with other timeshare owners. Again, they may not bring you the financial satisfaction you desire, but they will at least get you out of your timeshare ownership contract.

Use Auctions

Several companies have popped up in recent years that coordinate auctions of timeshare units. TRI West Timeshare, for instance, is a Los Angeles, California–based company that has been around since 1981 and that is promoted by the Timeshare User's Group consumer organization. TRI West specializes in timeshare resales, but also offers auction services for owners who prefer to go that route. There is a lot of good (and free!) information about auctions on its Web site, *www.triwest-timeshare.com*, that you can explore without having to commit to anything.

TRI West says that fully 90 percent of owners who follow the company's minimum bid recommendations and attend their timeshare auctions actually do make a sale. What are those recommendations? Perhaps not as much as you would hope, especially after factoring in TRI West's fees and commissions, but at least enough that you will walk away with a little bit of cash still in your pocket.

For example, the mid-range minimum bid recommendation that TRI West suggests for a two-bedroom, deeded timeshare unit is $2,000. This minimum bid recommendation is not necessarily the highest price your unit will bring at auction, but it is a price that you must be willing to accept if you enter into the auction process.

≡ FAST FACT

The minimum bid recommendations that TRI West promotes for timeshare auctions range from low to high. A deeded studio unit's minimum bid can be anywhere from $500 to $1,500, while a right-to-use two-bedroom unit's minimum can range from $1,000 to $2,000. The highest minimum bid that TRI West suggests is $2,500 for a two- or three-bedroom deeded unit, or $3,000 if the unit is in a five-star resort.

Now, you can subtract from that price the $225 listing fee that TRI West charges, along with the 15 percent commission the company will be due—which comes with a $950 minimum, as long as it does not exceed 50 percent of the final selling price. If you do the math, you will see that your $2,000 timeshare sale will actually leave you with a net return of just $825.

There are other auction companies out there, as well, that may give you different pricing suggestions. Timeshare Resales USA, for instance, has a site called *www.timesharesforauction.com* that is based in Florida, has been around since 1987, and falls under the reputable GMAC Real Estate banner.

If you like the idea of setting a minimum bid price for an auction but do not want to pay any fees or commissions, you can run your own auction on Web sites such as eBay. You are not likely to find as concentrated a group of dedicated timeshare customers there, nor will you have the benefit of a resale professional's expertise and closing assistance, but you just may luck out and end up getting the same price you would have at another auction—and pocketing virtually every penny.

Donate Your Unit to Charity

Another option, if you don't care about putting any cash immediately into your pocket, is to donate your timeshare unit to charity. In most cases, doing this will allow you to take a tax deduction at the end of the year—sometimes one that amounts to as much profit as you would have been left with after choosing the resale or auction route, after all of your advertising and marketing expenses. Plus, you will be helping a good cause in the process.

Donate For A Cause is one organization that can help you make a charitable donation fairly quickly and with minimal hassle. A broker started the company after thirteen years of seeing how difficult it can be for some timeshare owners to sell their units on the resale market, and how little cash the owners got back in the end. A tax deduction for the timeshare unit's value, the broker reasoned, is sometimes an easier and more financially intelligent way to go.

The Donate For A Cause Web site, *www.donateforacause.org*, includes online forms that you can fill out so that your unit can be evaluated for its donation potential. You then select a charity to receive the bulk of the unit's value. You can submit your own charity's contact information or choose from a list that includes:

- American Kidney Fund
- Florida Veterans Assistance Association
- International Hearing Dog
- National Foundation for Cancer Research
- Network Against Sexual and Domestic Abuse
- Great Beginnings Montessori School

Usually, the costs to you are minimal, potentially including the purchase of a replacement deed (about $25) or an affidavit of death (about $75) if the timeshare's owner has passed away. If your unit is accepted by the organization, the entire process usually takes four to six weeks. A subcontractor sells your unit on the open market and takes a 35 percent commission, while the remaining 65 percent of the sale price—minus a $190 title search fee—goes to the charity of your choice. All of the forms that you need to fill out for the Internal Revenue Service are on the Donate For A Cause Web site, as well.

There are many other groups that will accept your timeshare donation outright, but you will have to do a bit more legwork with the IRS and, possibly, an appraiser. You can find listings of some charities that accept timeshare units on the Timeshare User's Group Web site, *www.tug2.net*. And of course, if there is a charity you work with often, you can simply call and find out whether it accepts timeshare donations and try to work directly through the people you already know.

Return Your Unit to the Developer

In some cases, if you cannot sell your timeshare on the resale market, you will be able to give it back to the resort developer. This is not a sure thing, and you should not count on the service being available when you buy your timeshare in the first place.

The easiest way to facilitate the property transfer back to the developer is simply to transfer the deed, which usually requires a recording fee of less than $100 at the clerk's office in the county where your resort is located. If your developer accepts timeshare unit returns, he should be able to help you with this process.

You also can try calling the clerk's office directly, especially in places like Las Vegas, Nevada, and Orlando, Florida, where there are a bevy of timeshare units. The clerks, in some cases, will know more about the return process than the resort developers themselves.

E-ALERT

Returning your timeshare unit to the developer almost always means you are giving up any potential to make even a single dollar of your investment back. On the other hand, it can often be the path of least resistance in terms of getting yourself out of your contract.

Arrange a Permanent Swap

Members of the Timeshare User's Group have created a page on their Web site where fellow owners can look for timeshare units they may be interested in obtaining through a permanent swap, thus saving both unit owners the hassle of having to sell and purchase new timeshares altogether.

There is no legal assistance or contractual information offered in this section of the group's Web site, but there are plenty of units listed by region, everywhere from Hawaii to Tennessee. Points systems have their own section, too, so you can search for a similar value in that type of ownership scenario.

The "Wanted to Buy, Trade, Rent" page on the *TimeSharing Today* Web site also sometimes lists classified ads from timeshare owners who are looking to make permanent swaps. The page is not devoted to permanent swaps, as the Timeshare User's Group page is, but you can find opportunities at *TimeSharing Today*, as well, if you take the time to look.

▮ TRAVEL TIP

In many cases, arranging a permanent swap is simply a matter of transferring the deed at the county clerk's office and filling out a transfer of ownership form with the resort and/or exchange company. Some owners find this a far easier route than selling their timeshares on the resale market and then looking for another unit to buy.

Give Your Unit Away

Still another option for a timeshare unit that will not move on the resale market is gift giving. That's right: You can turn your timeshare into a present for a family member, close friend, or important business associate. In many cases, this means that you will still be invited to enjoy the resort from time to time—but without all of the annual maintenance fees and other expenses that go along with ownership.

Of course, your timeshare will have to be paid for in full in order for you to follow this path, and the person to whom you are transferring it will become responsible for those fees that you will no longer be paying. In many cases, though, the beneficiary of your gift will be thrilled to pay a few hundred dollars a year in maintenance fees in exchange for a $15,000 timeshare unit that she will be receiving for free.

 **E-QUESTION**

When might it be appropriate to give a timeshare unit as a gift?
Gift-giving occasions include as your children's wedding gift, as your parents' retirement gift, as a close friend's fiftieth birthday gift, as a longtime colleague's holiday bonus, or as a hard-working employee's reward for bringing in new business.

The process of giving a timeshare gift is similar to the process for making a permanent swap. You have to change the deed in the county clerk's office, as well as a transfer of ownership form with your resort developer and/or exchange company. Oh, and since you can't exactly tie a red ribbon around the timeshare itself, you may want to save a resort catalog to cover in gift wrap and a festive bow for the big presentation!

How to Recover from a Loss

If you went into timeshare ownership with realistic expectations— and not the assumption that you would make a profit on your unit in the long run—then recovering from a loss should be more of an emotional process than a financial one.

For starters, if you did not find timeshare ownership to be all that you had hoped, you may be kicking yourself for having bought a unit in the first place. All that money spent, you may think, for what you might have gotten at a cheaper rate by simply staying in hotels all along.

It's possible, of course, that this will be true, but in many cases, you will not have spent *that* much more money than hotels would have charged you. Even better, if you held onto your timeshare for a good five years before divesting it, you may even be in the break-even category when compared with the cost of hotel rooms. That's not such a bad thing when it comes to taking vacations, especially if you have enjoyed yourself in places that you found to be beautiful and relaxing.

If you managed to make all of your mortgage and maintenance payments on time, your credit rating should not be affected in any way by ending your timeshare ownership—even if you suffer a financial loss in the process. The whole thing is kind of like buying a new car for $25,000, keeping it for two years, and then having to sell it for $18,000. You aren't going to be thrilled about the whole deal, but no credit service is going to deny you a new MasterCard or Visa account because of it.

The real question you probably will end up asking yourself is this: Is investing in timeshare again something worth considering? In other words, was it the entire concept of timeshare that failed you, or just the unit and resort that you chose?

≡FAST FACT

When it comes to evaluating what you gained and lost during the course of your timeshare ownership, remember that you never set out to make money in the first place. Your goal all along should have been to save a little cash while investing in vacation memories, which you likely did, at least on some level.

This is something that only you will be able to answer after you sit back and reflect on why you bought your unit, how you used it, and why you decided to sell it. And if you do decide that it was your choice of unit—not timesharing itself—that left you so unhappy, your odds are much higher of faring better with a future purchase in a different resort. Live and learn, as they saying goes. And from now on, be sure to try to find bargains along the way.

CHAPTER 17

Unique, Nonproperty Timeshares

THERE IS NO DOUBT THAT when you think of timeshares, you most often think about a one- or two bedroom resort unit that is similar to a hotel in a vacation-friendly place. Yet there are far more timeshare opportunities out there, ranging from utmost luxury to easily afford-able. You can enter into timeshare contracts for everything from boats to campground space to recreational vehicles that will take you across the country and beyond. You simply have to learn where to find these offers—and know the right questions to ask about each.

You Have Options: Beyond Resorts

Used to be, say back in the 1950s, that people rarely bought any-thing they would not own outright. The great dream of the United States middle class was homeownership, and the notion of owning a secondary or vacation home on top of your family's primary resi-dence was reserved for only the wealthiest families in any commu-nity. People who knew that they could not afford vacation homes simply put the idea out of their minds altogether and went about the business of building their savings accounts. On occasion, they took a vacation, but they never imagined that there was any other way to own property other than 100 percent.

Today, of course, the consumer culture that exists in the United States demands ever-more-creative ways of offering people the options not just to buy things like vacation property, but to buy into usage contracts when total ownership is not financially possible. As the thinking now goes, just because you cannot afford something doesn't mean that you shouldn't have it.

≡FAST FACT

The concept of timeshare usage even reaches into the upper income levels of United States consumerism. Fractional ownership of luxury private jets, for instance, has increased more than 60 percent since the year 2000, according to some sources.

Timeshare units in beachfront and golf-course resorts are just one way that this consumer philosophy manifests itself. People who cannot afford a two-bedroom villa in Sedona, Arizona, may instead purchase a timeshare usage package with a campground in North Carolina. At the other end of the income spectrum, people who cannot afford their own Boeing 737 may buy a timeshare usage package with a private jet company simply so that they do not have to fly on commercial planes.

Often, when you get into the concept of timesharing aboard high-end airplanes, boats, and the like, the term *timeshare* is replaced with the phrase fractional ownership. In many cases, this is essentially the same thing—you are buying the right to own or use a fraction of something, just as you would a resort unit—but fractional ownership sounds far more substantial and, therefore, comes with a certain level of cachet.

It is important to remember that fractional ownership, in the world of timeshare resorts, is something different from straight weeks- or points-based timeshare. The phrase often refers to a deal in which you buy several months' worth of timeshare use at a time, at a far greater entry price than traditional timeshares require. Outside of the resort timeshare universe, though, fractional ownership can refer to the same thing as a weeks- or points-based timeshare, albeit for a boat, campground site, or recreational vehicle instead of for a resort unit.

Boats

The concept of timeshare has a history in the marine community that is questionable, at best. Traditionally, people who do not own boats but who want to use them for periodic vacations will charter them, or rent them, for a week or two at a time. Everything from a 30-foot sailboat to a 300-foot megayacht can be chartered, with prices ranging from less than $4,000 a week for a bareboat that you sail yourself to upward of $400,000 a week for a fully crewed luxury vessel.

The boats typically are found in the Caribbean and Mediterranean seas, though some are also available seasonally in places like New England, Alaska, the Chesapeake Bay, Florida, and the Bahamas. There are a few floating around for charter in Scandinavia, the South Pacific, and beyond, but because boats require provisioning and other shore-based services that can be very expensive in remote locations, they tend to be available for charters only in destinations where the broader masses of people typically like to vacation.

E-ALERT

The idea of fractional boat timeshare is different than the concept of using your timeshare points to obtain a cruise-ship vacation. With fractional boat timeshares, you are buying the rights to use a smaller boat, or sometimes even a private yacht.

Sounds a lot like hotel rooms, right? And since timeshares are succeeding as an alternative to buying hotel rooms all over the world, then wouldn't timeshare use of boats be a logical extension of the boat-charter market, too? You would think so—unless you knew a little bit about how boat charter works.

People who charter boats like to go from Point A to Point B, sailing where the wind and their imaginations take them. That's a lot different than returning to, say, the same vacation resort on the same stretch of beach year after year after year. If you want to sail from St. Martin to Antigua, for instance, but the guy who plans to be aboard the boat the week before you wants to sail from Tortola to St. Thomas, you are going to have a logistics problem. Hence the concern with offering boating timeshares. The people who own the boats do not want to have to pay the extra repositioning fees to get the boat from where the previous guy wanted it to where you want it. And so instead of offering timeshare usage plans—where you would have a say in where and when you get to go—the boats offer one-time charters, allowing them to take or turn down your vacation requests just the same way hotels do.

It is for this reason that timeshare has had such a hard time gaining a foothold in the boating industry. And yet there are a few companies trying a version of it that would seem to make sense for some types of boating vacations in the future: more-or-less fixed itinerary fractional ownership plans in which you start out and end up at the same base marina year after year after year, but you can sail wherever you want to during your annual week of boat usage.

🧳 TRAVEL TIP

One of the easiest vacation destinations for beginning American boaters to cruise is the U.S. Virgin Islands. The landmasses are close together, meaning that you spend minimal time under way, and everybody speaks English in case you need help. For these reasons, boating timeshare deals in the Virgin Islands make sense for first-timers.

The company Elite Island Yachts—a division of Festiva Resorts—is one firm that is trying this concept out in partnership with The Catamaran Company, a well-respected boating company that has been in the charter business for years. Elite Island Yachts will have a fleet of Lagoon 440s (which are 44-foot catamarans with four cabins apiece) based in Tortola, St. Martin, and St. Vincent, three distinct Caribbean cruising areas. You, the timeshare owner, will pay a one-time fee that will let you charter out of any of these home bases for a total of twelve to thirty-six weeks during the course of your twelve-year membership. You can use the Lagoon 440 on your own and act as the captain, or you can use three of the staterooms for yourself and hire a captain (through the company) to stay in the fourth cabin and take care of business along the way.

You cannot sail between the home-base destinations, as you might on a cruise ship, because they are simply too far apart for a smaller boat like a 44-footer to reach in a week's time. But you could alternate among the vacation destinations in much the same way that you would alternate among an exchange company's resorts—only without having to pay the per-vacation exchange fee on top of your cost of membership.

For more information about this timeshare opportunity on the water, go to *www.thecatamarancompany.com*. You also can look for additional companies' promotions in the top marine-industry magazines, such as *Power & Motoryacht* (*www.powerandmotoryacht.com*), *Voyaging* (*www.voyagingonline.com*), and *SAIL* magazine (*www .sailmag.com*).

Campground and Recreational Vehicle Sites

For some people, the idea of staying in a posh, five-star resort with a gourmet restaurant and a balcony overlooking the beach is nothing short of hell. Sure, it is a pretty enough environment with more than enough fun things to do, but the crowds and noise and fluorescent lights interfering with the stars in the night sky all add up to a vacation that some people would simply rather do without. Sometimes, getting away from it all means just that: getting away from everything and being one with the great outdoors.

If you are one of these nature buffs, then the odds are that you enjoy camping. And because there are plenty of other people out there in the world who think the same way that you do, there are companies trying to sell you ever more camping services. Hence the birth of the "campshare" idea—taking the principles of timeshare resort vacations and applying them to timeshare campground vacations.

E-ALERT

Campground timeshares are like resort timeshares in that you need to use your membership in order to make it a financially worthwhile purchase. If you simply want to camp once every couple of years, you might be better off sticking to inexpensive state parks or paying one-time fees at private facilities than joining a campground timeshare that is part of a network of private grounds.

The organizing structure behind timeshare campgrounds is that you pay a fee for use of your home campground (just as you would pay the price of a home-resort timeshare unit) and then get access to both your home campground and other campgrounds in the timeshare company's network. Sometimes, access to these other campgrounds is included in your membership, while at other times, your membership entitles you to discounted fees at campgrounds nationwide.

There are annual maintenance fees for your home campground, just as there would be for your home timeshare resort. There also are additional usage fees if you want to purchase extras like a deluxe cabin or a spot to park your recreational vehicle, which can run as little as $1 per foot of RV, per night. Some of the fancier timeshare campgrounds even have activities that are similar to those offered by timeshare resorts, such as family-friendly crafts and games.

One major difference, though, between timeshare resorts and timeshare campgrounds is that with resorts, you usually are able to purchase a time increment of just one week. With campground timeshares, you usually are forced to purchase shares that are more substantial—sometimes as much as eight weeks' time in a single share.

This is, in part, because people who like to camp often go for a month or two during the summer, packing up their tents in their recreational vehicle and heading out cross-country for weeks at a time. Other reasons that campground shares tend to be for longer usage periods than single-week resort timeshares include the fact that campgrounds themselves tend to be on the inexpensive side, so campground timeshare owners need to offer you, the buyer, a package of sorts instead of just a single week's worth of use.

▮ TRAVEL TIP

If you prefer to camp in a recreational vehicle, be sure to compare not just the annual membership fees of different campground timeshare networks, but also their campsites' nightly RV charges. They can range from $1 to $8—a significant difference during a two-month vacation.

Just as there are different timeshare resort exchange networks, there are also different timeshare campground networks. A few of the better-known companies are called Adventure Outdoor Resorts, Camperworld, Coast to Coast Resorts, and Resort Parks International.

Adventure Outdoor Resorts

Adventure Outdoor Resorts started out with just three properties in 1991. Today, the company's network boasts nearly 500 campgrounds and resorts throughout the United States and Canada. The company is similar to Resort Condominiums International or Interval International in that you must become a member through your home campground resort. You simply cannot call the company and sign up for an annual membership.

The nightly camping fee that members pay is $6 at all Adventure Outdoor Resorts, which you can search for by location through the company's interactive Web site. You are allowed to camp for as long as twenty-one nights in a row during low-demand seasons or for as long as fourteen consecutive nights during high-demand seasons. You actually get two fourteen-night stays during those high-demand periods, but you must wait seven nights before using the second fourteen-day period (meaning you cannot use the two fourteen-day periods back to back). Adventure Outdoor Resorts is based in Gunnison, Colorado. To learn more, you can check out the company's Web site at *www.whresorts.com*.

Camperworld

Camperworld is a smaller operation that is based in Salt Lake City, Utah. It has been operating since 1977. Its network of camping and recreational vehicle resorts includes what it calls ten of the finest sites in Utah, along with nearly a thousand other parks that you can access through affiliations that Camperworld has established with Adventure Outdoor Resorts, Coast to Coast, and Resort Parks International.

You can explore the Utah resorts that Camperworld recommends on its interactive Web site, *www.camperworld.com*.

 **E-QUESTION**

Is there a resale market for campground timeshares?
Yes. Just as you can often find a good deal on a resort timeshare through the resale market, you can also find less-expensive campground timeshares up for sale. They are fewer and farther between, but a World Wide Web search for "campground timeshares" will often lead you to at least a handful of classified ads.

Coast to Coast Resorts

Since its founding in 1972, Coast to Coast Resorts has helped more than a million families vacation at close to a thousand outdoor resorts and campgrounds in the United States, Canada, and Mexico. It also boasts a network of "Good Neighbor Parks" that are privately owned, open to the public, and available at discounted rates for Coast to Coast members.

Membership in Coast to Coast gives you some of the benefits that you might find with your timeshare resort exchange company, such as hotel and motel discounts, travel services, recreational vehicle insurance and financing, and condominium rentals. Like Adventure Outdoor Resorts, you must join Coast to Coast through your home campground resort. You cannot simply call and purchase an annual membership.

The Coast to Coast Web site, *www.coastresorts.com*, includes an interactive map through which you can search for affiliated campgrounds all over the United States. Company contact information is on the site, as well.

Resort Parks International

Resort Parks International, founded in 1981, calls itself North America's premier network of private-membership RV networks and resorts. The company is based in Long Beach, California, and it boasts more than 100,000 members. As with Adventure Outdoor Resorts and Coast to Coast Resorts, membership in Resort Parks International is available only through your home campground resort. You cannot simply call the company and sign on for an annual membership.

The Resort Parks International Web site, *www.resortparks.com*, has an interactive map that will let you search for its affiliated campground resorts. It also has a separate update page that you can click on to see the latest campground additions to the Resort Parks International network.

Recreational Vehicles

In addition to timeshares that allow you the use of recreational vehicle timeshares, you sometimes can find a program that will let you purchase a timeshare in the RV itself. As with a boating timeshare, you would almost never own an actual share in the vehicle, but rather the right to use it for a certain amount of time each year.

⚡ E-ALERT

Most people who buy recreational vehicles want to have their own space and stuff with them while they are on vacation. For this reason, recreational vehicle timeshares historically have attracted a smaller number of people than other kinds of timeshares. This may affect the long-term viability of any plan you purchase, since it is possible that your RV management company could go out of business altogether.

Some RV timeshare programs are run by recreational vehicle manufacturers themselves, while others are organized through RV rental companies or even by RV owners who want to form individual shared-use partnerships when buying a new, high-end recreational vehicle. In some cases, you can even use timeshare resort points through a company like Resort Condominiums International to purchase a week of RV vacation.

Why not just rent? Some people argue that RVs made available to renters are not always in the best of shape, while timeshare recreational vehicles are better models to begin with that benefit over time from more stringent maintenance schedules.

A typical recreational vehicle timeshare can cost as little as $5,000 or more than $150,000, depending on the RV model and usage benefits—plus the maintenance fees that you would pay for any other kind of timeshare. With a recreational vehicle timeshare, you often will be entitled to four weeks or more of annual vehicle use, with a weekly limit on the number of miles that you are allowed to drive (say, in the 1,000-mile-per-week range). You may be charged a monthly maintenance fee instead of an annual one, as you would be with a resort timeshare unit.

As recreational vehicles, like all vehicles, have a limited lifespan, there usually will be an end date for your timeshare term. When that date comes, the RV may be sold or taken back by its manufacturer, sometimes with at least part of the income from any sale being given back to you and the other RV timeshare owners. Some companies will let you cash out or reinvest that money in another recreational vehicle timeshare, whichever you prefer. Other companies may keep the entire bankroll, as part of your original buy-in agreement.

American QuarterCoach, based in Burr Ridge, Illinois, is one company that offers recreational vehicle timeshares under the name "fractional ownership." It has offered the program since 2003. You pay an initial buy-in fee, just as you would with a timeshare resort unit, and then you pay additional monthly management fees to cover maintenance, insurance, and other expenses.

Different buy-in rates allow you different amounts of RV usage in the American QuarterCoach system. A one-half plan will allow you twenty-four weeks of use a year, a one-quarter plan gives you twelve weeks annually, and a one-eighth plan will include five weeks of RV use for you and your family each year.

 **E-QUESTION**

How does RV timeshare compare with outright ownership in terms of price?
American QuarterCoach offers this breakdown: Buying your own rec-reational vehicle will run you at least $220,000, not including insur-ance and other costs. A one-half timeshare membership is just less than $140,000, a one-fourth timeshare membership costs just under $70,000, and a one-eighth membership is about $35,000.

The company says that fractional ownership makes sense for many people because typical recreational vehicle owners use their RVs only about three weeks each year. And, as a bonus to its fractional ownership members, the company will even provide pickup and delivery of its recreational vehicles—with the goal of making RV vacation travel as hassle-free as possible.

As with any timeshare purchase, you will want to ensure that you are dealing with an upstanding company before you sign anything. Your safest course of action is to ask your attorney to take a look at the contract, specifically the terms of usage and the rights you have to getting any money back after the end date of your timeshare period.

CHAPTER 18

If They Had It to Do Again

ONE OF THE IDEAL PLACES to learn about the best and worst of timesharing is from people who have a great deal of experience in the industry. The folks quoted in the following pages are not developers or salesmen; they are people just like you, who want to buy timeshares and then enjoy fantastic vacations. Some of these people have probably been buying, using, renting, and selling timeshares for longer than you may even have known the option existed, and they have a bevy of great stories and insights to share.

Buying New Timeshares

Some longtime, experienced timeshare owners believe their new-from-the-developer purchases have been worth every penny—proving that sometimes you get what you pay for even if the price is a high one. George M., who bought his first timeshare back in 1994, is one of those people. He now owns four weeks of timeshare at three different resorts and has visited more than thirty other resorts through exchanging, but one of the purchases that has made him happiest was of a new unit from a developer at the St. James's Club on the Caribbean island of Antigua.

"We visited the resort on a timeshare trade, and it had top-notch service," he remembers. "After going on the timeshare tour, we knew we wanted to own there. Now, we had already been timeshare owners for eight years, and we knew we would only buy a resale. However, the resort was offering a very good price on some weeks, so we purchased one but fully intended on getting home and using the rescission period to find a resale and cancel the developer purchase.

"During the rest of our stay, we heard nothing but praise for the management from other owners. We arrived home and searched every resale Web site we could find, called dozens of resellers, and never found one unit on the resale market. Some resellers told us they never had seen one for sale.

"We kept our purchase and, when we visited the next year, we were so impressed again with management that we bought a second week."

E-ALERT

Do plenty of research before you buy anything, and think twice before buying your first unit from a developer. A good number of the developers' units are overpriced, and you can find far better deals on the resale market, where you will have less financial and emotional strain if you end up making a mistake your first time out.

George says he sees many things in his units at the St. James's Club that novice buyers should look for when dealing directly with a timeshare developer. First of all, the resort management is owner-friendly. For example, there are no charges to owners for internal trades (trading for a different unit within the same resort), and owners receive discounted meal plans at the restaurants the resort operates.

Also, George's contract limits annual maintenance-fee increases to 5 percent, per year. His two-bedroom unit's annual maintenance fee is $450 per year, which he says shows, when combined with the limited possible increases, that the resort is well run and is not wasting any of the timeshare owners' money. He cites this as one possible reason for the lack of resale units, as well, and the corresponding high value that his units have retained since he first bought them.

Lastly, the managers offer personal service. George recalls having trouble getting a restaurant reservation and mentioning as much in passing to the timeshare manager on site. "He told me if it ever happens again, to call him," George says. "That we are owners, and they will make sure we get the reservation whenever we want. I own at other resorts with higher fees that don't even come close to the service of this resort."

All in all, George agrees that the advice to buy resale is correct about 99 percent of the time—but that his experience tells him that in a handful of cases, buying from the developer will be the only way you can get what you want. And that's not necessarily a bad thing.

Buying Resale Timeshares

Chris N., who has been buying new and resale timeshare units since 2000, says there are great deals out there to be had if you simply have some patience and look around for opportunities.

"In 2001 I bought my first resale: a Marriott in Fort Lauderdale," he says. "The location is great, it is a top trader, and the price was unbelievable. I believe it was from a couple in the middle of a divorce."

Finding a unit like that on the resale market is easier than you might imagine, as there are far more people looking to sell their timeshares than there are people seeking to buy them. An unfortunate fact of supply and demand is that you almost always will be able to profit from the misfortune of others, which you may or may not feel so bad about when you are sitting in your bargain-basement-priced timeshare balcony right next to another person who paid full price from the developer for the same experience.

Aside from finding a person so desperate to sell that you can get a good deal, you need to pay attention to the resort itself when sifting through the countless units on the resale market. One thing that longtime owner George M. says to look for when evaluating resale units is how many of them are for sale in any given resort. "Are there a lot of units for sale? If so, why are so many owners selling?"

Often, he says, it's because maintenance fees have increased dramatically or because a special assessment is being considered to cover general renovations and repairs—indicating that maintenance fees were either set too low in the first place or that owners' money is not being handled wisely.

≡FAST FACT

One timeshare owners' group estimates that there are as many as 500,000 timeshare units available on the resale market at any given time, all around the world.

Using Timeshares

Charles K. started out in timesharing just four years ago, but he already owns seven weeks of timeshare in South Africa, almost always has nearly two dozen confirmed exchanges in the works, and usually has three or four additional weeks on deposit in an exchange company's space bank, awaiting trades.

Charles says that when you are just starting out in the world of timeshares, you have to take other people's opinions cautiously when discussing how best to make use of your investment. For instance, he says the Timeshare User's Group—of which he is a member—is a great consumer organization with combined knowledge that is "light years ahead of any other source and an excellent reference." On the other hand, Charles warns that most of the group's members (like most people the world over) have strong opinions about what works best for them, based on their own experiences—which may be drastically different from your own personal situation.

"There are many ingrained prejudices and pet theories floating around there," Charles says. "It seems that everyone has a system that works for them, and they defend it to the death."

Having said that, there are some tips that current timeshare owners offer for newcomers. Chris, for instance, says he prefers to use timeshares at brand-name resorts because they give him more amenities to choose from.

"One of the best features of the newer hotel-based timeshare properties is that they are often located on the same property as one of their luxury hotels," Chris explains. "Examples are Marriott's Canyon Villas, which are adjacent to the J.W. Marriott Desert Ridge Resort and Spa in Phoenix, and Starwood's Harborside Resort, which is adjacent to the Atlantis Resort and Casino on Paradise Island, Bahamas.

"As a guest at these timeshares, you normally get full access to the hotel's amenities in addition to the amenities exclusive to the timeshare. The timeshare amenities typically include things like a pool, workout facility, and a small convenience store—enough to have a nice, relaxing vacation. But by sharing the amenities of an adjacent resort hotel, you also get access to fabulous restaurants, spas, golf, mega-sized pools, and water slides."

▣ TRAVEL TIP

The key to using your timeshare is figuring out what system works best for you, be it returning to the same place year after year, gaming the system to travel the world, or some combination of the two.

Exchanging Timeshares

Bill and Nancy G. bought their timeshare a couple of years ago through the Disney Vacation Club, a points-based system. They are allowed to use their points for stays of varying lengths at multiple Disney properties, or they can bank them into the Resort Condominiums International system to trade for other timeshares or for things like rental cars, cruises, and the like.

Overall, Bill says that he has been thrilled with the developer, but not so much with the exchange company. The value of his points have actually gone up—since new timeshare owners are being charged more than he was in order to buy the same number of points—but when he tries to use those points outside the Disney system, he often feels stymied.

"We have been pleased with the Disney point system," he explains. "We have been able to tailor the number of days we spend at their resorts, and have had no scheduling problems. We do, however, avoid the peak periods such as Christmas because we want to avoid the crowds.

"After having had good experiences with Disney, we paid to convert our membership into the RCI points system. We have found the RCI system to be pretty much useless. There is no flexibility to select a few days here or there, as we had been led to believe. For example, we put in for any days in San Francisco from January 1 to April 1 this past January. There wasn't a single day available, even though this was the off-season. We have tried other locations, always without success."

E-ALERT

If you're a first-time buyer, consider sticking with a brand-name developer such as Disney or Marriott, where you can use your points at various developer-owned timeshares without using an exchange company, or simply to buy a timeshare in a resort where you hope to return year after year.

Chris N., the man who has been buying timeshares since 2000, is not quite so down on trying to make exchanges through a company like Resort Condominiums International. However, he says that timeshare exchanging is an art, not a science, and that everyone should be prepared to learn from trial and error.

The two things Chris says are most important to keep in mind are that you are dealing with the laws of supply and demand, and that everyone is trying to trade "across or up," as opposed to seeking out smaller, less-desirable units than the one they already own. "Be realistic with your expectations," Chris says. And do your homework—especially when looking for resale units for the sole purpose of exchanging them.

"Thanks to advice on TUG, several years ago, I purchased a great resale at a resort in the mountains of North Carolina," Chris explains. "At the time, the resort had several repossessed weeks; they were reacquired from owners frustrated by a recent dispute between the resort and the management of nearby recreational facilities. This dispute jeopardized the existing agreement for owners to use these facilities. At the same time, the resort had instituted a three-year special assessment to fund some large improvements and maintenance to the resort. As a result, owners would have to pay an additional $140 a year for three years and face the possibility that [much] of the nearby recreation would now be off-limits.

"When several owners walked away from their weeks, the resort was left holding them with no owner to pay the annual fees. I was able to buy an annual late-April week for $500, with the annual maintenance fee being $400. In the last three years, I have consistently traded this week into the top-rated resort in Cancun. If I were to buy a week at the Cancun resort, it would cost me $20,000 with an annual maintenance fee of $650.

"I have never been to North Carolina, and I will probably never visit my home resort," he says. But given the purchase price, annual fees, and trading power of the unit, it has been a good deal in the long run. "I would never think about vacationing in a twenty-year-old condo on a North Carolina lake," Chris says, but "it is very popular with folks within driving distance."

Renting Timeshares

Bill Rogers, who created the Timeshare User's Group after he exchanged his unit one year for another that was promised to be just as nice but turned out to be quite lousy, says that if he were starting out in the universe of timesharing all over again, he wouldn't buy a unit at all—new from the developer or on the resale market.

"I'd rent one for a while," he says. "That way, I could see if I liked it, and I wouldn't have any of the financial obligations. It can be very inexpensive, too. I've rented timeshares for less than the cost of the annual maintenance fee."

Selling Timeshares

Chris N. was one of the lucky ones when it came to selling his time-share. In May 2000, he paid $26,000 for a shoulder-season week at Starwood's Harborside Resort in the Bahamas, adjacent to the Atlantis Resort and Casino. "I admit I was dazzled," he recalls, perhaps a bit concerned in retrospect about the amount he paid for his first-ever timeshare unit.

FAST FACT

Incentives can be helpful in selling your timeshare unit, and they don't have to be expensive. Consider offering anyone who buys your timeshare a free subscription to a timeshare magazine, or a year's worth of suntan lotion for the adjacent beach, or a free golf lesson at the resort course. You will spend a little, but you may gain a lot in terms of closing the deal quickly.

"Luckily for me this resort became one of the most-sought-after locations, and the prices continued to rise over the years," he explains. "Being from the West Coast, my wife and I realized that the total cost (airfare, meals, spending money) of each annual trip was much more than we had planned. We sold the timeshare in 2003 to someone else for exactly what we paid—rare in timesharing!"

The Bottom Line

Overall, what all of these timeshare owners have in common is the belief that research and experience are truly the only things that will help you find out exactly how to make the timeshare world work best for you. Everyone has different tastes in resorts, in vacation lengths, and in vacation styles, and for that reason the universe of timeshares offers a seemingly endless array of choices. Making those options fit the vacationing choices that you and your family most covet is a challenge that only you will be able to fulfill—by asking questions, doing research, and making the smartest possible purchases along the way.

The experiences these owners have shared in this chapter are just the first few stories in a virtual encyclopedia of other people's experiences that you can find by visiting chat rooms, attending sales presentations, and joining consumer groups. Your job is to make friends, take notes, and learn everything you can beyond the basics that you already have taken the time to explore. Should you find your personal path in the world of timeshares, the vacations you enjoy for many years to come will be a wonderful reward. Enjoy them, as you will have earned them!

CHAPTER 19

Consumer Groups and Additional Research Options

IT IS SURPRISING, GIVEN the number of people out there who own timeshares, that so few consumer groups have popped up around the industry. In the United States, for instance, just two organizations have come to dominate the consumer-news and chat scene (though a third, launched in 2004, is hoping to make inroads). Meanwhile, at the industry level, well-known organizations such as the National Association of Realtors and the Better Business Bureau continue to be a good source of information for protecting yourself against fraud.

United States–Based Consumer Groups

A substantial World Wide Web presence has given the United States–based consumer groups a broader worldwide following. The good news is that in an effort to grab online readers' attention across the globe, all three of the consumer-based groups listed below make a great deal of their Web site content available for free to nonmembers. This gives you the chance to learn a great deal about timeshares without forking over a single penny, and also to decide which group's information you find most helpful before signing up for their members-only sections. Even better news is that, should you decide to join any of these groups, the membership fees are quite reasonable—in all cases less than $25 and in some cases less than $10.

Hiatus magazine

This quarterly magazine was launched in 2004 with the goal of simplifying timeshare shopping for consumers. It is produced by Bigfish Publications, a six-year-old company in Scottsdale, Arizona. *Hiatus* takes great pains to point out that its publisher, editor, and writers neither invest in nor maintain any personal stake in firms whose products and services are reviewed in the magazine.

Its biggest claim to fame thus far is the publication of the *2005 Hiatus Buyer's Guide to Vacation Ownership*, which evaluates 245 timeshare resorts in side-by-side comparisons of things like suite amenities, resort facilities, recreation, and guest activities. *Hiatus* says that no resort appearing in the guide paid any money to be listed, meaning that you, the consumer, should be getting an unbiased look at each property. The resorts are listed by United States region, and there is an international section, as well.

═FAST FACT

Membership in an online consumer group usually allows you access to online chat rooms where you can talk with other timeshare owners about their personal experiences with specific resorts and exchange companies. In many cases, this is the most honest information you will find anywhere about timeshare use and value.

Hiatus magazine itself offers articles about timeshare ownership, general travel and destination features, resort comparisons, and more. Many of its past-issue features are available for free at its Web site, *www.gohiatus.com*, where you can surf the links to see whether the magazine's tone and offerings are right for you.

The Timeshare Beat magazine

This online publication has been on the World Wide Web since 1999. It publishes daily, Monday through Friday, offering news and information about everything from timeshare resorts to new opportunities in timesharing, including boats. The site claims that about 230,000 different people see it every thirty days, for a total of more than 2.7 million individual users per year.

The majority of people reading *The Timeshare Beat* are from the United States, specifically from Virginia, Oregon, California, Tennessee, and Georgia (though there are other nationalities and states represented, as well). The site has classified ads for everything from timeshare industry jobs to timeshare financial services, along with useful information for timeshare owners such as calendar weeks, a worldwide clock, and timeshare contract terminology. To explore *The Timeshare Beat* online, go to *www.thetimesharebeat.com*.

Timeshare User's Group

The Timeshare User's Group was started in 1993 by Bill Rogers after he and his wife traded a timeshare unit in a very nice resort for a unit that he describes as being in a "rundown converted motel." He thought there should be a place where timeshare-unit owners could go to find independent information and talk about their experiences, and so he launched the Web-based group that is now found at *www .tug2.net*.

Timeshare User's Group has information about more than 2,000 resorts on its Web site, along with resort ratings, chat rooms, resale values, classified ads for timeshare resales, display ads for timeshare resort services, and more. One of the best things about the site—if you are new to timeshares and have a lot to learn—is that much of its instructional information is viewable for free. You can learn about everything from buying to selling to exchanging your timeshare in articles written by other timeshare-unit owners who have had good and bad experiences alike.

Some other Web-based consumer groups claim that the world's largest exchange company, Resort Condominiums International, gets more than a fair shake on the TUG Web site (with complaints being taken off the chat room listings, and such), but for the most part TUG has an excellent reputation as a source of unbiased, user-friendly timeshare information. The membership fee is $15, which you can pay online, or by telephone, fax, or snail mail.

TimeSharing Today Magazine

This magazine's tagline states that it is "The Trusted Independent Voice of Vacation Ownership Since 1991." *TimeSharing Today* is published every other month, with fifty-four pages full of information about resorts, timeshare use and exchanges, classified ads, display ads from industry business, and general industry information.

📁 TRAVEL TIP

The TimeSharing Today Web site is chock-full of helpful information, much of it available to nonmembers for free. You can view all the content, including resort reviews and timeshare resale documents, by signing up to receive the magazine (twelve issues for $24) or simply the online edition (nine issues for $12).

The magazine promotes the fact that the major exchange company Resort Condominiums International has banned *TimeSharing Today* advertisements in its own corporate magazines, perhaps because *TimeSharing Today* aggressively promotes and assists the timeshare resale market. If you are looking to buy on the resale market, you might find it helpful to sign up for a subscription at *www.tstoday.com*—if only to gain access to what other timeshare owners are saying about certain resorts.

United Kingdom–Based Consumer Groups

The beauty of the Internet is that it can bring people of like minds together across great distances. Such is the case with timeshare owners, many of whom are using consumer-created Web sites in the United Kingdom to voice the same kinds of concerns as owners in the United States are sharing on Web sites such as *www.tug2.net* and *www.tstoday.com*.

There are of course other Web sites in Europe and elsewhere abroad that are devoted to the sharing of timeshare information among unit owners, but these British sites are posted in English, making them easiest for the majority of Americans to comprehend.

Brits tend to be a bit more colorful in their complaints than their Yankee counterparts across the pond, and it can be fun to join their chat rooms (with names like "Shark Alley") just to hear about how they got "brassed off" after "sussing out" the details of a "five-hour ear bashing" timeshare sales pitch. Of course, you may come away with lots of valuable consumer information, as well, and some valuable contacts should you ever decide to look into exchanging your timeshare unit in the United States for one overseas.

Crimeshare

The name of this lone-gunman organization says it all about his motives for creating the Crimeshare Web site: to list timeshare scams and frauds that have occurred since 1998. The site offers some valuable insights into the types of schemes and scandals that can befall unwary timeshare buyers and users. The Crimeshare "black list" is more than arm's length, offering you nonspecific information about companies that the Web site creator has deemed unsavory. The "Timeshare Sh*t of the Year Award" page delivers news and information in a way that is colorful, to say the least. If you want to learn more about this unorthodox site, log on to *www.crimeshare.cc*.

E-ALERT

The challenge of this Web site is that virtually all of the information is one-sided with no rebuttal or even fair comment from the resort developers or exchange companies coming under fire. For this reason, the Crimeshare Web site creator has been referred to on other timeshare Web sites as "one pissed-off guy."

Timeshare Consumers Association

The Timeshare Consumers Organization is a donation-funded group that works to offer timeshare advice, create discussion forums among timeshare owners and users, help owners realize the full benefits to which they are entitled, publicly expose illegal and unethical practices, lobby governments for better timeshare laws, and more.

Much of the information posted on the group's Web site is viewable for free, even by nonmembers. It includes warnings about timeshare scams, general advice on buying and selling timeshares, and information on making the most of your exchange club membership. The forums are viewable by anyone, but you must be a member to post a message. Some of the topics open for discussion include dealings with specific developers and resale companies—invaluable firsthand experiences that you can use to protect yourself (and your money) throughout the duration of your timeshare ownership. To read more from this group, log on to *www.timeshare.org.uk.*

TimeshareForums.com

This Web site is strictly about forums and chat rooms, with no additional content posted. It was conceived as a cyberspace meeting place where timeshare owners, exchangers, and renters could share their experiences. Positive and negative comments alike are welcome, and the forums range from timeshare economics to horror stories and personal experiences at specific timeshare resorts worldwide.

There are also forums about individual exchange companies, including Resort Condominiums International, Interval International, and a handful of their smaller competitors. Additional forums are designed for owners of brand-name resort units, including those at Disney, Marriott, Hyatt, Starwood, and Fairfield resorts. You can post a timeshare for resale here or look for one to buy or rent. To get into the chatting action, log on to *www.timeshareforums.com.*

Timeshare Talk

This Web site calls itself the United Kingdom's premier forum for timeshare owners. It has several good features, including its resale classified ads, but perhaps its best link is to chat forums where members speak frankly about their experiences at good and bad timeshare resorts alike.

The "Shark Alley" forum is full of conversations about rip-offs and scams that people have experienced when trying to buy timeshare units. Even if you do not intend to buy a timeshare from any of the resorts being discussed, the scams themselves are interesting to read about because they follow the same patterns as unscrupulous deals all over the world. You can protect yourself by learning about how other people have been suckered. Log on to *www.timesharetalk .co.uk* to check out the details.

Voice

Voice is an acronym that stands for Vacation Owners Independent Coalition In Europe. It is a nonprofit organization created to safeguard the interests of timeshare owners, consumers, and industry players. It was cofounded by a consumer group and a trade group, and it includes articles that offer introductory information about buying, selling, and using timeshare units.

≡FAST FACT

There are no chat rooms or forums on this Web site, so you cannot communicate directly with other Voice members about your experiences. You can, however, scroll through many pages of frequently asked questions to get a basic understanding of how timeshares evolved and are used today. The group's Web site is *www.voice.eu.com*.

Industry Organizations

Aside from consumer-run timeshare groups, there are several industry organizations that lend credibility to the resort developers, resale brokerage firms, and exchange companies that are allowed to become members. No system of industry oversight can be perfect, of course, but a company's membership in one of the following groups shows that, at a minimum, the company knows that there are rules and regulations out there in the world.

American Resort Development Association

Know by the acronym ARDA, the American Resort Development Association is based in Washington, D.C. It was created in 1969 and now claims about a thousand members, some that are small, private firms and others that are worldwide conglomerates. Some members are timeshare homeowners' associations, while others are resort management companies and developers.

ARDA's goals include advocating for governmental policies that encourage timeshare industry growth, doing media and other out-reach to spread the word about the growth of the timeshare industry, and providing educational materials for consumers and developers who want to enter the timeshare industry. It also enforces a Code of Standards and Ethics that consists of timeshare solicitation, sales, and general requirements. Sanctions can be levied against ARDA members who fail to comply with the code.

E-ALERT

Although companies may not follow the industry's rules and regulations, seals of approval from reputable groups and organizations are a good sign that the company is at least trying to take an ethical and legal approach to working with its colleagues, its competitors, and, ultimately, you—the timeshare consumer.

One of the best consumer-oriented features on the ARDA Web site is a searchable database of members, broken down into categories. Some of those categories include real estate brokerage, vacation club/travel club, travel services/tour operators, timesharing, resale brokers (licensed), and auctioneering—all things you may want to look into when buying, using, or selling a timeshare unit. To learn more about the American Resort Development Association, check out its Web site, *www.arda.org.*

National Association of Realtors

The National Association of Realtors has been around since 1908 and now has more than a million members. Its core purpose is to help Realtors become more profitable and successful, but its benefit to you—the consumer—is that it promotes a Code of Ethics that is no fewer than eight pages long and that lays out in strict detail the way ethical real estate transactions should be made.

A nice feature on the group's Web site is a searchable database that will allow you to find a Realtor in your area who specializes in what the organization defines as resort area/second home sales—including timeshares. You can type in your city and state of residence, and a list of certified Realtors will pop up complete with contact information. To learn more about the National Association of Realtors, log on to its Web site, *www.realtor.org.*

State and Federal Government Organizations

Usually, the sale of timeshares is regulated—at least in the United States—by the Real Estate Commission in the state where the timeshare resort is located. You can look this up by going to *www.us.gov,* the official portal of the United States government. The site index page, which has a clearly marked tab for you to click on, will lead you to a link called "State Government." Click on that link, and you will see a listing of all fifty states, plus the territories and outlying areas of American Samoa, Micronesia, Guam, the Midway Islands, Puerto Rico, and the U.S. Virgin Islands. You can click on any of those state or territory links to get to the home page of that state or territory. From there, the individual state and territory Web sites should lead you to their own Real Estate Commissions, or at least to a telephone number you can call if you have any further questions.

The Federal Trade Commission does not regulate the sales of timeshares in any way. It does, however, work to prevent fraudulent, deceptive, and unfair business practices—including false advertising and shady marketing schemes. For this reason, the Federal Trade Commission can sometimes be a good place to file a complaint in regard to timeshare sales. You can be as broad or as specific as you would like, complaining about everything from the general timeshare buying process to the behavior of a single telemarketer or salesperson. Learn more at the Federal Trade Commission's Web site, *www .ftc.gov*.

 **E-QUESTION**

How else can I find the commission that is in charge of my state?
The fastest way is often by typing the state's name, plus the phrase "real estate commission," into a search engine like *www.google.com*.

The Better Business Bureau

The Better Business Bureau is pretty much a household name, having provided everything from dispute resolution to truth-in-advertising reports since 1912. Today, the bureau receives all of its funding from businesses, but it is well-known as a place where consumers will be treated fairly should there be a need to lodge a complaint.

More than two million businesses are on file with the bureau, and you can research many of them online—for free—just by typing in their names. A Reliability Report will pop up for any company in the nationwide database, and the report will tell you not only how long the company has been a Better Business Bureau member, but also whether it has a satisfactory rating and how many complaints have been filed against it. Major timeshare companies, including Resort

Condominiums International and Interval International, are included in the database, as are some developers such as Disney Vacation Development (all three companies have satisfactory ratings, by the way). Learn more about all the Better Business Bureau offers by logging on to *www.bbb.org*.

🧳 TRAVEL TIP

You can use the Better Business Bureau to file a complaint if you believe you have been the victim of a timeshare scam— an important step that will perhaps save other people from the same fate in the future.

Chambers of Commerce

Local, state, and national chambers of commerce, like the Better Business Bureau, are a place where you can look to help assess the reputation of any resort developer or timeshare exchange company. If a business has gone to the trouble of joining a chamber of commerce, the action alone improves the odds that it is run by a reputable person.

The national Chamber of Commerce is not a parent organization of the countless state and local chambers across the United States, nor does it give out the names of its members to consumers. Instead, your best bet for finding out if a business is a member of any chamber is to ask your contact at the company, or to call the local chamber in the state where the business is based. For more general information about the Chamber of Commerce system, log on to *www.uschamber.com*.

Timeshare Developers, Exchange Companies, and Resale Brokers

WHETHER YOU WANT TO buy direct from a timeshare resort developer, sign up with an exchange company to make trades on your unit, or work with a resale broker on purchasing, selling, or even renting a timeshare unit, the companies listed in the following pages will be a good place for you to begin your search.

Brand-Name Timeshare Developers

You read about these companies more extensively in Chapter 1, and some of their resorts have been highlighted throughout the book, as well. The following listing of contact information is provided for easy reference.

Club Intrawest
The Landing
326-375 Water Street
Vancouver, British Columbia
V6B 5C6, Canada
(800) 649-9243
✐ www.clubintrawest.com

Disney Vacation Club
Disney Vacation Development, Inc.
200 Celebration Place
Celebration, FL 34747-9903
(800) 800-9100
✐ www.disneyvacationclub.com

Fairfield FairShare Plus
Fairfield Resorts, Inc.
8427 SouthPark Circle
Suite 500
Orlando, FL 32819
(800) 251-8736
✐ www.fairfieldresorts.com

Four Seasons Residence Club
2701 Loker Avenue West
Suite 110
Carlsbad, CA 92008
(800) 343-1270
✐ www.fourseasons.com

Hilton Grand Vacations Club
Hilton Grand Vacations Company, LLC
6355 MetroWest Boulevard
Suite 180
Orlando, FL 32835
(800) 230-7068
www.hiltongrandvacations.com

Hyatt Vacation Club
Hyatt Vacation Ownership, Inc.
450 Carillon Parkway
Suite 210
St. Petersburg, FL 33716
(800) GO-HYATT
www.hyatt.com

Marriott Vacation Club International
6649 Westwood Boulevard

Suite 500
Orlando, FL 32821-6090
(800) 259-1104
www.vacationclub.com

Starwood Vacation Ownership
9002 San Marco Court
Orlando, FL 32819
(800) 553-0464
www.starwoodvo.com

WorldMark by Trendwest
9805 Willows Road
Redmond, WA 98052
(800) 772-3487
www.worldmarktheclub.com

Exchange Companies

You learned about the two major exchange companies, Resort Condominiums International and Interval International, as well as many of the smaller exchange companies in Chapter 1. The following list of contact information is provided for easy reference use.

Resort Condominiums International
RCI North America Office
9998 North Michigan Road
Carmel, IN 46032
(317) 805-9000
Member services—weeks:
(800) 338-7777
Member services—points:
(877) 968-7476
www.rci.com

Interval International
Box 431920
6262 Sunset Drive
Miami, FL 33243-1920
(800) 843-8843
www.intervalworld.com

Dial an Exchange
2845 Nimitz Boulevard, Suite E
San Diego, CA 92106
(800) 468-1799
www.daelive.com

Hawaii Timeshare Exchange
Box 1077
Koloa, HI 96756
(866) 860-4873
www.htse.net

Interchange Timeshare
Box 179
Broadbeach, Queensland 4218
Australia
(011) 61 7 5531 6100
www.interchange-timeshare.com.au

Internet Exchange Services
16310 Highway 19
Suite One
Hudson, FL 34667
(888) 431-9868
✍ www.internet-ies.com

Intervac
Intervac USA
30 Corte San Fernando
Tiburon, CA 94920
(800) 756-4663
✍ www.intervacusa.com

OwnerTrades.com
OwnerTrades.com is a Web-based
company created by a timeshare-unit
owner. There is no associated mailing address or telephone number.
✍ www.ownertrades.com

Platinum Interchange
1300 North Kellogg Drive, Suite B
Anaheim, CA 92807
(800) 854-2324
✍ www.platinuminterchange.com

San Francisco Exchange Company
185 Berry Street
Suite 5411

San Francisco, CA 94107
(800) 739-9967
✍ www.sfx-resorts.com

Timex Direct Exchange System
Timex is a Web-based company
created by a timeshare-unit owner.
There is no associated mailing
address or telephone number.
✍ www.timex.to

Trading Places International
23808 Aliso Creek Road
Suite 100
Laguna Niguel, CA 92677
(800) 365-1048
✍ www.tradingplaces.com

TUG Direct Exchange
Timeshare User's Group
Box 1442
Orange Park, FL 32067
(904) 298-3185
✍ www.tug2.net

VacationEarth
Box 740016
Boynton Beach, FL 33474
(954) 978-9097
✍ www.vacationearth.com

Resale Brokers

Legitimate timeshare resale brokers are licensed in the same way that legitimate
Realtors are licensed. Never, ever, do business with someone claiming to be a
resale broker if she cannot produce a valid license, and always check with the
Better Business Bureau and the American Resort Development Association to
ensure that the broker you are working with is a member of one or both groups.

The well-respected Timeshare User's Group and *TimeSharing Today* magazine accept advertisements from many legitimate resale brokers. To help get you
started, the listing below is culled from those groups' advertisements and then
expanded with additional information. You can also see promotions from these
resale brokers by going to *www.tug2.net* and *www.tstoday.com*.

Advantage Vacation

Advantage Vacation is a licensed real estate company that is a member of the National Association of Realtors and the Better Business Bureau. The company's Web site has specialized links to timeshares that are located in Hawaii, California, Florida, Arizona, New York, Nevada, Utah, Virginia, Mexico, and the Caribbean. Timeshare units in other locations are available, as well. The company offers a free newsletter that includes timeshare properties for sale, as well as articles about timeshare buying, selling, and usage. Learn more by logging on to *www.advantagevacation.com*.

Holiday Group

The Holiday Group is based in Seattle, Washington, and has been in business since 1992. It is one of the timeshare resale brokerage companies that does offer you a rescission period, or cooling-off time, after making a purchase. You will have seven days to change your mind and get your money back, whether because of budgeting difficulties, new-found information, or a simple decision that a particular timeshare unit is not for you.

This company belongs to the Better Business Bureau and promises to abide by the Code of Ethics of the National Association of Realtors. It deals with individual people's units, or with units that have been foreclosed or repossessed (not with resorts that are in financial trouble). On any given day, it usually has hundreds of worldwide properties available for resale purchase. Learn more at *www.holidaygroup.com*.

Timeshare Locators

This licensed real estate company has been doing business for twenty-one years. It is based in Solana Beach, California, and its Web-site property listings include dozens of timeshare units from all over the world, and in all price ranges. If you are a seller, the company will *not* charge you an up-front listing fee.

The company's Web site offers bare-bones information about the timeshares in its database and instead asks you to provide information about yourself in order to receive additional information about specific properties. Be prepared to be contacted by a sales representative if you want to work with this resale broker. Go to *www.timesharelocators.com* for more information.

Timeshare Resale Alliance

This company specializes in California timeshare resorts. It has been operating since 1968 and is a member of both the Better Business Bureau and the National Association of Realtors. Its headquarters are in San Diego.

Buyers pay nothing until they decide to make a purchase, at which point a minimum $500 credit-card charge is requested along with signed paperwork. Timeshare-unit sellers pay commissions, but no up-front charges for listing a unit for sale. All sales go through an escrow process, offering safeguards for buyers against unpaid liens, and title insurance is part of every deeded-property transaction. Learn more about the Timeshare Resale Alliance at the company's Web site, *www.resaletimeshare.com*.

Timeshare Resales U.S.A.

Timeshare Resales has been working to buy and sell units since 1987. It is part of the GMAC Real Estate group, a well-known and highly reputable national corporation. Timeshare Resales U.S.A. is also a member of the American Resort Development Association, the Better Business Bureau, and the Orlando (Florida) Chamber of Commerce.

You can search the company's online database for timeshares that are for sale as well as for rent. You also can click the link to *www .timesharesforauction.com,* an affiliated Web site where you can search geographically for timeshare units that are going up for auction. Learn more at *www timesharecresaleusu.com.*

Timeshare Wholesalers

This Des Moines, Washington–based company claims more than three decades in the timeshare business, and it lists timeshare units for sale all over the world. Timeshare Wholesalers is a licensed real estate brokerage that has a good frequently-asked-questions section on its Web site to help get you started in the timeshare ownership process.

Its Web site allows you to search for available properties by geographic region (using the same style of color-coded map that Resort Condominiums International provides on its Web site). Learn more at *www.timesharewholesalers .com.*

The Timeshare Store

The Timeshare Store is located in the heart of the theme-park universe in Orlando, Florida. It has a division dedicated to resales of Disney Vacation Club timeshares, and it even encour-ages Disney Vacation Club members to stop by on their way to their time-shares, since there is a Publix grocery store in the same shopping center.

Most of the properties this company lists for sale are in its home state of Florida. A nice feature on this company's Web site is a search engine that lists properties by price. You can search only properties that are $3,000 or less, only properties that are $15,000 or more, and pretty much everything in between. You also can search through properties by resort name if you already have an idea about where you want to buy. The Timeshare Store's Web site is *www.timesharesale.com.*

TRI West Real Estate

This licensed real estate firm is a member of the National Association of Realtors, the American Resort Development Association, and the Real Estate Broker Alliance. The company is based in Los Angeles, California, and maintains an online "blue book" database that you can search through to try to find out what timeshares have sold for in the resorts where you are considering making a purchase. Not all resorts are listed in the database—one search for any resort with the word "Disney" in the title came up empty—but you just may get lucky and find some valuable historical information before you make your opening bid.

TRI West has been in business since 1981 and claims to be the largest and oldest timeshare resale and rental broker on the West Coast. It takes a 15 percent commission from the time-share seller on every unit sold. Contact TRI West by logging on to *www .triwest-timeshare.com.*

Vacation Calendars

NO MATTER WHICH TIMESHARE exchange company you work with, you will have to arrange for weeklong trades in keeping with the calendar of weeks that is standard to the industry. Most resorts fall under this system. Some allow check-in on Fridays, while others make the first day of your weeklong stay a Saturday or Sunday. You can ask the resort of your choice which check-in day it uses, and then use the calendars in this section to determine exactly which dates would correlate to your timeshare week.

YEAR 2007

Week	Friday to Friday	Saturday to Saturday	Sunday to Sunday
1	Jan. 5–Jan. 12	Jan. 6–Jan. 13	Jan. 7–Jan. 14
2	Jan. 12–Jan. 19	Jan. 13–Jan. 20	Jan. 14–Jan. 21
3	Jan. 19–Jan. 26	Jan. 20–Jan. 27	Jan. 21–Jan. 28
4	Jan. 26–Feb. 2	Jan. 27–Feb. 3	Jan. 28–Feb. 4
5	Feb. 2–Feb. 9	Feb. 3–Feb. 10	Feb. 4–Feb. 11
6	Feb. 9–Feb. 16	Feb. 10–Feb. 17	Feb. 11–Feb. 18
7	Feb. 16–Feb. 23	Feb. 17–Feb. 24	Feb. 18–Feb. 25
8	Feb. 23–March 2	Feb. 24–March 3	Feb. 25–March 4
9	March 2–March 9	March 3–March 10	March 4–March 11
10	March 9–March 16	March 10–March 17	March 11–March 18
11	March 16–March 23	March 17–March 24	March 18–March 25
12	March 23–March 30	March 24–March 31	March 25–April 1
13	March 30–April 6	March 31–April 7	April 1–April 8
14	April 6–April 13	April 7–April 14	April 8–April 15
15	April 13–April 20	April 14–April 21	April 15–April 22
16	April 20–April 27	April 21–April 28	April 22–April 29
17	April 27–May 4	April 28–May 5	April 29–May 6
18	May 4–May 11	May 5–May 12	May 6–May 13
19	May 11–May 18	May 12–May 19	May 13–May 20
20	May 18–May 25	May 19–May 26	May 20–May 27
21	May 25–June 1	May 26–June 2	May 27–June 3
22	June 1–June 8	June 2–June 9	June 3–June 10
23	June 8–June 15	June 9–June 16	June 10–June 17
24	June 15–June 22	June 16–June 23	June 17–June 24
25	June 22–June 29	June 23–June 30	June 25–July 1
26	June 29–July 6	June 30–July 7	July 1–July 8
27	July 6–July 13	July 7–July 14	July 8–July 15
28	July 13–July 20	July 14–July 21	July 15–July 22
29	July 20–July 27	July 21–July 28	July 22–July 29
30	July 27–Aug. 3	July 28–Aug. 4	July 29–Aug. 5
31	Aug. 3–Aug. 10	Aug. 4–Aug. 11	Aug. 5–Aug. 12
32	Aug. 10–Aug. 17	Aug. 11–Aug. 18	Aug. 12–Aug. 19

Week	Friday to Friday	Saturday to Saturday	Sunday to Sunday
33	Aug. 17–Aug. 24	Aug. 18–Aug. 25	Aug. 19–Aug. 26
34	Aug. 24–Aug. 31	Aug. 25–Sept. 1	Aug. 26–Sept. 2
35	Aug. 31–Sept. 7	Sept. 1–Sept. 8	Sept. 2–Sept. 9
36	Sept. 7–Sept. 14	Sept. 8–Sept. 15	Sept. 9–Sept. 16
37	Sept. 14–Sept. 21	Sept. 15–Sept. 22	Sept. 16–Sept. 23
38	Sept. 21–Sept. 28	Sept. 22–Sept. 29	Sept. 23–Sept. 30
39	Sept. 28–Oct. 5	Sept. 29–Oct. 6	Sept. 30–Oct. 7
40	Oct. 5–Oct. 12	Oct. 6–Oct. 13	Oct. 7–Oct. 14
41	Oct. 12–Oct. 19	Oct. 13–Oct. 20	Oct. 14–Oct. 21
42	Oct. 19–Oct. 26	Oct. 20–Oct. 27	Oct. 21–Oct. 28
43	Oct. 26–Nov. 2	Oct. 27–Nov. 3	Oct. 28–Nov. 4
44	Nov. 2–Nov. 9	Nov. 3–Nov. 10	Nov. 4–Nov. 11
45	Nov. 9–Nov. 16	Nov. 10–Nov. 17	Nov. 11–Nov. 18
46	Nov. 16–Nov. 23	Nov. 17–Nov. 24	Nov. 18–Nov. 25
47	Nov. 23–Nov. 30	Nov. 24–Dec. 1	Nov. 25–Dec. 2
48	Nov. 30–Dec. 7	Dec. 1–Dec. 8	Dec. 2–Dec. 9
49	Dec. 7–Dec. 14	Dec. 8–Dec. 15	Dec. 9–Dec. 16
50	Dec. 14–Dec. 21	Dec. 15–Dec. 22	Dec. 16–Dec. 23
51	Dec. 21–Dec. 28	Dec. 22–Dec. 29	Dec. 23–Dec. 30
52	Dec. 28–Jan. 4	Dec. 29–Jan. 5	Dec. 30–Jan. 6

YEAR 2008

Week	Friday to Friday	Saturday to Saturday	Sunday to Sunday
1	Jan. 4–Jan. 11	Jan. 5–Jan. 12	Jan. 6–Jan. 13
2	Jan. 11–Jan. 18	Jan. 12–Jan. 19	Jan. 13–Jan. 20
3	Jan. 18–Jan. 25	Jan. 19–Jan. 26	Jan. 20–Jan. 27
4	Jan. 25–Feb. 1	Jan. 26–Feb. 2	Jan. 27–Feb. 3
5	Feb. 1–Feb. 8	Feb. 2–Feb. 9	Feb. 3–Feb. 10
6	Feb. 8–Feb. 15	Feb. 9–Feb. 16	Feb. 10–Feb. 17
7	Feb. 15–Feb. 22	Feb. 16–Feb. 23	Feb. 17–Feb. 24
8	Feb. 22–Feb. 29	Feb. 23–March 1	Feb. 24–March 2
9	Feb. 29–March 7	March 1–March 8	March 2–March 9
10	March 7–March 14	March 8–March 15	March 9–March 16

Week	Friday to Friday	Saturday to Saturday	Sunday to Sunday
11	March 14–March 21	March 15–March 22	March 16–March 23
12	March 21–March 28	March 22–March 29	March 23–March 30
13	March 28–April 4	March 29–April 5	March 30–April 6
14	April 4–April 11	April 5–April 12	April 6–April 13
15	April 11–April 18	April 12–April 19	April 13–April 20
16	April 18–April 25	April 19–April 26	April 20–April 27
17	April 25–May 2	April 26–May 3	April 27–May 4
18	May 2–May 9	May 3–May 10	May 4–May 11
19	May 9–May 16	May 10–May 17	May 11–May 18
20	May 16–May 23	May 17–May 24	May 18–May 25
21	May 23–May 30	May 24–May 31	May 25–June 1
22	May 30–June 6	May 31–June 7	June 1–June 8
23	June 6–June 13	June 7–June 14	June 8–June 15
24	June 13–June 20	June 14–June 21	June 15–June 22
25	June 20–June 27	June 21–June 28	June 22–June 29
26	June 27–July 4	June 28–July 5	June 29–July 6
27	July 4–July 11	July 5–July 12	July 6–July 13
28	July 11–July 18	July 12–July 19	July 13–July 20
29	July 18–July 25	July 19–July 26	July 20–July 27
30	July 25–Aug. 1	July 26–Aug. 2	July 27–Aug. 3
31	Aug. 1–Aug. 8	Aug. 2–Aug. 9	Aug. 3–Aug. 10
32	Aug. 8–Aug. 15	Aug. 9–Aug. 16	Aug. 10–Aug. 17
33	Aug. 15–Aug. 22	Aug. 16–Aug. 23	Aug. 17–Aug. 24
34	Aug. 22–Aug. 29	Aug. 23–Aug. 30	Aug. 24–Aug. 31
35	Aug. 29–Sept. 5	Aug. 30–Sept. 6	Aug. 31–Sept. 7
36	Sept. 5–Sept. 12	Sept. 6–Sept. 13	Sept. 7–Sept. 14
37	Sept. 12–Sept. 19	Sept. 13–Sept. 20	Sept. 14–Sept. 21
38	Sept. 19–Sept. 26	Sept. 20–Sept. 27	Sept. 21–Sept. 28
39	Sept. 26–Oct. 3	Sept. 27–Oct. 4	Sept. 28–Oct. 5
40	Oct. 3–Oct. 10	Oct. 4–Oct. 11	Oct. 5–Oct. 12
41	Oct. 10–Oct. 17	Oct. 11–Oct. 18	Oct. 12–Oct. 19
42	Oct. 17–Oct. 24	Oct. 18–Oct. 25	Oct. 19–Oct. 26
43	Oct. 24–Oct. 31	Oct. 25–Nov. 1	Oct. 26–Nov. 2

Week	Friday to Friday	Saturday to Saturday	Sunday to Sunday
44	Oct. 31–Nov. 7	Nov. 1–Nov. 8	Nov. 2–Nov. 9
45	Nov. 7–Nov. 14	Nov. 8–Nov. 15	Nov. 9–Nov. 16
46	Nov. 14–Nov. 21	Nov. 15–Nov. 22	Nov. 16–Nov. 23
47	Nov. 21–Nov. 28	Nov. 22–Nov. 29	Nov. 23–Nov. 30
48	Nov. 28–Dec. 5	Nov. 29–Dec. 6	Nov. 30–Dec. 7
49	Dec. 5–Dec. 12	Dec. 6–Dec. 13	Dec. 7–Dec. 14
50	Dec. 12–Dec. 19	Dec. 13–Dec. 20	Dec. 14–Dec. 21
51	Dec. 19–Dec. 26	Dec. 20–Dec. 27	Dec. 21–Dec. 28
52	Dec. 26–Jan. 2	Dec. 27–Jan. 3	Dec. 28–Jan. 4

YEAR 2009

Week	Friday to Friday	Saturday to Saturday	Sunday to Sunday
1	Jan. 2–Jan. 9	Jan. 3–Jan. 10	Jan. 4–Jan. 11
2	Jan. 9–Jan. 16	Jan. 10–Jan. 17	Jan. 11–Jan. 18
3	Jan. 16–Jan. 23	Jan. 17–Jan. 24	Jan. 18–Jan. 25
4	Jan. 23–Jan. 30	Jan. 24–Jan. 31	Jan. 25–Feb. 1
5	Jan. 30–Feb. 6	Jan. 31–Feb. 7	Feb. 1–Feb. 8
6	Feb. 6–Feb. 13	Feb. 7–Feb. 14	Feb. 8–Feb. 15
7	Feb. 13–Feb. 20	Feb. 14–Feb. 21	Feb. 15–Feb. 22
8	Feb. 20–Feb. 27	Feb. 21–Feb. 28	Feb. 22–March 1
9	Feb. 27–March 6	Feb. 28–March 7	March 1–March 8
10	March 6–March 13	March 7–March 14	March 8–March 15
11	March 13–March 20	March 14–March 21	March 15–March 22
12	March 20–March 27	March 21–March 28	March 22–March 29
13	March 27–April 3	March 28–April 4	March 29–April 5
14	April 3–April 10	April 4–April 11	April 5–April 12
15	April 10–April 17	April 11–April 18	April 12–April 19
16	April 17–April 24	April 18–April 25	April 19–April 26
17	April 24–May 1	April 25–May 2	April 26–May 3
18	May 1–May 8	May 2–May 9	May 3–May 10
19	May 8–May 15	May 9–May 16	May 10–May 17
20	May 15–May 22	May 16–May 23	May 17–May 24
21	May 22–May 29	May 23–May 30	May 24–May 31

Week	Friday to Friday	Saturday to Saturday	Sunday to Sunday
22	May 29–June 5	May 30–June 6	May 31–June 7
23	June 5–June 12	June 6–June 13	June 7–June 14
24	June 12–June 19	June 13–June 20	June 14–June 21
25	June 19–June 26	June 20–June 27	June 21–June 28
26	June 26–July 3	June 27–July 4	June 28–July 5
27	July 3–July 10	July 4–July 11	July 5–July 12
28	July 10–July 17	July 11–July 18	July 12–July 19
29	July 17–July 24	July 18–July 25	July 19–July 26
30	July 24–July 31	July 25–Aug. 1	July 26–Aug. 2
31	July 31–Aug. 7	Aug. 1–Aug. 8	Aug. 2–Aug. 9
32	Aug. 7–Aug. 14	Aug. 8–Aug. 15	Aug. 9–Aug. 16
33	Aug. 14–Aug. 21	Aug. 15–Aug. 22	Aug. 16–Aug. 23
34	Aug. 21–Aug. 28	Aug. 22–Aug. 29	Aug. 23–Aug. 30
35	Aug. 28–Sept. 4	Aug. 29–Sept. 5	Aug. 30–Sept. 6
36	Sept. 4–Sept. 11	Sept. 5–Sept. 12	Sept. 6–Sept. 13
37	Sept. 11–Sept. 18	Sept. 12–Sept. 19	Sept. 13–Sept. 20
38	Sept. 18–Sept. 25	Sept. 19–Sept. 26	Sept. 20–Sept. 27
39	Sept. 25–Oct. 2	Sept. 26–Oct. 3	Sept. 27–Oct. 4
40	Oct. 2–Oct. 9	Oct. 3–Oct. 10	Oct. 4–Oct. 11
41	Oct. 9–Oct. 16	Oct. 10–Oct. 17	Oct. 11–Oct. 18
42	Oct. 16–Oct. 23	Oct. 17–Oct. 24	Oct. 18–Oct. 25
43	Oct. 23–Oct. 30	Oct. 24–Oct. 31	Oct. 25–Nov. 1
44	Oct. 30–Nov. 6	Oct. 31–Nov. 7	Nov. 1–Nov. 8
45	Nov. 6–Nov. 13	Nov. 7–Nov. 14	Nov. 8–Nov. 15
46	Nov. 13–Nov. 20	Nov. 14–Nov. 21	Nov. 15–Nov. 22
47	Nov. 20–Nov. 27	Nov. 21–Nov. 28	Nov. 22–Nov. 29
48	Nov. 27–Dec. 4	Nov. 28–Dec. 5	Nov. 29–Dec. 6
49	Dec. 4–Dec. 11	Dec. 5–Dec. 12	Dec. 6–Dec. 13
50	Dec. 11–Dec. 18	Dec. 12–Dec. 19	Dec. 13–Dec. 20
51	Dec. 18–Dec. 25	Dec. 19–Dec. 26	Dec. 20–Dec. 27
52	Dec. 25–Jan. 1	Dec. 26–Jan. 2	Dec. 27–Jan. 3

Index

Everything® You Need for a Family Vacation

**The Everything®
Family Guide to Hawaii**
1-59337-054-7
$14.95

**The Everything®
Family Guide to New York
City, 2nd Ed.**
1-59337-136-5, $14.95

**The Everything® Family
Guide to Washington D.C.,
2nd Ed.**
1-59337-137-3, $14.95

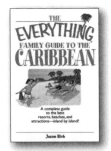

**The Everything® Family
Guide to the Caribbean**
1-59337-427-5
$14.95

**The Everything® Family
Guide to Cruise Vacations**
1-59337-428-3
$14.95

**The Everything® Family
Guide to Mexico**
1-59337-658-8
$14.95